Law and Literature

Edited by

Patrick Hanafin
Adam Gearey
Joseph Brooker

Blackwell
Publishing

BLACKWELL PUBLISHING
9600 Garsington Road, Oxford OX4 2DQ, UK
350 Main Street, Malden, MA 02148-5018, USA
550 Swanston Street, Carlton, Victoria 3053, Australia

First published 2004 by Blackwell Publishing Ltd as a special issue of *Journal of
Law and Society*

Library of Congress Cataloging-in-Publication Data applied for

ISBN 1-4051-1930-6 (paperback)

A catalogue record for this title is available from the British Library.

Set in the United Kingdom
by MHL Production Services Limited

The publisher's policy is to use permanent paper from mills that operate a
sustainable forestry policy, and which has been manufactured from pulp processed
using acid-free and elementary chlorine-free practices. Furthermore, the publisher
ensures that the text paper and cover board used have met acceptable
environmental accreditation standards.

For further information on
Blackwell Publishing visit our website:
www.blackwellpublishing.com

Contents

JOURNAL OF LAW AND SOCIETY
VOLUME 31, NUMBER 1, MARCH 2004
ISSN: 0263-323X, pp. 1–2

Introduction: On Writing: Law and Literature

PATRICK HANAFIN,* ADAM GEAREY,* AND JOSEPH BROOKER*

Law and literature have always lived together, trespassed on, and infiltrated each other. The recent growth of intellectual studies of their relationship has simply been the overdue recognition of this fact. If literature has laws, law also has a literary dimension. It has been argued by a number of critical legal theorists that law has historically repressed its written character, refusing to draw the full implications of that character. Our theory of writing must have an important effect on our theory of law. Law, in so far as it exists as text, cannot evade ambiguities and arguments over interpretation – with which literary scholars are well familiar. Law has been reconceived as figuration, as representation, as narrative, as 'framing'.

This collection has no single agenda. We have not sought to impose one academically safe way of practising law and literature. Instead we aim to create a space where these two disciplines can interfere with one another, and form the occasion for new thought, within or beyond the laws of academic discipline. In editing this collection, we have not attempted to prescribe in advance all the ways in which law and literature can be thought together. We have encouraged our contributors to approach this conjunction in their own chosen ways: to tie or untie many different kinds of knot between the two discursive threads. Some contributors have chosen to analyse the representation of law and legal process in literary works, as part of the cultural history of representations of law. Others have focused not only on literature's representation of law, but on law's representation of literature. Literary studies, despite some important recent developments, still remain insufficiently alive to the impact that law has had on literary history – not least in terms of censorship and the forms of self-censorship that follow upon it.

Contributors have been encouraged to explore the complex terrain of particular histories. Rather than reducing law and literature to a singular relationship, they have investigated the diverse articulations which obtain in different historical and geographical loci. For instance, what effects do

* *Birkbeck College, University of London, Malet St., London WC1E 7HX, England*

1

colonial and post-colonial conditions have on these relationships? In the encounter between law and the political how does literature engage with a law conceived as politics and power?

Contributors have also sought to approach both literature and law as concepts. What do they share, and what can they learn from each other? Literature, certainly, has its own laws: the laws of genre, the rules of art, the great systems of classification and taxonomy which have been proposed from the classical world to Northrop Frye and Roland Barthes. Is our practice of literary value bound up with, or by, laws – explicit or otherwise? Can preferences be translated into laws – or does the act of judgment seek, precisely, to evade the binding of law and represent a particular experience in all its uniqueness? In this sense, law and the aesthetic are more closely interwoven than one may think. What this collection suggests is a strange play in which literature unsettles the law. The writing that names itself 'law and literature' is of itself strange and unsettling. This writing tends to spill out of any frame imposed upon it. The exciting new work in this collection assumes diverse inflexions and styles in attempting to test and extend the boundaries of law and literature scholarship.

JOURNAL OF LAW AND SOCIETY
VOLUME 31, NUMBER 1, MARCH 2004
ISSN: 0263-323X, pp. 3–14

The Writer's Refusal and Law's Malady

PATRICK HANAFIN*

In this piece I want to (re)pose the relation of writing to law and politics, by interrogating the sense of a writing which is simultaneously an unwriting or undoing of legal and political discourse through Maurice Blanchot's involvement in the movement against the French colonial war in Algeria and, in particular, his framing of the Declaration of the Right to Insubordination in the Algerian War *in 1960. The piece analyses how the sense of the event of the Declaration continues to call us to acknowledge a 'disastrous responsibility' to a non-community beyond the time of law and politics.*

INTRODUCTION

Begin to write. Not with your last ounce of strength, but with all the strength you have no longer.[1]

This piece attempts to examine the relation of the writer to the juridico-political sphere by analysing Maurice Blanchot's appearance before the law after he had taken part in the movement against the French war in Algeria. Blanchot was the principal author, along with Dionys Mascolo, of *The Declaration of the Right to Insubordination in the Algerian War.*[2] This Declaration, more commonly known as the Manifesto of the 121 set forth a right to refuse to take arms against the Algerian people. It placed individuals before a

* *School of Law, Birkbeck College, University of London, Malet St., London WC1E 7HX, England*

I wish to thank Julia Chryssostalis for her incisive comments on an earlier draft of this piece.

1 A. Smock, 'Disastrous Responsibility' (1984) 3 *L'Esprit Créateur* 5, at 10.
2 This text was first published in *Vérité-Liberté* on 6 September 1960. The authorities seized the edition of the review and the publisher was charged with inciting soldiers to desert. The text is also known as the Manifesto of the 121, after the number of its signatories, who included Simone de Beauvoir, Pierre Boulez, Andre Breton, Marguerite Duras, Henri Lefebvre, J.-B. Pontalis, Alain Resnais, Alain Robbe-Grillet, and Nathalie Sarraute.

3

solitary responsibility, not to a *patria*. It called for a questioning of the actions which the state perpetrated in the name of the People. As the Manifesto states:

> *Chacun doit se prononcer sur des actes qu'il est désormais impossible de présenter comme des faits divers de l'aventure individuelle, considérant qeux-memes, a leur place et selon leurs moyens, ont le devoir d'intervenir, non pas pour donner des conseils aux hommes qui ont a décider personnellement face à des problémes aussi graves, mais pour demander a ceux qui les jugent de ne pas se laisser prendre a l'équivoque des mot et des valeurs.*[3]

This act of writing questioned the very relation of the sovereign power to the citizenry. It called for an absolute right to refuse to accept the acts of war which the state purported to carry out in the name of the people.

The event of the Manifesto enacted many of Blanchot's fictional and critical concerns, such as the contest between the law and its other; the play between power and transgression; and the notion of responsibility. This incident and the context to which gave rise to it raise questions of ongoing import, namely the (a)political role of the writer and the right to refuse the way in which legal language taxonomizes the subject. In his essay 'Intellectuals under Scrutiny' Blanchot expresses the difficulty for the writer of answering the call to responsibility for an unknown other:

> There is ... for the person whose vocation is to remain in retreat, far from the world ... the pressing necessity to expose himself to the 'risks of public life' by discovering a responsibility for someone who, apparently, means nothing to him, and by joining in the shouting and the clamour, when, on behalf of that which is closest, he has to give up the sole exigency that is properly his own: that of the unknown, of strangeness and of distance.
>
> When the ... writer ... declares himself ... [h]e absents himself from the only task that matters to him ... It would be easy for him to remain on the sideline. What then is this command from without, to which he must respond and which obliges him to take his place in the world again and assume an additional responsibility which may lead him astray.[4]

This additional responsibility led the writer 'astray' in the eyes of the law, which in turn made of him an outlaw. It is as Ann Smock has termed it a 'disastrous responsibility'.[5] This is a responsibility which assumes one's inability to be responsible. Yet the recognition of the inability to be responsible makes it all the more imperative. This giving up of the self in the service of an impossible responsibility is similar to the effacement of the self which, for Blanchot, was writing. In both cases, the self is given in order to respond to a call to be responsible for one's inability to be responsible for the unknown other. As he noted elsewhere, one must respond to the impossibility to be responsible.[6] It is this very call to be responsible to an unknown other that

---

3 *Déclaration sur le droit a l'insoumission dans la guerre d'Algérie*, <http://www.bok.netpajol/manif121.html>.

4 M. Blanchot, 'Intellectuals under Scrutiny' in *The Blanchot Reader*, ed. M. Holland (1995) 217.

5 Smock, op. cit., n. 1, p. 5.

6 M. Blanchot, *L'Ecriture du Désastre* (1983) 46.

4

informed Blanchot's framing of the *Declaration of the Right to Insubordination in the Algerian War.*

THE MAGISTRATE'S MALADY

In his own encounter with the law after the state instituted criminal legal proceedings against the co-authors of this insubordinate document, Blanchot experienced how legal language purported to rob the individual of his own speech. Blanchot appeared before an examining magistrate during the course of the proceedings in order to give a statement. In Blanchot's account of his encounter with the magistrate, he challenges directly the magistrate's own legitimacy. He remarked to the magistrate that the then Prime Minister, Michel Debré, had, in a speech delivered two or three days before Blanchot's appearance before the magistrate, declared that the 121 signatories of the Declaration would be severely punished. Blanchot claimed that in so doing, the Prime Minister had already pronounced judgment and made the magistrate's role superfluous. The reaction of the magistrate was one of acute anger. He bellowed at Blanchot: 'There are things that one does not say here!'[7] Blanchot, in reply, observed that therefore the magistrate's chambers constitute a space in which the citizen cannot freely express himself and likened it to the space in which the pre-revolutionary monarch dispensed justice. To this provocation the magistrate replied, confirming Blanchot's suspicions, 'Don't forget that for such words I can send you to prison'.

The second point of discord between Blanchot and the magistrate concerned the tradition in civil law jurisdictions that a magistrate take the deposition of the accused and then dictate it in his own (the magistrate's) words to the legal clerk. When he began to do this, the magistrate was interrupted by Blanchot who said 'you will not substitute your words for mine. I don't doubt your good faith but your phrasing of my words is unacceptable'. After some argument the magistrate finally relented and allowed Blanchot to speak his statement directly to the clerk. In referring to this incident Blanchot notes:

> There is a seriously deficient point in this affair, which is the debate between a man with a wealth of legal expertise at his fingertips and another who has perhaps few words and does not even know the sovereign value of speech, of *his* speech. Why is it that the judge has the right to be sole master of language, dictating (in what is already a *diktat*) the words of another, as seems appropriate to him, reproducing them not as they were said, stuttering, meagre and unsure, but made worse, because finer, more consistent with the classical ideal, and, most of all, more definitive.[8]

7 M. Blanchot, 'Pre-texte: Pour L'Amitie' in *A la recherche d'un communisme de pensée*, ed. D. Mascolo (1993) 11.
8 id.

The reductive violence of legal discourse is all too manifest here. The law wants to make of Blanchot an object, a pure mask resounding with the magisterial voice, the perfect persona. It attempts to impose its language on his words. However, his words fight back leave a trace, even in the violent discourse of law. The combat between the words of law and those of the individual without traces leaves traces, both on the law and its agents.

Here there is a conflict of languages between the citizen and the representative of the law, an attempt to discipline, to suppress the unruly words of the citizen called before the law to explain himself. In this sense, Blanchot's appearance before a representative of the law mirrors the position of the narrator in his novel, *The Madness of the Day*, who is similarly asked to explain himself to the representatives of power/knowledge, namely, the psychiatrist and the ophthalmologist. Like his narrator in the novel, Blanchot interrupts his own representation by the law. This reveals a law which is not so much secure and self-assured but under siege, driven by a terror of being displaced, a trauma which undoes its hold on the power over discourse. In Leslie Hill's terms, 'the law always expresses itself as an irreducible double bind.'[9] In this sense, the sense of law is its own undoing; law is vulnerable to the contradictions which lie at the heart of its discourse. Legal discourse reveals a space in which power and transgression are at play. It is these infintesimal moments of interruption which expose the limits of legal discourse, which display fleetingly the law of another community not bound by law's word. Blanchot as outlaw, as disruptive force, exposes law's limiting discourse. He seduces the magistrate and reveals a law which, though authoritarian and oppressive, is fallible. The magistrate who questioned Blanchot had subsequently to take sick leave for what he termed moral exhaustion, a monstrously appropriate malady for a servant of the law to be afflicted with.[10] For what Blanchot did in his performance was to expose the very moral exhaustion of the law, a law which no longer respected the autonomy of the citizens on whose behalf it purported to speak. What instead it did was to force words out of the citizen, only then to transform them into the acceptable speech of law.

Blanchot himself was in a sense enchanting the law, calling it forth from within itself to address its own irresponsibility, exhausting its limits, just as the other figure of law in *The Madness of the Day* states:

9 L. Hill, *Maurice Blanchot: Extreme Contemporary* (1997) 101.
10 In his autobiographical collection of musings, *Angélique ou L'Enchantement* (1987) 204, Alain Robbe-Grillet makes an interesting comparison between Blanchot's appearance before the magistrate and the weakness of the magistrate in front of the seductive character of the young woman in Robbe-Grillet's film, *Glissements Progressifs Du Plaisir*. This undoing of the law by a seductive law beyond law is enacted again through the character of Blanchot in his appearance before the magistrate. Blanchot also manages to undo the magistrate, to seduce or bewitch him. Perhaps here we see the play between power and transgression, between law's repressive face and its seductive other face, a compearing of two beings to form a communion.

6

The truth is, we can no longer go our separate ways. I will follow you everywhere, I will share the same roof, we will enjoy the same sleep.[11]

This double figure appears again in Blanchot's *Unavowable Community* where he speaks of two opposing versions of socio-political formation. One is exemplified by immanence, homogeneity, and a repressive law, while the second version is heterogeneous, fluid, and interrupts the law. This figure is the intruder or outsider who 'perturbs the untroubled continuity of the social bond and does not recognise prohibitions'.[12] Thus, the law in its repressive mode is constantly interrupted by this alter ego. The law tried to impose its power over language to deny Blanchot of his speech. Yet through his passive resistance he exposes the law's own fragility. He interrupts or contests the law's representation of itself as well as its representation of him, and in so doing evokes the law of the Other beyond all law.

This performance of the interruption of law evokes the play between law and its subversion. Nothing is ostensibly changed: the institutions continue, but something will never be the same. This is the imperceptible moment of subversion, which, as workless, as pure excess, achieves nothing, but this is its very force. It counterposes worklessness to the work of power, non-identity to identity, responsibility to one's own non-responsibility. Thus, Blanchot appears before the law as writing appears before the work or the book. For Blanchot, 'To write is to produce the absence of the work (worklessness)'.[13] Writing, for Blanchot, is the 'relation to the other of every book, to what in the book would be de-scription, a scriptuary exigency outside discourse, outside language. Writing on the edge of the book, outside the book'.[14]

Like the writer who goes beyond the book, the work, towards a certain worklessness, Blanchot, as apolitical writer, is impelled to intervene in the political in the name of an unavowable community.[15] The relation of writing to the law of the book mirrors the relation of Blanchot as citizen to the law of the state. As Hill notes in this regard:

> The relation between writing and the law is a relation of non-relation; and it is from this that derives the 'transgressive' demand … of writing, writing that is always other than the law, not because of its superior power or legitimacy in the face of the law, but rather because of its refusal, on grounds of impotence, impossibility, and weakness, to allow itself to be addressed by the language of

11 M. Blanchot, *The Madness of the Day* (1981, tr. L. Davis) 15.
12 M. Blanchot, *La Communauté inavouable* (1983) 70.
13 M. Blanchot, *The Infinite Conversation* (1993) 424.
14 id., p. 427.
15 In speaking of how he saw his role in authoring this document, Blanchot has noted:

> I signed this text … as an apolitical writer who felt moved to express an opinion about problems that concern him essentially … One of the main purposes of the Declaration is to bring out the particular responsibility of intellectuals: when the democratic order is corrupted or decays, it falls to them, independent of any purely political allegiance, to say in simple terms what seems to them just.

(M. Blanchot, 'The Right To Insubordination' in op. cit., n. 4, p. 196.)

7

the law and constituted by the law as a subject or hostage of that law ... preceding the discourse of law, lacking all unity, presence, and identity, writing is a challenge to any authority whatsoever, including of course its own.[16]

Both the act of writing the Declaration and Blanchot's encounter with the magistrate play out this tension evoked in his writings on writing. Like the one who writes, Blanchot in his persona as apolitical writer is called by a responsibility to an unknown other to refrain from silence and intervene or interrupt the operation of politics and law. This lack of unity, presence, and identity which he performs unsettles both the political machine and the machinery of justice. Like Melville's Bartleby, his not saying, his passivity, his persistent just being there is enough to disrupt. His is a fading before the law which widens law's limit point. Even though the law tries to order the voice of the citizen, what in effect occurs is that law's power is always already undone in this move.[17] It is vital from the point of view of legal and political elites that the insubordinate citizen is *seen* to be managed, through repressive legal intervention, despite the fact that such insubordination can never be managed or repressed, given its intimate bond with the law. This insubordinate performance may point to that space of resistance wherein is traced 'the flashing line that causes the limit to arise'.[18]

In this moment the play between power and transgression is clear. Alterity rather than identity marks the law's relation to itself. In engaging in dissent, the insubordinator finds himself at the mercy of the laws of the state which attempt to punish him for his temerity and crush his act of insubordination, by a prison sentence but more invidiously by taking his language and forming it into the classical speech of law which allows for no protest. However, it is the law that is perplexed and at the mercy of Blanchot after the encounter. The law is revealed as the perpetrator of its own transgression. It struggles to impose itself while the transgressor remains within, yet beyond, its grasp, a state of affairs expressed eloquently in the image of the oil-soaked rag in Blanchot's novel, *The Most High*. The stain remains, this trace which lives on after the process, which points to this coming politics, beyond the time of politics and the repressive law.[19] It is in the empty space between utterance and recording that Blanchot's words leave their trace. At the end of the

16 Hill, op. cit., n. 9, pp. 187–8.
17 As Hill notes (id., p. 215):
   the language of power [is] ultimately always vulnerable: vulnerable not to the challenge that might come from a rival code of values ... but vulnerable instead to the infinite scepticism affirmed by the language of writing itself.
18 M. Foucault, 'A Preface To Transgression' in *Language, Counter-Memory, Practice: Selected Essays and Interviews*, ed. D.F. Bouchard (1977, tr. D.F. Bouchard and S. Simon) 35.
19 As Blanchot reminds us: 'There is not, to begin with, law, prohibition, and then transgression, but rather there is transgression in the absence of any prohibition, which eventually freezes into Law, the Principle of Meaning'. (M. Blanchot, *The Writing of the Disaster* (1980, tr. A. Smock) 75.)

8

encounter between Blanchot and the magistrate, it is the law which is temporarily disarmed. This subversive moment provokes not a new state or a different elite but, rather, the power of a withdrawal, a haunting, a seduction. Law's discourse is disrupted by his insubordinate being there before it. This presence, which the law attempts to make absent by imposing on him the force of its language, in his very persistence disturbs, makes ill, literally, the law.

EXSCRIPTIONS: UN(WR)ITING COMMUNITIES

Like Blanchot's appearance before the law, the Declaration penned by him performed an interruption in the time of politics. Its counter-declaratory power called for a solitary responsibility to an unknown other. Just as Blanchot's words unsettled the magistrate, so did this document unsettle the stabilized political order. It points to what an alternative politics might be, without telling us explicitly, like a secret that can never be uttered, unavowable. The Declaration, instead of imposing a community of citizens bound together by force of law and state power, called for an effacement of the sense of community built on identity. This community of singularity without identity threatened the very putting to work of the nation in the rhetoric of the Fifth Republic. The personification of the nation in the body of de Gaulle and the construction of an immanent French identity was at odds with a document which saw the cause of Algeria as the cause of all free men.

In de Gaulle's France, the dominant politics of communal identity conceived of the community as having an identity that was immanent to it and that needed to be brought out and put to work. The community as subject necessarily implies the community as subject-work; one's true or higher being or universal self is found in one's communal identity. This conception of politics as work relies upon and follows from the conception of community as immanent identity. The hollow and parodic language of the legal document attempts to construct or put to work the polity. It creates the textual illusion of a community founded on a being in common. It creates the textual boundaries which enclose the citizen in the state. In this regard, law can be seen as a stabilizing instrument, a means of suspending in abstract ghostly form identifiable citizens who are simultaneously citizens with an identity, this identity being the invisible bond which fixes the citizenry in an illusory commonality. In other words, the text of law creates or provokes a symbolic unity where none exists in order to secure the state in its territorial and textual space. This illusory wholeness or togetherness is permanently under siege in the paranoiac discourse of the security state. However, this grounded commonality of the state shares discursive space with a formless community, which constantly interrupts it, as the possibility of community beyond the juridico-political state form.

9

Jean-Luc Nancy[20] discusses the putting to work of a community's immanent identity in terms of areality, a word which is an archaic French term meaning the nature or the property of an area, an *aire*. The word however also suggests a lack of reality or else a suspended reality. Perhaps it is such a becoming areal of the nation that provokes such fears for its disappearance, explaining why a call to refusal such as Blanchot's, coming from a community without grounding or identity, threatened the French state so much. As areal, the nation is exscribed, revealed as a community without ground. This thinking of a politics beyond the grounded community of the nation-state can be located for Nancy in poetry. He states that 'poetry is a cadastre, or else a geography'.[21] He writes:

> The poet can be recognised by a certain surveyor's step, by a certain way of covering a territory of words, not in order to find something, or to plant a crop, or to build an edifice, but simply to measure it.[22]

This taking measure of speaks more of an exscription than of an inscription. The writer disappears but paradoxically leaves an indelible trace, like the event of Blanchot's encounter with the law. Blanchot's performance, then, in the events surrounding the Declaration could be described, (ab)using Nancy's words, as an (a)political gesture that:

> takes the form of an effacement: a gesture which itself is, after all, commonplace, which indicates your place, mine, yet another's, and which withdraws.[23]

This is an event of being in common as different, of being together as apart. The poetic nature of Blanchot's gesture is to be seen in its compearing of singular beings. It is a making that is simultaneously an unmaking. Blanchot's Declaration pares away the layers of rhetoric to reveal the non-identity and groundlessness occluded by legal writing.

REFUSING RIGHTS

Blanchot in describing the rationale behind the Declaration elaborated on the importance of the use of the term 'right' to insubordination in this context:

> I believe that the whole force of the Declaration, its whole power of disturbance, comes from the authority with which it utters the single word insubordination, a solemn word, signifying utmost refusal: the Right to insubordination. I say Right and not Duty ... an obligation refers to a prior moral code that shields, guarantees, and justifies it; wherever there is duty, all that is necessary is to close one's eyes and carry it out blindly; everything is

---

20 J.-L. Nancy, *Corpus* (2000) 39–40.
21 J.-L. Nancy, *The Birth to Presence* (1993) 308.
22 id.
23 id., pp. 308–9.

then quite straightforward. The right to do something, on the other hand, refers only to itself, to the exercise of that freedom of which it is the expression; a right is a free power for which each individual, for himself and with regard to himself, is responsible and which binds him completely and freely: nothing is stronger, nothing is more serious. That is why it is essential to say: the right to insubordination: each person takes their own sovereign decision.[24]

In writing elsewhere of an absolute right, Blanchot defines it as:

> a right which no real power doubles or reinforces ... a right, then, detached from power and duty, a madness required by reasonable integrity and which, moreover, seems to succeed quite often.[25]

This notion of right destabilizes the limiting language of universal human rights which is authorized by some transcendental power or value. In this counter-declaration of right, individuals take their own sovereign decision. It performs or prefigures a right to refuse which is so powerful because not given by some divine power or moral code. It is a right to resist not granted by the law.

Thus, it is in counter-opposition to the rather ironic right to resistance found in, for example, Article 20 of the Constitution of the German Federal Republic which, in the event of an attempt to overthrow the established legal order, all German citizens have a right to resist if other less extreme remedies are not possible. This legalized form of the right to resistance remains a last resort when the very legal order itself is under threat and provides not so much a right but imposes a duty on the German citizen to resist the overthrow of the state, yet another method of protection for the security state.[26] However, through its very institutionalization, the right to resist in the German Constitution, becomes nothing but a contingent duty leaving untroubled the normal role of the citizen as ineffectual critic. It is this very role which Michel Foucault rejects in another counter-declaration of rights in the following terms:

> We must reject the division of tasks which is all too often offered to us: it is up to individuals to become indignant and speak out, while it is up to governments to reflect and to act. It is true that good governments like the hallowed indignation of the governed, provided it remains lyrical. I believe that we must realise how often, though, it is the rulers who speak, who can only and want only to speak. Experience shows that we can and must reject the theatrical role of pure and simple indignation which we are offered.[27]

Blanchot in his Declaration turns the type of legal formulation found in the German Constitution around and speaks of a right to refuse, not in

24 Blanchot, op. cit., n. 7, p. 11.
25 M. Blanchot, *The Space of Literature* (1982, tr. A. Smock) 105.
26 See, further, G. Agamben, *Stato di eccezione* (2003) 21.
27 Cited in T. Keenan, *Fables of Responsibility: Aberrations and Predicaments in Ethics and Politics* (1997) 157.

answer to a need to protect the specific type of legal order the Constitution establishes, but a right to refuse based on a call to responsibility to an unknown other. There is no duty here to protect an identifiable politico-territoral space, but instead, an absolute right based on an impossible responsibility to the other to whom we may have no duty to defend. In this sense, another counter-declaration of right issued some twenty years later by Michel Foucault, no stranger to the works of Blanchot, bears certain traces of similarity. In 1981, Foucault together with activists from Medecins du Monde and Terre des Hommes, issued a press declaration at the Intercontinental Hotel in Geneva on the need to intervene to protect Vietnamese boat people from international pirates. Thousands of stateless people who had fled the war in Vietnam but who were not granted refugee status elsewhere had been preyed on by pirates in the Gulf of Thailand and raped, tortured, and murdered while international governments and international organizations failed to intervene. In language strikingly similar to that of the Manifesto of the 121, Foucault's document, published after Foucault's death as *Face aux gouvernements, les droits de l'Homme*, declares:

> We are here only as private individuals, who have no other claim to speak, and to speak together, than a certain shared difficulty in accepting what is happening ...
> ... Who ... has commissioned us? No one. And that is precisely what establishes our right.
> ... People's misfortune must never be a silent remainder of politics. It founds an absolute right to rise up and to address those who hold power.
> ... [this new right is] that of private individuals actually to intervene in the order of international politics and strategies.[28]

This attempt by Foucault to use the rhetoric of rights to subvert its normal functioning in the hands of the disciplinary state, again draws out the tension or aporia between power and its transgression. Perhaps what Foucault like Blanchot was enacting was this absolute right deprived of the law's force, a right dislodged from the repressive state apparatus, which was impossible to conceive, by virtue of its very ungroundedness. Indeed, as Tom Keenan has observed, what Foucault in this gesture did perform was the definition of:

> A radical theory of rights as such. Not the classical rights of individuals, the inalienable rights of man, or the rights said to find their ground in human nature, but rather a theory of rights as the condition of a radically democratic politics, rights without limit and end, rights as the irreducible claim and gesture of the political as such.[29]

Thus, both Blanchot and Foucault call for a right beyond state power, an interruption which neither destroys nor recreates but leaves the present not quite what it was. This event, this interruption in the present order will, as

28 id., pp. 156–7.
29 id., p. 173.

12

Keenan reminds us, 'have already violently interfered with the presence of our present and our position(s) within it'.[30] It is such an ephemeral writing of dissent that silently calls to a time beyond the political which leaves a stain on the present 'stabilized' order. This is, then, in counter-opposition to the writing or inscribing of a community through the written constitution, call it an exscribing, an unwriting, an undoing. It calls for another politics, a politics beyond the time of the political, made not of inscribed, clearly delineated subjects but of ghosts, traces, people without qualities, people without identity, whatever singularities. The Declaration performs a thinking of another politics beyond the political time of the present. Giorgio Agamben provides an eloquent mode of helping us to think towards this new politics when he observes:

> *The novelty of the coming politics is that it will no longer be a struggle for the conquest or control of the state, but a struggle between the state and the non-state (humanity), an insurmountable disjunction between whatever singularity and the state organization.* This has nothing to do with the simple affirmation of the social in opposition to the state ... Whatever singularities cannot form a *societas* because they do not possess any identity to vindicate nor any bond of belonging for which to seek recognition. In the final instance the state can recognise any claim of identity ... What the state cannot tolerate in any way, however, is that the singularities form a community without affirming an identity, that humans co-belong without any representable condition of belonging ... The state ... is not founded on a social bond, of which it would be the expression, but rather on the dissolution, the unbinding it prohibits. For the state, therefore, what is important is never the singularity as such, but only its inclusion in some identity, whatever identity (but the possibility of the *whatever* itself being taken up without an identity is a threat the state cannot come to terms with) ...
> Whatever singularity ... [which] rejects all identity and every condition of belonging, is the principal enemy of the state. Wherever these singularities peacefully demonstrate their being in common there will be a Tiananmen, and sooner or later, the tanks will appear.[31]

CONCLUSION

The events surrounding the Declaration revealed a disjunction between the time of politics and the time of the coming community. This workless interruption opposes the law of the book, the law of inscription. As Blanchot observed in writing about a similar hiatus between the time of politics and that of the promise of another radical politics, the events of May 1968:

> In May there is no book about May: not for lack of time or the need to 'act', but because of a more decisive impediment: it is all being written elsewhere, in a world without publication; it is being distributed in the face of the police and

30 id., p. 169.
31 G. Agamben, *The Coming Community* (1996) 84–6.

13

in a way with their help, violence pitted against violence. This stop put to the book, which is also a stop put to history, and which, far from taking us back to a point preceding culture, is what is most provocative to authority, to power, to the law. May this bulletin prolong that stop, while preventing it from ever stopping. No more books, never again, for as long as we remain in contact with the upheaval of the break.

... The only mode in which revolution is present is that of its real possibility. At that moment, there is a stop, a suspension. In this stop, society falls apart completely. The law collapses: for an instant there is innocence; history is interrupted.[32]

Power unmasked momentarily, like the unmasking of the gas-masked enforcer of law's order in a street protest, before the blows of the baton rain down on the unmasker. This moment when the interruption flickers and fades through a haze of gas, smoke, and fire is the very sense of this faceless community.

The right to refusal calls us to think beyond the state and our role in the biopolitical matrix. It involves a questioning of why it is that the law presumes to be in control of language. It involves a certain refusal to submit to the law, to be insubordinate. It is that other law of writing that is without foundations as opposed to the writing of law which purports to found the community. It is a call to suspend the dialectical closure of representational politics, as well as the essential complicity of government and legal opposition deriving from it, in order to affirm a different kind of politics, no longer dependent on the law of possibility. As Blanchot suggests in *The Unavowable Community*, it involves a thinking beyond the reliance on received political concepts such as those of project or subject.[33] Perhaps this ephemeral tracing of a non-community is best exemplified by the electrical blackout in New York in August 2003, where citizens reacted in a temporary coming together, a provisional friendship created in times of adversity, a spontaneous compearing. As the writer and, (co)incidentally, translator of Blanchot, Paul Auster noted in a newspaper interview at the time, this was 'a poetic response to disaster'.[34] It could be seen as a coming (together of) community in adversity rather than a closing down of community against the invader. An inoperative community in an inoperative city? Auster's description of the response as poetic is important here, in that in an America where there is a profound sense of putting the nation to work against the latest provisional enemy (for enemies are always provisional), there exist, nonetheless, fleeting glimpses of a coming community.

32 Blanchot, 'Disorderly Words' in op. cit., n. 4, p. 205.
33 See Hill, op. cit., n. 9, pp. 217–18.
34 A. Monda, 'La città ha vinto con poesia'. Lo scrittore Paul Auster racconta' *La Repubblica*, 17 August 2003, 3.

JOURNAL OF LAW AND SOCIETY
VOLUME 31, NUMBER 1, MARCH 2004
ISSN: 0263-323X, pp. 15–37

Estopped by Grand Playsaunce: Flann O'Brien's Post-colonial Lore

JOSEPH BROOKER*

This article seeks to extend our understanding of the Irish writer Flann O'Brien (Myles na gCopaleen, Brian O'Nolan) by reading him from a Law and Literature perspective. I suggest that O'Nolan's painstaking and picky mind, with its attention to linguistic nuance, was logically drawn to the languages of law. In this he confirmed the character that he showed as a civil servant of the cautious, book-keeping Irish Free State. The Free State, like other post-colonial entities, was marked at once by a rhetoric of rupture from the colonial dispensation and by a degree of legal and political continuity. I suggest that O'Nolan's writing works away at both these aspects of the state, alternating between critical and utopian perspectives.

After establishing an initial context, I undertake a close reading of O'Nolan's parodies of actual legal procedure, focusing on questions of language and censorship. I then consider his critical work on the issue of Irish sovereignty, placing this in its post-colonial historical context. Finally I describe O'Nolan's treatment of Eamon de Valera's 1937 Constitution. I propose that his attention to textual detail prefigures in comic form the substantial rereadings of the Constitution that have been made in the last half-century.

From its first appearance in the *Irish Times* on 4 October 1940, Myles na gCopaleen's *Cruiskeen Lawn* column was one of the ways that independent and neutral Ireland talked to itself, or at least was talked at.[1] Among the column's characteristic modes was the Catechism of Cliché. The following instance leads appropriately enough into the subject of law and its representation:

* *Birkbeck College, University of London, Malet St., London WC1E 7HX, England*

1 On the column, see S. Young, 'Fact/Fiction: *Cruiskeen Lawn*, 1945–66' in *Conjuring Complexities: Essays on Flann O'Brien*, eds. A. Clune and T. Hurson (1997) 111–8; and J. Brooker, *Flann O'Brien* (2004) ch. 6.

What physical qualities have all barristers in common?
Keenness of face and hawkiness of eye.
Their arguments are –
Trenchant.
Their books?
Dusty tomes; but occasionally musty old legal tomes.
In what do they indulge?
Flights of oratory.
If they are women, what is their description?
They are Fair Portias.[2]

That is only the beginning of the text's depiction of the legal world, which sketches its outline through the fixed verbal forms associated with it. The mode is exemplary of its author's attention to the nuances of language, including its tendency to become typecast. But this particular instance of the column is also a hint at the importance that law had for its author. The oeuvre of (the columnist) Myles na gCopaleen, (the novelist) Flann O'Brien, (the civil servant) Brian O'Nolan, and their other aliases is yet to receive all the attention it merits.[3] But even what has been published on this writer – such as Sue Asbee's monograph, Keith Hopper's extended study, and the essay collection *Conjuring Complexities*[4] – has not found time to remark on the persistence of the legal in his texts. At different moments O'Nolan's work conjures alternative scenarios of law-making and law-enforcement; it ponders paradoxes raised by legal and constitutional texts; it immerses itself in the language of the law; and it reimagines the territory and sovereignty of Ireland.

This essay will seek to offer a detailed analysis of some of these moments. But it will also seek to look up from these musty old tomes, and consider the larger meaning of O'Nolan's fascination with the law. I particularly want to explore how it fits into Irish society and history – more specifically, the context of post-independence Ireland in which O'Nolan did his work, and which in some respects that work exemplified.[5] It is thus necessary to begin by considering the importance to independent Ireland of the British connection and the colonial history that had shaped the policy and character of the new state.

2 M. na Gopaleen (Flann O'Brien), *The Best of Myles*, ed. K. O'Nolan (1977) 204–5.
3 I have discussed some of the issues of identity and authorship that he raises in J. Brooker, 'Mind That Crowd: Flann O'Brien's Authors' in *New Visions: The Writer in Literature and Criticism*, eds. P. Mackay and K. Hadjiafxendi (2004). I generally refer to him as 'O'Nolan', unless the context bids otherwise.
4 See S. Asbee, *Flann O'Brien* (1991); K. Hopper, *Flann O'Brien: A Portrait of the Artist as a Young Post-modernist* (1995); A. Clune and T. Hurson (eds.), *Conjuring Complexities: Essays on Flann O'Brien* (1997).
5 See S. Deane, *Strange Country: Modernity and Nationhood in Irish Writing since 1790* (1997) 157–63. See, also, D. Kiberd, *Irish Classics* (2000) ch. 28, especially 500–1, 515–7.

RUPTURE AND CONTINUITY: POST-COLONIAL LAW AND SOCIETY IN IRELAND

Most laws are contested at one time or another, but law in colonial societies has a particularly fraught status. To the extent that the whole apparatus of the colonial state is regarded as a foreign imposition, it is an object of contention rather than consensus. The law of the colonial state needs to enforce agreement and stability; but in so far as it is viewed as the language of a contested power, that which needs to be the medium of resolving contention is itself highly contentious. Part of the mission of law is to naturalize itself: to seek legitimacy as a given rather than mere convention, and to be in principle timeless rather than a temporary convenience. Yet this legitimacy is likely to be placed in question more powerfully and insistently in a colonial setting than elsewhere. If colonial power is viewed not as benevolent reign but as illegitimate occupation, then colonial law ceases to be a solution and becomes part of the problem. Indeed, the law in such conditions may even be regarded as *illegal*.[6] In the generations preceding Irish independence, the starkest example of this phenomenon was the struggle over the ownership and tenantship of land. The policy of withholding rent and ostracizing landlords, as in the celebrated case of Captain Boycott in 1880, was a vivid example of a challenge to colonial law with mass appeal. So too was the Sinn Féin policy of unilateral autonomy from Britain, including British courts as well as Westminster.

If colonial law is in this sense a problem, post-colonial law raises different questions. In relation to the colonial regime, it is likely to be caught between the two poles of rupture and continuity. On one hand, the end of the colonial era implies a radical break, involving the many forms of culture as much as politics. In the case of the Irish Free State, a strong political emphasis was laid upon the definition of the state as separate from Britain. R.F. Foster comments that:

> what matters most about the atmosphere and mentality of twenty-six-county Ireland in the 1920s is that the dominant preoccupation of the regime was self-definition against Britain – cultural and political. Other priorities were consciously demoted.[7]

The founding text of such a policy had been Douglas Hyde's lecture 'The Necessity for De-Anglicizing Ireland' in 1892. Hyde had diagnosed Ireland as a nation of imitators, 'lost to the power of native initiative and alive only to second-hand assimilation'. He appealed instead 'against this constant running to England for our books, literature, music, games, fashions, and

---

6 In colonial Ireland a good deal of symbolic importance was accordingly invested in the Gaelic Brehon law which had been ousted by the British system. For a brief discussion, see R.H. Grimes and P.T. Horgan, *Introduction to Law in the Republic of Ireland* (1981) 17–20.

7 R.F. Foster, *Modern Ireland 1600–1972* (1989) 516.

ideas', in order that the Irish race might 'develop in future upon Irish lines': 'we must strive to cultivate everything that is most racial, most smacking of the soil, most Gaelic, most Irish'.[8] Hyde's thinking is one of the sources of the Free State's attempt to resist imported English publications via the imposition of tariffs. This protectionist strategy was promoted by Fr. R.S. Devane in 1927:

> We are at present engaged in an heroic effort to revive our national language, national customs, national values, national culture. These objects cannot be achieved without a cheap, healthy and independent native press. In the face of English competition such a press is an impossibility ... Against such propaganda of the English language and English ideas the present effort at national revival looks very much like the effort to beat back an avalanche with a sweeping brush.[9]

In a polemic like this it is made clear that mere native creativity and individual endeavour are insufficient for the preservation of national culture and character: what is required is authentically post-colonial legislation. The protectionism of independent Ireland is part of an attempt to establish the state's difference with what has gone before: a politics of discontinuity.

Yet it is simultaneously difficult to avoid the converse of this: the fact that the machinery of the post-colonial state is inherited from the former occupying power. This includes government buildings, institutions and structures, personnel – and also the law itself. As Basil Chubb comments apropos of the Irish case:

> the political legacy of the departing imperial power in the shape of traditions, habits and institutions as well as patterns and levels of public services was enormous and could not be wiped out by a treaty leading to the emergence of a new sovereign state.[10]

The point can be generalized, as Ray Ryan notes:

> A state, any state, cannot proclaim a spectral or millenarian relationship to history; it cannot enact a sudden, magical, divine intervention that would transform the existing order, which like the rebels of 1916 would forego mundane compromises and transform colonial dullness into exhilarating freedom.[11]

Chubb further elaborates on life after 1922:

> The governmental institutions, devices and practices that were adopted were those in use in the United Kingdom, the Westminster and Whitehall models. The articles in the Irish Free State Constitution that dealt with the machinery of government were 'a bold attempt to capture the essential elements of

8 D. Hyde, 'The Necessity for De-Anglicizing Ireland' in *Poetry and Ireland since 1800*, ed. M. Storey (1988) 82, 83.
9 Quoted in T. Brown, *Ireland: A Social and Cultural History 1922–1985* (1985) 70.
10 B. Chubb, *The Politics of the Irish Constitution* (1991) 10.
11 R. Ryan, 'Introduction: State and Nation: The Republic of Ireland, 1949–99' in *Writing in the Irish Republic* (2000) 4.

18

cabinet government and squeeze them into the phraseology of constitutional clauses' ... The marked tendency from the beginning to work the British system in undiluted form was confirmed when de Valera assumed office. Evidently, it could also accommodate his very different style of government. Although his Constitution, Bunreacht na hÉireann, involved a radical revision of the constitutional status of the state and its relationships with the British Crown and Commonwealth, it largely confirmed what already existed so far as the machinery of government was concerned.[12]

J.J. Lee has sought to offer a nuanced view of the question of 'the British legacy'. He points out that 'there was no single monolithic "British legacy"', and more concretely points to a raft of legislative and constitutional issues on which the question of whether Ireland was following British precedent is at best ambiguous. Thus the formation of an unarmed police force might be seen to follow the British example, while the RUC were armed as the Royal Irish Constabulary had been. And again: 'Was Mr De Valera being "un-British" in trying to persuade the Irish people to send PR "back from where it came from" in 1959, and to replace it by the existing British system?'[13]

Among the clearest British legacies in the machinery of the state was the civil service. As Chubb notes:

> the civil service which had been taken over and retained intact in 1922 was hardly affected by the crucial political change of 1932: neither in 1922 nor 1932 was there a purge of the public service or a spate of political appointments.[14]

Lee confirms that the civil service was 'the main British institutional legacy' in the 'public sphere': 'Irish public administration closely and consciously imitated the English model'.[15] These salient points may be qualified by the countervailing fact that the civil service was also a locus of de-Anglicization or Gaelicization, in that competence in the Irish language was made a prerequisite for successful candidates. This element of the new state's machinery is of particular pertinence here, as it was Brian O'Nolan's primary livelihood from 1935 to 1953. O'Nolan, like other applicants, had to pass an oral examination in Irish to attain his post: he can have had no difficulty in doing so, as he had spoken Irish since birth.[16] His years in the civil service also produced much of his most compelling work, including *At Swim-Two-Birds*, the unpublished manuscript of *The Third Policeman*, *An Béal Bocht*, and over a decade of *Cruiskeen Lawn*.

12 Chubb, op. cit., n. 10, p. 12.
13 J.J. Lee, *Ireland 1912–1985: Politics and Society* (1985) 88.
14 Chubb, op. cit., n. 10, p. 13.
15 Lee, op. cit., n. 13, p. 89.
16 See A. Cronin, *No Laughing Matter: The Life and Times of Flann O'Brien* (1989) 74. On O'Nolan's childhood knowledge of Irish, see p. 9.

NOTWITHSTANDING ANY COLLOQUIALISM: FREE STATE, CIVIL SERVANT

The precise contribution of his civil service career to O'Nolan's literary career and creative make-up has yet to be fully explicated. I shall here make three general observations about this relationship. Firstly, O'Nolan's post made it difficult for him to put his own name to texts in public. The job was a factor in prompting the confetti of pseudonyms and false identities that littered his career – though these are overdetermined, as he could undoubtedly have managed with fewer alter egos.[17] Secondly, the job gave him a proximity to the business of the state, which he found both intriguing and appalling. In a retrospective essay of 1956 he recalled that it had been his destiny 'to sit for many hours everyday in Dáil Éireann, though not as an elected statesman, and the agonies entailed are still too fresh in my memory to be recalled without emotion'.[18] Yet to regard him simply as disdainful of the machinery of legislation is to miss his fascination with government. This is a man who actually ran for the Senate in 1957; it is a pity for literary history that he never managed to follow W.B. Yeats into it.[19] O'Nolan may have been disgusted with the servants of the state, but that attitude presupposed a commitment to it. As Cronin comments,

> he did not have a problem in relation to nationalism because basically and instinctually as well as by heredity he was a nationalist, at least of sorts. He was not a Francophile or an Anglophile and his elaborate critique of Ireland was based on the rough premise that, with all its shortcomings, it was as good a place as anywhere else: as Myles na Gopaleen or otherwise he was always very quick to resent insult to his country or implications that other countries were inherently superior.[20]

The claim that 'he did not have a problem in relation to nationalism' is somewhat too simple: the qualifications 'at least of sorts' and 'with all its shortcomings' are more telling. But the general picture is valid. O'Nolan was a pugnacious defender of the value of Ireland as a well as a sarcastic critic of the nation, and only a figure as steeped in political process as he could have produced the peculiar political writing that he did.

That leads to the third point, which takes us closest to the heart of O'Nolan as a writer. The civil service suited O'Nolan because he was a pedant. As Cronin sees, his 'love of order and discipline, of clearly set-out and satisfying routines ... must have helped him' in his early years in the service. His first reports were favourable: 'Mr O'Nolan', wrote his superior John Garvin in 1937, 'is an efficient and painstaking officer [who] displays marked application to his duties'.[21] Even O'Nolan's solitary complaint

17 See Brooker, op. cit., n. 3.
18 Cronin, op. cit., n. 16, p. 65.
19 id., p. 192.
20 id., p. 52.
21 id., pp. 77–8.

20

against his employers in these early years demonstrates not his unsuitability for the post but the meticulous qualities that he brought to it. Having sat the entrance exam as Brian Ó'Nualláin, he now complained that

> During my recent absence from the office, I received two letters addressed to B. Nolan. This is not the name under which I entered the Civil Service, nor is it the English transliteration in use by my family. My own name is one of the few subjects upon which I claim to be an authority and notwithstanding any colloquialism countenanced for the sake of convenience in the Office, I would be glad if my own predilection in the matter be accepted in official correspondence in future. I also desire that my name be correctly entered in any future edition of the telephone guide or any similar circular.[22]

This is the appropriate language for a bureaucrat speaking to bureaucrats. But it is also an idiom with affinities to O'Nolan's creative work. To take just one example from *Cruiskeen Lawn*, occasioned by a controversy over a picture in the Municipal Gallery:

> Impertinent as the expression of individual opinions must be in such a situation, it is a gross outrage that this Board of the Municipal Gallery, having formed opinions desperate and dark of hue, should decide that the citizens of Ireland should not be permitted to form any opinion at all. By what authority does this bunch take custody of the community's aesthetic conscience?
>
> The members of the Corporation are elected to discharge somewhat more physical tasks, such as arranging for slum clearance and the disposal of sewerage. Here there is scope for valuable public service, a vast field of opportunity confronts the eye. Why must the members trespass in other spheres where their intellectual equipment cannot be other than inadequate?[23]

A few words here signal that this is not to be treated as an ordinary public pronouncement: 'opinions desperate and dark of hue' is an alliterative touch of purple excess, 'this bunch' is excessively colloquial. But the overriding idiom is not far from the precise and extensive language of the state, with which O'Nolan was so familiar in his other day job. The subject matter is the remit of the state's public work – 'arranging for slum clearance and the disposal of sewerage' – and its limits. O'Nolan, in the guise of Myles na gCopaleen, seeks to circumscribe excessive state intervention in civil society and cultural experience. Granting himself a legislative power – the column begins with the assertion that 'I know that many readers will look to me for an authoritative pronouncement'[24] on the issue – he bids to set rules for the limits of public bodies. The column is in part a parody of the official discourse that O'Nolan knew well; but it also simultaneously appears to be a serious judgment on a public issue. We cannot find Myles na gCopaleen either wholly inside or wholly outside the language of the bureaucrat: his writing relies heavily on what it mocks. Much of O'Nolan's writing is in this vein: particularizing, hairsplitting, obsessed with form and formula. This is a

---

22 Quoted in id., pp. 78–9.
23 na Gopaleen, op. cit., n. 2, pp. 236–7.
24 id., p. 235.

21

major part of what drew him to the discourses of law, as we shall see more clearly a little later on.

The mixture of rupture and discontinuity in post-colonial state-building leaves the new dispensation in an ambiguous position. Michael Collins's triumphant arrival at Dublin Castle is at once an emblem of radical change that would have seemed unlikely not long earlier, and a sign that the ticking business of the modern state is about to carry on in safe hands. Too timid a continuity with the past places the value of the revolution or triumph over colonial rule in doubt. The extent of constitutional continuity described by Chubb may reasonably provoke the nationalist reflection that society has stayed fundamentally the same while the post-boxes have been painted green.[25] Yet too radical a rupture threatens to damage the conception of law as a given, a system whose origins are in nature rather than in contingent decision-making. It may also risk losing the sympathy and tacit support of the citizenry if the transition involves making new legislation which is thought to be oppressive. The Irish Free State can be seen in both these lights. If the new state was cautious and unadventurous, the triumph of the Gaelic and de-Anglicizing ethos could also be an onerous force – not least for those writers and intellectuals of Brian O'Nolan's generation. 'Many intellectuals', writes Dermot Keogh, 'felt themselves ground to bits in de Valera's new Ireland'.[26] Anthony Cronin confirms this analysis in his account of the formation of O'Nolan's generational group at the UCD of the 1930s: 'it was they who were most irked by the Catholic triumphalism, the pious philistinism, the Puritan morality and the peasant or *petit bourgeois* outlook of the new state'. He adds, however, that any such dissidents were in an ambiguous position: 'in the first place they were themselves inheritors of whatever privileges were going, and in the second they found it almost impossible to break with formal Catholicism, either in belief or practice'.[27]

Brian O'Nolan was a product of this ambiguous situation, in which a rhetoric of national renewal was accompanied by the persistence of pre-revolutionary processes and institutions. The civil service itself is a good enough illustration of this process, with its Gaelic requirements and residual British structure. If O'Nolan's penchant for the pedantic created a certain continuity between his work as a civil servant and his writing, this analogy can be extended to the relationship between O'Nolan and the Free State as a whole. In Cronin's words:

> The outlook of the Government was legalistic and fanatically Catholic although it had a certain reverence for the book-keeping virtues of the Protestant business community which had continued to thrive after independence. Its greatest fear, other than the spread of godless, atheistic

---

25 For this motif see D. Kiberd, *Inventing Ireland* (1995) 265.
26 D. Keogh, *Twentieth-Century Ireland: Nation and State* (1994) 75.
27 Cronin, op. cit., n. 16, p. 48.

communism to Ireland, was deficit financing. The Free State scrupulously paid its debts and expected everybody else to pay theirs.[28]

O'Nolan was not fanatically Catholic, though he remained quietly so. It is telling that his final novel, *The Dalkey Archive* (1964), is prefaced by a cautious dedication to 'my Guardian Angel, impressing upon him that I'm only fooling and warning him to see to it that there is no misunderstanding when I go home'.[29] More significant here is the analogy that O'Nolan's career suggests with the 'book-keeping virtues' of the state. The publican and publisher John Ryan recalled O'Nolan's bitterness at the fact that he had to make two requests to the Commissioners of the Inland Revenue for a tax assessment form.[30] Declan Kiberd well captures this aspect of the writer, but also grasps the larger paradox of which it is only one half:

> O'Brien himself was in the strictest sense a Free State author, disabled by that very culture that had nurtured him, yet strangely addicted to many of its practices. He was one of those law-abiding bourgeois souls who actually paid their taxes in advance, and whose journalism was motivated by a concern that ratepayers get value for their pound; but he consorted with the city's bohemian set in bars before slipping away to catch the bus home to Blackrock. If the cultural debates of the time pitted Irish-speaking suburban inheritors of the national culture against the roaring dissidence of a Patrick Kavanagh, O'Brien found himself on the cusp between the two groups. The intellectual stasis of the civil servants was replicated in his art as surely as the formal energies of the bohemians.[31]

If O'Nolan's writing is in this sense double-sided, his satire and critique also turns on two contradictory aspects of independent Ireland which we have already noted: the language of rupture and the experience of continuity. On one hand he is a critic of overblown rhetoric and nationalist exaggeration, swift to scorn exorbitant claims on behalf of the new state. On the other hand, his work reacts against the sense of stasis and entrapment in that state, with a utopian vein of fantasy. We shall see both these tendencies at work in O'Nolan's treatment of the issue of national sovereignty. But first let us consider more directly his treatment of the Irish legal system.

AGRO AND OTHER RELIEF: THE CRUISKEEN COURTS

> Owing to (pressure) (of work) in the courts of justice, withdrawal of judges, electric heaters, bicycle-crime and other matters, the public-spirited Myles na gCopaleen Central Research Bureau has persuaded several impatient litigants to bring their differences before the Cruiskeen Court of Voluntary Jurisdiction.[32]

---

28 id., p. 47.
29 F. O'Brien, *The Dalkey Archive* (1993 [1964]) 5.
30 Cronin, op. cit., n. 16, p. 190.
31 Kiberd, op. cit., n. 5, p. 516.
32 na Gopaleen, op. cit., n. 2, p. 137.

So begins the first of Myles na gCopaleen's wartime courtroom dramas. Myles's alternative court is to handle the overspill from Ireland's crowded legal system. Unsurprisingly it produces its own kind of overspill – a surreal surfeit of jargon and rhetoric. The cases tried by the Cruiskeen Court are the most central instances of O'Nolan's imagination of the law. They allow him to probe at some issues of social import, and to create a fantastic version of Irish legal proceedings. More immediately and self-evidently, though, they demonstrate the appeal that the languages of law had to his mind, attracted as it was to elaborate phraseologies and verbal formulas:

> In the first case the plaintiffs sought a plenary injunction for trespass, a declaration of fief in agro and other relief. The defence was a traverse of the field as well as the pleadings and alternatively it was contended that the plaintiffs were estopped by grand playsaunce.
>
> Mr Juteclaw, for the defendants, said that at the outset he wished to enter four caveats *in feodo*. His statutory declarations were registered that morning and would be available to the plaintiffs on payment of the usual stamp duty. He asked for a dismiss.[33]

One can almost see O'Nolan chuckling behind his clacking typewriter. Myles does not do much to the legal language here: he just accumulates it for its own sake. The Latinate idiom gains a certain autonomy, a condition of pure linguistic exuberance: simply in marshalling technical terms the writer indulges his attraction to the recondite word ('estopped', 'playsaunce') and savours the queerness of the official idiom. Elsewhere, though, Myles intervenes more noticeably in the language of the court.

Thus, when the prosecuting counsel, Mr Juteclaw, protests that his client's loss of two fingers while at school 'had reacted somewhat against his client's ability as a wage-earner in later life', the judge protests:

> His Honour: Re-acted, Mr Juteclaw? Come now. Surely the word we seek here is 'militated'?
> Mr Juteclaw: I accept your Honour's correction.[34]

At the close of this case, the successful counsel for the defence asks for a clarification:

> Mr Faix, thanking his honour, asked for guidance as to the meaning of the phrase 'the parties to pay their own costs'.
> His Honour: It means what it says.
> Mr Faix: In a lifetime at the bar I have never heard the phrase. I have frequently heard the phrase 'abide their own costs'. I respectfully ask for guidance.[35]

Elsewhere, in a column detailing the dealings of the District Court, a defendant confesses to the linguistic grounds that lie beyond his failure to abscond:

33 id., p. 137.
34 id., p. 139.
35 id., p. 140.

24

If I had failed to appear in this court at the time appointed, too well I knew that my bail would not be *confiscated*. Neither would it be *impounded*. (Here defendant became moved.) Neither would it be *declared forfeit* – or even *forfeited*. It would not be *attached*. It would be ... (Here defendant broke down and began to weep.) ... My bail would be ... ESTREATED.[36]

The work done upon language in these examples is more flagrantly evident in the following incident. When the counsel for the defence leaves the court in protest, he soon returns:

Mr Juteclaw re-appeared and said he wished to apologise for a serious solecism he had unwittingly committed. When felt compelled by the dictates of honour to quit the court, he had merely lifted his papers and left. As a lawyer of long standing, he knew that the correct and accepted thing was to *gather up* his papers and withdraw. He then renewed his apologies, gathered up his papers, and withdrew.[37]

This stages as solemn farce one of Myles na gCopaleen's most insistent concerns: the role of cliché in public discourse. The presiding judge, Twinfeet J., is apt to correct the lawyers, not on what might be thought substantive moral grounds, but on purely idiomatic points. The gravest error that a counsel can make in the Cruiskeen Court is a linguistic one. The clichéd terms are less often legal language proper than those which have become the standard form in court reports. Mr Faix is unable to understand the meaning of 'pay their own costs', so used is he to the formula 'abide their own costs'. More drastically, Juteclaw's failure to *gather* his papers and *withdraw*, rather than lifting them and going, is recognized as a 'serious solecism'. In this case not only the form of words is wrong: the same action must be repeated under the correct name. The idiom in which the courts have been shrouded thus not merely dictates the thoughts of the legal representatives, but scripts their physical actions and movements too.

The tracking of such prescripted language and ready-made phrases was a major dimension of *Cruiskeen Lawn*. Myles uses a number of methods to expose the presence of such discourse, of which we have already glimpsed the most extensive: the Myles na gCopaleen Catechism of Cliché.[38] The catechism is characteristic of O'Nolan, in its rationalistic pursuit of the logic of something that does not deserve to be treated so logically. The most banal locutions Myles can find are solemnly treated not as isolated infelicities but as a connected system; an alternative intellectual world becomes founded on error or poverty of imagination. Crucially, all its materials are recognizable – more than that, are overly recognizable, are precisely the kind of sentences one is most likely to employ should one pluck up the self-importance to write to the *Irish Times*. The unhappy joke of the Catechism of Cliché is not

36 id., p. 153.
37 id., p. 138.
38 I have discussed the catechism, and other methods by which Myles pursues cliché in the column, in Brooker, op. cit., n. 1, ch. 6.

25

so much that we can imagine a world like this, as that this is our world, day in day out.

There are two sides to the catechism. It revels in repetition, and attacks it. Certainly the clichés are savoured even as they are criticized. Yet the note of disdain for them is persistent. This can be visceral: 'This murder of my beloved English language is getting in under my nails'.[39] The catechism is also described as:

> [a] unique compendium of all that is nauseating in contemporary writing. Compiled without regard to expense or the feelings of the public. A harrowing survey of sub-literature and all that is pseudo, mal-dicted and calloused in the underworld of print.[40]

Elsewhere, with what looks a rare degree of unqualified seriousness, Myles reasons that '[a] cliché is a phrase that has become fossilised, its component words deprived of their intrinsic light and meaning by incessant usage'.[41] What is striking in the present context is that the clichés of the Cruiskeen Court are *not* treated in this manner. The note of joy in the ravelling of discursive stereotypes is present; the note of exasperation is absent. It is as though Myles grants the law its right to cliché: as though it goes without saying that the law is a matter of cliché. It relies, after all, on precedents, rules, formulas; it aims to be consistent rather than creative. The clichés of the courtroom do not suggest a degraded tongue but a social ritual. Law thus escapes Mylesian censure, but at the cost of being rendered as performance. In particular, Myles's columns emphasize the discursive channels through which legal activity runs, the persistence of the letter in the legal. Peter Goodrich writes that:

> Law is a literature which denies its literary qualities. It is a play of words which asserts an absolute seriousness; it is a genre of rhetoric which represses its moments of invention or of fiction; it is a language which hides its indeterminacy in the justificatory discourse of judgment; it is procedure based on analogy, metaphor and repetition and yet it lays claim to being a cold or disembodied prose.[42]

Cruiskeen Lawn itself, we might add, was a literature whose literary status was never clear.[43] But in its treatment of the courtroom it can be seen to insist on that literary and rhetorical quality in the law to which Goodrich points. We shall see later that a similar insistence on the letter of the law underpins Myles's approach to the Constitution.

Language can also be at stake in a more specific sense. As well as recalling the counsel to their proper clichés, Twinfeet J. also seeks to hold the line against their foreign-sounding 'jargon': 'Justice is a simple little lady

---

39 na Gopaleen, op. cit., n. 2, p. 207.
40 id., p. 202.
41 id., p. 227.
42 P. Goodrich, *Law in the Courts of Love: Literature and other Minor Jurisprudences* (1996) 112.
43 See Young, op. cit., n. 1, pp. 117–18.

26

... not to be overmuch besmeared with base Latinities'.[44] Twinfeet is not easy to pin down. He may suddenly break into Hiberno-English:

> Twinfeet J., mounting the bench, remarked that 'That was a hardy one'.
> Mr Faix, speaking on behalf of the Dublin Bar, agreed that the day was cold.
> His Lordship: how did ye all get over the Christmas.
> Mr Faix: Er – suitably, my Lord.
> His Lordship: Do you know what it is, there is a lot of bad stuff going around.
> If ever one of the criminals responsible is brought before me, I warrant you
> that I will make an appalling example of him. But pray let us to business.[45]

Like much of Myles na gCopaleen's output, this turns on a collision of idioms, whose most sustained form is the series of columns recounting the schemes of 'the Brother'. There is some glee in the depiction of a presiding judge whose discourse belongs not to the accredited profession but to the Dublin working class. Mr Faix is evidently disconcerted. Equally disconcerting is Twinfeet's lurch back into respectable speech within a couple of sentences, as though he has switched on the translation device that will produce the idiom appropriate to this arena. We may read this as a further confirmation of the artificiality of legal discourse posited by Goodrich. Yet one odd feature remains in the language of the court: the predominance of English. Twinfeet J. declares at one point that:

> indecencies are ... possible in the sphere of Saxon grammar. One must not
> mate our gentle tongue with Negroid importations from regions barbarous of
> character, of situation transalpine.[46]

The 'gentle tongue' here is English. What, we might wonder, has happened to the nation's proclaimed first language, Irish?

It is possible to see it making a disguised return elsewhere, in a District Court report. An elderly man who gives his name as Myles na gCopaleen is 'charged with begging, disorderly conduct, using bad language and with being in illegal possession of an arm-chair'.[47] He claims to be a 'republican soldier', who was 'holding a political meeting in Capel Street when he was savagely assaulted by the Sergeant'; later, 'in the course of a long address', he calls himself 'a Southern Irishman' who cannot accept the suggestion that he should reside in Belfast, 'a steel iron town of aspect unendearing of populace contumacious'.[48] The bulk of his statements are incomprehensible to the court: as the Sergeant guarding him complains, he is 'continually conversing in this strain, leaving us all as wise as if he were speaking double dutch'.[49] The reason that they are in Latin. The irony is that we might expect such a character's linguistic defiance to consist of speaking Irish.

---

44 na Gopaleen, op. cit., n. 2, p. 137.
45 id., pp. 142–3.
46 id., p. 141.
47 id., p. 148.
48 id., p. 152.
49 id.

27

A real-life precedent is offered by *Attorney-General* v. *Joyce and Walsh* (1929), a murder trial in which:

> nine prosecution witnesses and both of the accused gave their evidence in the Irish language, which was interpreted, for the benefit of the judge, the jury and others concerned in the case by an official interpreter provided by the State, whose version of the evidence, in English, was taken down by the official stenographers and formed the record of the witnesses' and the accused's evidence.[50]

The work of the law thus involves an act of translation. Kennedy CJ noted that any witness should be 'allowed to give evidence in the language which is his or her vernacular language, whether that language be English or Irish, or any foreign language'.[51] But he also noted that Irish was a special case:

> The Irish language, however, is not merely the vernacular language of most, if not all, of the witnesses in question in the present case, but it holds a special position by virtue of the Constitution of the Saorstat, in which its status is recognised and established as the national language of the Saorstat, from which it follows that, whether it be the vernacular language of a particular citizen or not, if he is competent to use the language he is entitled to do so. Therefore it may be said that all those who gave their evidence in the Irish language in the present case had, as it were, a double right to do so: first, on general principles of justice as their vernacular language; and, secondly, as a matter of constitutional right.[52]

The 'double right' that the judge seeks to define is not exercised in the District Court. The 'republican soldier' frustrates the court by speaking not in his native tongue but in a foreign one too obscure for most of his listeners. He thus becomes, in part, a strange rewrite of a figure of whom James Joyce had written in an essay of 1907, 'Ireland at the Bar'. This 'bewildered old man ... a deaf-mute before his judge', unable to understand English, had been tried and sentenced to death through an interpreter. Joyce read him as an emblem of Ireland's plight in the face of an uncomprehending world.[53] The old man's name was, of all things, Myles Joyce.

The parallels between the two cases are inexact; the Myles who appears in the *Cruiskeen Lawn* scenario is able to speak English when he chooses, and indeed moves in and out of Hiberno-English ('Yez are all leppin' because I didn't skip'[54]). But the comparison points up the oddity of O'Nolan's figure, in whom Latin has come to take the place of Irish. The dead language subtly works as a ghost of the native tongue. The effect is incongruous, as the scene plays itself out in a queerly different yet parallel way from how it might have proceeded in the era of Joyce's essay. The defendant exercising what in

50 *Attorney-General* v. *Joyce and Walsh* [1929] I.R. 526, reprinted in *Irish Cases on Evidence*, ed. J.S.R. Cole (1972) 126.
51 id.
52 id., p. 127.
53 J. Joyce, *Occasional, Critical, and Political Writing*, ed. K. Barry (2000) 144–5.
54 na Gopaleen, op. cit., n. 2, p. 151.

independent Ireland has become his 'double right' (Kennedy CJ) is replaced by the author-surrogate, exercising his right to an erudition that will frustrate the Irish court just as an Irish speaker would once have frustrated its colonial predecessor. The old republican who refuses to speak English and does not retreat into Irish either may indeed be seen as making what the Sergeant calls 'a farce of the language movement'.[55]

One final case deserves attention for its direct pertinence to the law and policy of the Free State. Here a shopkeeper, 'a member of the Gaelic League, a fluent speaker of Irish and a graduate of Cardinal Newman's university', is tried 'for "exposing" for sale a book which, while not indecent, was in its general tendency indecent'.[56] The establishment of literary censorship at the start of the 1930s was a major piece of 'Gaelicizing' and Catholic legislation. The Censorship Board would become a major component of the draconian public policy of the state for decades to come.[57] Myles's column is thus not teasing at a minor or marginal matter. The mockery takes two main forms. One is an amused indictment of the judge's hypocrisy. 'Gentlemen', he asks the court, 'is this book you have there any good? I mean, is it . . . very bad? Is it disgusting, I mean?'. Mr Lax, prosecuting counsel, informs him that it is 'filthy', then admits that he has not read it: 'I would not soil my eyes with such nefarious trash, my Lord'.[58] Lax embodies the paradoxical position of the Censorship Board and its supporters: in order to condemn a book it might be necessary to read it, but to read it was to lay oneself open to its corruptive influence. The Catholic commentator, Shane Leslie, writing on *Ulysses* in the *Dublin Review* in 1922, had found an ingeniously simple way around this crux, assuring his readers that Joyce's book 'may safely be repudiated, before reading, by the Irish people'.[59]

Twinfeet J's position is slightly different. His solicitous inquiries as to whether the book is 'any good', which is to say 'very bad', prime us for his subsequent retreat to his chamber for one hour to read the book in private. This echoes another incident in which he insists on taking a plaintiff's landlady to his chamber for questioning overnight.[60] The broad joke is that the masters of suppression are the most given to temptation: the censor secretly relishes the material he denounces. But a more surprising twist awaits when Twinfeet returns with the book. It purports to be a copy of *Madame Bovary*, whose cover image of its heroine 'not dressed for the street', but 'withal attired', Twinfeet judges acceptable. The book's contents are thus incongruous:

55 id., p. 148.
56 id., p. 141.
57 See M. Adams, *Censorship: The Irish Experience* (1968), and J. Carlson (ed.), *Banned In Ireland: Censorship and the Irish Writer* (1990).
58 na Gopaleen, op. cit., n. 2, p. 142.
59 S. Leslie, '*Ulysses*' in the *Dublin Review*, clxxi (September 1922) 112–9; reprinted in *James Joyce: The Critical Heritage*, ed. R.H. Deming (1997) 201.
60 na Gopaleen, op. cit., n. 2, p. 144.

29

The tone throughout is elevated, urbane, even technical. It appears to be 'An Outline of Irish Grammar' and is the work of the Irish Christian Brothers. The work bears no obvious relation to the illustration I have mentioned. The case must be dismissed with costs.[61]

How we should read this is not quite self-evident. A possible interpretation is that the judge has substituted the Irish Grammar into the covers of the book and kept Flaubert's novel for himself. But perhaps the correct interpretation is that the joke is a piece of inversion. The pious shopkeeper has been reading a book by the Christian Brothers, and has been so ashamed of this that he has felt the need to disguise it as *Madame Bovary*. One is reminded of the joke in which a teenage boy is too ashamed to ask for a Crystal Palace shirt and ends up with something that was less embarrassing to request at the counter, a packet of condoms. It is not Flaubert, but the tastes of the Gaelic Leaguer and language revivalist, that are really obscene.

'TO LEAVE THE SO-CALLED EMPIRE': SOVEREIGNTY AND BEYOND

The question of national sovereignty was among the most central and most vexed in political, legal, and cultural debates in independent Ireland. At a commemoration of the Easter Rising in 1933, the new Taoiseach, Eamon de Valera, publicly placed the term at the centre of his political and constitutional strategy:

> Let it be made clear that we yield no willing assent to any form or symbol that is out of keeping with Ireland's right as a sovereign nation. Let us remove these forms one by one, so that this state we control may become a Republic in fact; and that, when the time comes, the proclaiming of the Republic may involve no more than a ceremony, the formal confirmation of a status already attained.[62]

If that de facto Republic was by definition to cover the whole territory of Ireland, then this was wishful thinking on de Valera's part. Indeed, he himself knew as well as most nationalist leaders the intractability of the Northern question.[63] The 1937 Constitution itself would include a claim to the whole national territory which was, however, no sooner staked than deferred.[64] It was owing to the nuances of territorial aspiration that de Valera's 1937 text did not, in fact, define Ireland as a Republic. Instead, Article 5 defined Ireland as 'a sovereign, independent, democratic state'. Personally presenting the new document to the Irish population in a radio

61 id., p. 142.
62 Eamon de Valera, quoted in R. Fanning, 'Mr de Valera Drafts a Constitution' in *De Valera's Constitution and Ours*, ed. B. Farrell (1988) 34–5.
63 See Chubb, op. cit., n. 10, pp. 22–6.
64 See P. Hanafin, 'Legal Texts as Cultural Documents: Interpreting the Irish Constitution' in Ryan, op. cit., n. 11, pp. 159–61.

broadcast, de Valera assured his listeners that 'sovereignty resides in them the people as their inalienable and indefeasible right'.[65]

The word 'sovereign' itself had an added potency in relation to the Ireland in which Brian O'Nolan grew up: it would have referred most immediately to money, and by symbolic extension to the British monarch. Ireland's relation to the Crown was of course pivotal in the arguments which attended the birth of the Free State: the anti-Treaty side were more vocally offended by the prospect of an oath of allegiance to the King than by the partitioning of Ireland. As R.F. Foster puts it, the Irish conceived sovereignty and allegiance to be the 'real' questions, and 'the position of the Crown in Irish affairs remained the crux'.[66] Vital to Ireland in the years after independence, then, was to establish its own sovereign character: to demonstrate that the new state, which hardline republicans had called so meagre, indeed possessed an independent status and identity. In that sense the intensity of official enthusiasm for Gaelicization may be interpreted as a result of the Civil War.

I have suggested that O'Nolan was an emblematic figure for the Free State: but despite his own idiosyncratic love for the Irish language, this does not apply to the Gaelicizing tendency. In his own way, O'Nolan was one of the period's most penetrating critics of Irish pride. I have analysed elsewhere the way that he chisels away at the nation's inflated account of itself in some of his earliest work – specifically an article in the magazine *Blather* which he produced with friends in 1934 and 1935.[67] The jest here is that the agitation for:

> proper Atlantic ports at Galway, Killybegs and elsewhere, has in no small measure displeased *Blather*. Why? The reason is very simple. The pre-eminent claims of Bettystown have been passed over, and it is the sheerest folly on the part of those concerned to imagine that *Blather* is going to stand for it.[68]

The magazine's pursuit of Bettystown's strategic potential rebounds on those places whose nautical claims really were being exalted at a time when, as Joseph Lee bluntly notes, 'For practical purposes, Ireland had neither an air force nor a navy'.[69] *Blather*'s comedy hints that Ireland's proud strides towards securing its sovereignty are equivalent to the vital task of developing Bettystown harbour. The piece is thus an act of comic belittling, which undercuts the rhetoric of sovereignty with the reality of political continuity and material limitation.

Yet we can see a countervailing impulse elsewhere, in the conveniently direct form of alternative nautical fantasies. In the *Blather* of January 1935,

---

65 Quoted in Chubb, op. cit., n. 10, p. 22.
66 Foster, op. cit., n. 7, p. 505.
67 See J. Brooker, 'Children of Destiny: Brian O'Nolan and the Irish Ready-Made School' (2004) 2 *Precursors and Aftermaths*.
68 'Whither Bettystown? Progress or Decay? Our Stern Attitude' *Blather*, October 1934, reprinted in *Myles Before Myles*, ed. J. Wyse Jackson (1988) 106.
69 Lee, op. cit., n. 13, p. 236.

three months after the plea for Bettystown, O'Nolan, under the guise of the magazine's proprietor, the O'Blather, proposes the fancy that Ireland should be sawn off from its moorings and allowed to float. To counter the risk that it should 'edge over to England on a dark night and be anchored to her for the rest of time, like Wales', the Shannon would be diverted to the back of the country so as to propel it forward. The whole nation, the O'Blather proposes, can now go abroad for the winter: languish in the Mediterranean, grow tropical fruits, bait arctic bears and Russian wolves. 'We can give the British hell', he concludes, 'as often as we feel like it by steaming past her coast and ruining the country with gigantic tidal waves. The possibilities are endless'.[70]

This was not the last time that O'Nolan would exploit this conceit. In a *Cruiskeen Lawn* column of July 1945, he offers a lengthy reworking. The piece begins in politico-legalistic vein, punningly offering 'posed war plans for the land of May had option', in the light of the fact that:

> Readers will be aware of the constitutional position. We are in the Empire but not Ovid. Distinguished British statesmen resident in Co. Belfast have seen fit to make discourteous references to your republic, even suggesting that it would be no harm if you packed up and clear doubt! I ... I wonder would Mister Churchill really like it that way?[71]

What is most striking about this is its anticipation of Ireland's actual departure from the Commonwealth four years later. It was Mister Attlee, not Mister Churchill, who in the House of Commons in November 1948 would have cause to express regret at Ireland's repeal of the External Relations Act.[72]

Yet the post-war establishment of the Republic, the result of a piqued decision by Taoiseach John Costello while on an official visit to Canada, was a scuffling, haphazard business, as Ray Ryan notes: 'There were no ringing declarations of the nation's geography, history or identity, no mention of the people, no heroic acts of defiance, parades, speeches or flags'.[73] Myles na gCopaleen's imagined republic is different:

> Suppose ... suppose I were to tell you that I have devised a system of ... land migration, a system based on liquefaction and pumping such as would enable the sovereign republican government of your Ireland to ... literally to run the country, have it go and come as they please? Suppose you were, early one morning, to leave the so-called Empire in the most devastatingly literal sense, simply disappear bag and baggage? Wouldn't the British be just a little bit sorry? Know for the first time what you so patiently put up with from the Atlantic Ocean?[74]

70 'Balm for Ireland's Ills' *Blather*, January 1935, reprinted in Jackson, op. cit., n. 68, pp. 150–2.
71 M. na gCopaleen, *Cruiskeen Lawn*, 28 July 1945, reprinted in F. O'Brien, *At War*, ed. J. Wyse Jackson (1999) 166.
72 See Chubb, op. cit., n. 10, p. 15.
73 Ryan, 'Introduction', op. cit., n. 11, p. 1.
74 O'Brien, op. cit., n. 71, p. 167. Ellipses in original.

Ireland, it seems, can be moved. When Myles writes of the possibility of leaving the Empire 'in the most devastatingly literal sense', he puts a finger on a major source of his own comedy, which so often relies on the literalization of the figurative. Here the notion of 'leaving the Empire' is made concrete. The result propels Ireland away from the mutually paralysing circuit of Anglo-Irish relations, into a broader orbit: 'And where to go? Well, *there* is one idea. Set up house in the middle of the mild blue Mediterranean, become hot Latin persons'. At this point Myles provides a hand-drawn map, showing Ireland in its new southern location. The colonial relation – and the enduring post-colonial relation – of British economic and cultural superiority is suddenly transformed:

> Observe, reader, the bare forsaken aspect of England and Scotland on that map. Do they want it that way? Do they *really* want to traverse the Bay of Biscay and squeeze in through the tortuous portals of Gibraltar just to have a steak in Dublin? Do they seek a situation wherein a visit to Ireland even for the purpose of collecting debts involves an expensive ocean voyage? I doubt it very much. And let me add that if your somewhat severe governors think that there is much to be said against the South of France as a latitude unsuitable for your Ireland, why – [He provides another map, showing Ireland zig-zagging across the North and South Atlantic.] – there are other places. What's wrong with being anchored off New York harbour? Would not that substantially reduce the expenses of emigration? *And* if that ultimately bores, there are, as I have shown on my map, other places. (And still others – I understand that the climate is very temperate around Japan?)[75]

Sovereignty is redefined here, not as territorial integrity but as the capacity for spatial mobility. The reference to New York harbour points to the already-existing mobility of the Irish, as a diasporic nation that might not be defined merely by its location on the map. In this sense Myles's fantasy anticipates the alternative sense of space and place more recently proffered by Fintan O'Toole, when he notes that diasporic history has already meant a premature encounter with the challenges of modernity:

> What is history for the New York Irish is news for the Irish Irish, balanced, in a global society, between the ins and outs, the victims and the victimisers. There is a sense of moving back to the future, of the newest and most astonishing changes – mass media, virtual reality, the fusion of cultures – being a repetition of what is, in the history of emigrants, old hat. There is also a sense that what is most alien, most foreign, is also a kind of homecoming.[76]

Myles na gCopaleen's scheme to set Ireland into physical motion makes literal some of what O'Toole would consider as 'astonishing changes' fifty years later.

These two articles from O'Nolan, over ten years apart, play upon the same fantasy. What both offer is, in a sense, the opposite of satire. It is a utopian gesture – literally so, in the elastic or fluid sense of space and place that it

---

75 id., pp. 167–8.
76 F. O'Toole, *The Lie of the Land* (1997) 165.

involves which seeks to set Ireland free from the actual limits of the Free State, and propel it into a more fantastic realm of possibility.[77] Where the campaign for Bettystown turns on the smallness of Irish concerns, the O'Blather's plan and Myles's proposal seek to enlarge them, in an imaginative movement that would set Ireland in motion. They thus try to laugh their way beyond mere political continuity, into a rupture more generously conceived than that of the Gaeligores. If in the first piece sovereignty is shown to be a petty affair, in the other two it is given impossibly dynamic reality.

'THE IRISH VERSION PREVAILS': REREADING THE CONSTITUTION

In a later column, Myles na Gopaleen turns his attention more directly to the language of the state. We have already observed his declared aversion to official political discourse. But this distaste could express itself as forensic analysis:

> I regret to announce that the Constitution, your ultimate and fundamental statement of your Irish identity and destiny, is an unconscionably careless document. Some of the English is bad and most of the Irish is disgracefully bad. More, the two languages frequently express dissimilar and mutually repugnant meanings in stating what purports to be the same Article.[78]

It needs to be emphasized how significant a target the Constitution was. A national constitution, notes Chubb, is customarily 'the fundamental law of the land' and also 'a kind of higher law'.[79] Yet as McWhinney, cited by Chubb, emphasizes, the constitution of a democracy must also at least claim to be rooted in actual life and common social practice:

> A normative constitution is not only valid in a legal sense, but it must be faithfully observed by all and have integrated itself into the state society: ... its norms govern the political process; or the power process adjusts itself to the norms ... the constitution is like a suit that fits and is actually worn.[80]

Basil Chubb declares that de Valera's Constitution 'quickly became and remains a "normative" constitution'[81] in precisely this sense. To the extent that the text did reflect the unusually homogeneous religious and social views of the twenty-six-county state, Chubb is justified in viewing the law as

---

77 Perhaps what is most fantastic about the *Cruiskeen Lawn* diagrams is that the whole island of Ireland becomes mobile: there seems to be no Unionist veto over the scheme.

78 F. O'Brien (Myles na Gopaleen), *Further Cuttngs from Cruiskeen Lawn* (1988) 137.

79 Quoted in Chubb, op. cit., n. 10, p. 1.

80 E.M. McWhinney, *Constiution-making: Principles, Process, Practice* (1981) 7, quoted in id., p. 2.

81 Chubb, id., p. 30.

consensual. But his judgement is too complacent. The issue of gender is the most glaring site of discontent and contestation. Yvonne Scannell, while boldly proposing that the Constitution as reinterpreted in subsequent decades can actually 'advance the cause of women's rights', still confesses that the Constitution was 'rooted in a patronising and stereotypical view of womanhood'.[82] More recently, Patrick Hanafin has been more severely critical of the framers of the original Constitution, arguing that:

> the value placed in women in postcolonial society lies almost completely in their reproductive function. Woman's social role as mother is cherished more than any notion of individual female autonomy. A woman's value, as constitutionally predicated, lay only in what she could contribute to the greater good by her role as mother ... [The Constitution's provisions in Article 41.2] represent an outmoded and patriarchal view of societal organization.[83]

These feminist perspectives are not what power Myles na gCopaleen's treatment of the Constitution. O'Nolan was in some respects a conservative thinker, nervous of novelty and swift to scorn progressive schemes; and this is nowhere more evident than in his treatment of the claims of feminism.[84] Indeed, on this issue there is some basis for viewing Eamon de Valera himself as a more progressive figure. The Taoiseach had at least had the grace to acclaim Constance Markiewicz as 'colleague and comrade', and as the 'soldier of Ireland' the world knew, upon her death in 1927.[85] Myles's contribution to the debate over the Constitution is different: a matter less of content than of form, less of positive political and legal proposals than of textual insubordination.

He picks on the example of the age limit for the Presidency of Ireland. 'People think', he writes, 'that one must be at least thirty-five years old, a figure apparently arrived at by an arbitrary bisection of the Biblical three score and ten'. He then looks at the text of the Article. In English, it reads, 'Every citizen who has reached his thirty-fifth year of age is eligible for election to the office of President'. Myles responds:

> Consider the utter carelessness of that term 'reached'. First, it can be argued that the absence of the complementary term 'or passes' restricts candidature in the case of any individual to one year. Secondly, the word 'reached' establishes clearly that one need not be thirty-five but merely thirty-four! When one has reached one's thirty-fourth birthday, one has then reached one's thirty-fifth year. Was this then what the authors of the Constitution intended? Let us turn (puts on second pair of glasses over first) let us turn for enlightenment to the Irish version.[86]

---

82 Y. Scannell, 'The Constitution and the Role of Women' in Farrell, op. cit., n. 62, p. 134.
83 Hanafin, op. cit., n. 64, p. 158.
84 See, for instance, O'Brien, op. cit., n. 78, pp. 99–103.
85 See C. Markiewicz, *Prison Letters of Countess Markiewicz* (1987) 118–9.
86 O'Brien, op. cit., n. 78, p. 137.

Myles gives a literal translation of the Irish version – which he finds 'colossally inelegant' – as 'Every citizen who has completed thirty-five years, he is electable to the office of President'. 'Thus, you see', he concludes,

> you must have concluded your thirty-fifth year – reached your thirty-fifth birthday – to be eligible according to the Irish version. According to the English form of the Article first cited, you are game ball at thirty-four! The Irish version prevails. The English version of the Article, which is the only one many people can read, is false and repugnant to the Constitution![87]

This is a characteristic comedy of pedantry. A line has been isolated, a small point magnified. But the little joke hints at larger issues. Myles's starting point is what 'people think' – the everyday assumption which the law underwrites at the same time as it draws authority from it. Yet the discovery he flaunts is that this assumption is in conflict with the law. He points to a problem of legitimacy, identifying a discrepancy between law and life. In this sense the 'normative' quality of the Constitution, its successful integration with social practice, is minutely but pointedly eroded. And this discrepancy arises on a matter central to questions of political authority in a country which has escaped the oath to the British Crown: the means by which the head of state is selected.

The law, let alone not squaring with actual practice, does not even agree with itself. The post-colonial Constitution is bilingual: but the two languages, according to Myles's wilfully problematizing exegesis, are in conflict. The law concerning the head of state is fractured along the most broadly symbolic line imaginable: the language which the new state has promoted as its true tongue, and the one left over – left everywhere – by the old dispensation. Article 8 of the Constitution declares that the Irish language is 'the national language' and 'the first official language'; English is 'recognised as a second official language'. Should the two texts of the law conflict, 'the text in the national language shall prevail'.[88] 'The Irish version prevails', Myles thus notes in a line whose brisk rendition of official dogma is perhaps his article's comic peak. Yet if this seems to end the legal stand-off, it raises problems of its own. For one thing, as he notes, most people are unable to read this version, authoritative though it may be. For another, in a final irony, he reports that the Irish version is atrociously written anyway. The implication is that the self-appointed custodians of the language are the last people who should be trusted with it. However the crux is resolved, it seems, the law is flawed.

Norton writes that constitutional documents should not be confused with constitutions themselves, but 'can more appropriately be considered as a form in which the constitution is expressed rather than as a definition of the term itself'.[89] This view, notes Chubb, is convenient for the British with their

---

87 id., p. 138.
88 Quoted in Chubb, op. cit., n. 10, p. 30.
89 Quoted in id., p. 2.

36

lack of a written constitution.[90] Arguably it seeks to remove constitutions from textual expression. But this is the manoeuvre against which Myles na gCopaleen is working. His critique of the constitution is precisely a reading, which presupposes that the constitution will necessarily take textual form. Myles's pedantry is in a sense a materialism, refusing the consolations of a disembodied constitution beyond textual debate and criticism.

In this respect – in its tenacious determination to read and problematize the constitutional text – it is a comic forerunner of the very serious interpretations of the Constitution that have taken place over the last half-century. As Brian Farrell notes:

> de Valera had built in the mechanism for change in the provisions for formal amendment and for judicial review. He could scarcely have envisaged how adventurously Irish courts might come to relish that role. ... In fact, it is mainly through judicial review that de Valera's document is becoming our Constitution. It is not just a historical description of the institutions of government as established but a living organism that can grow to protect the lives, liberties and interests of citizens through changing times.[91]

Whether the Irish Constitution has actually done this to an adequate extent, in Irish times that have changed significantly even since Farrell's essay was published, one may doubt. But as Hanafin indicates, it is through reinterpretation that:

> the Constitution of national identity has been read otherwise as an opening to the other, to difference, and as an instance of the nation to come ... The Gaelic Romantic tradition of the constitution has now become the 'minor literature' of the Irish constitutional space. The dominant discourse has now been identified as the Irish Enlightenment tradition ... The Constitution now stands, ironically, as a site of resistance to that ethos upon which it was founded.[92]

In this sense the process of rereading may also imply a tacit process of rewriting. And Brian O'Nolan, as one of modern Ireland's most dogged readers, may be enlisted to this story. Simultaneously state employee and critic of national development, O'Nolan produced an idiosyncratic immanent critique of independent Ireland. His fascination with formula, his pedantic, painstaking approach to the languages of law, comprise an element of that work with which we have not hitherto made a reckoning. It was not only in conjuring a trinity of impossible policemen that Brian O'Nolan set his imagination to work on Ireland's law.

90 id., p. 30.
91 Farrell, op. cit., n. 62, p. 204.
92 Hanafin, op. cit., n. 64, p. 162.

JOURNAL OF LAW AND SOCIETY
VOLUME 31, NUMBER 1, MARCH 2004
ISSN: 0263-323X, pp. 38-59

'Tell All the Truth, but Tell it Slant':
A Poetics of Truth and Reconciliation

ADAM GEAREY*

There is a voice that tries to speak the truth. This essay will suggest that the discourse on the South African Truth and Reconciliation Commission [TRC] has perhaps ignored this most invisible of things, and has looked for the truth of the Commission everywhere except where it might be found, if indeed it can be found at all. To the extent that it is possible to oppose the truth of the voice to another truth, it may be useful to make use of a notion of poetics; even a sublime poetics.

INTRODUCTION

> The Truth must dazzle gradually
> Or every man be blind –[1]

But how can we speak of truth and reconciliation? Can there ever be a correct register?

The first problem: how could an aesthetics of truth and reconciliation come about in South Africa? There is a certain risk with this thesis, as it imposes a categorization on a kind of scholarship that is eclectic and mercurial. Perhaps it is wrong to isolate one of its elements, a certain

* *School of Law, Birkbeck College, University of London, Malet Street, London WC1E 7HX, England*

The author wishes to gratefully acknowledge grants from the Central Funds of the University of London and Birkbeck College that enabled a study visit to South Africa in the summer of 2003. Also, thanks to the Faculties of Law at the University of Pretoria, University of South Africa, Rand Afrikaans University, and the University of the Western Cape for making me most welcome. The hospitality and intellectual engagement of Karin van Marle, Johan Van der Walt, Wessel Le Roux, Dani Brandt, Dirk Hanekom, Thepo Madlingozi, and Duard Klein must also be celebrated in print! A version of this paper was delivered at the Critical Legal Conference, Rand Afrikaans University, Johannesburg, South Africa, September 2003.

1 Emily Dickinson, alluded to by Archbishop Desmond Tutu in the foreword to TRC, *'Truth and Reconciliation Committee of South Africa Report* (1998).

aesthetic leaning, and to see this as its predominant mode of argumentation. Whilst accepting this problem, it is still possible to maintain that an aesthetics does run through certain responses to truth and reconciliation, and does at least allow one to see correspondences between the work of different scholars. It may be helpful, therefore, to sketch a putative genealogy that links South African work with the developing body of aesthetic jurisprudence. In doing so we will also have to account for the metamorphosis of the field, and describe the distinctive use of poetics and aesthetics by South African scholars. In taking this novel turn, it is not the suggestion that legal aesthetics simply abandon its underpinnings and constituting philosophies; rather, the time has come for a study of the transformation of legal aesthetics, as it becomes, perhaps most properly, a legal poetics.

To bring these themes together, we will study Archbishop Desmond Tutu's reference to Emily Dickinson's poem 1129 in the foreword to the report of the Truth and Reconciliation Commission (TRC). We will then try to read the 'grain' of the voice that speaks in the foreword, and attempts to reflect on its own mandate; the authority that allows it to talk, or the position from which it talks. We will need to deal with the idea of truth that was deployed by the Truth and Reconciliation Commission. Polyvocal, reflexive, and complex, there is no way that this can be criticized as a naïve approach to the manifold difficulties of the task with which the Commission had been charged. However, is there perhaps another way of thinking about the truth; a sense that communicates with the allusion to Emily Dickinson? Perhaps this is different. We might call it a sublime truth; a truth that is warranted by the events that have summoned it; or even a truth in/adequate for any way of talking about the momentous process, the work in progress that is the transition to democracy in South Africa.

TOWARDS A POETICS OF TRUTH AND RECONCILIATION

The voice can be approached from the perspective of a legal aesthetics.[2] No attempt will be made here to summarize the legal aesthetics, other than to argue the following point. Aesthetics is not primarily concerned with a theory of the beautiful; maybe it would be more accurate to refer to a legal poetics,[3] a term that is perhaps far more useful in considering the South

---

2 P. Goodrich, 'Europe in America: Grammatology, Legal Studies, and the Politics of Transmission' (2001) 101 *Columbia Law Rev.* 2033–84, at 2075.
3 If aesthetics is the philosophy of the beautiful, then it would seem that aesthetic jurisprudence must have some concern with revealing the beauty of law. Although some have taken this approach, see E. J. Weinrib, *The Idea of Private Law* (1995), it represents a narrow interpretation of the possibilities offered by thinking through aesthetics. Aesthetics is much more than a theory of the beautiful. Building on the etymology of the term aesthetics, it appears more concerned with a quality of experience and sensation; perhaps aesthetics even extends into an account of human

African scholarship that will orientate our reading. Our argument will attempt to locate the South African scholarship within the broader discourse of legal aesthetics, before turning to a more focused discussion of the poetics of truth and reconciliation.

For the South African scholar, aesthetics could never be orientated towards disinterested reflection. Aesthetics provides a publicly orientated discourse of political possibility.[4] It is concerned with the question of how a new beginning is possible. A commitment to the politics of legal scholarship does not necessarily make South African work distinctive; rather, the originality of the position, the great difference with the predominant forms of Anglo American scholarship, is a rejection of the intellectual bankruptcy of the legal philosophy of the old apartheid order, a sense of the need to articulate a robust democratic culture: a need to start afresh. It would be interesting to study the broader social underpinnings of this generation of scholars, the institutional alliances and intellectual genealogies of those scholars who have turned to aesthetics, but space is limited here.[5] We need to focus on what makes South African scholarship different, and the way in which truth and reconciliation is thematized within a broadly aesthetic framework.

The appearance of truth and reconciliation as a theme within legal aesthetics has made for a certain reworking of the underpinnings of the field. There are, of course, immediately problems with how one even begins to think of legal aesthetics, and we at least have to acknowledge this before we return to our main point. How does legal aesthetics relate, for instance, to a 'jurisprudence of appearances'[6] or other cross-disciplinary forms of legal scholarship and social theory? Even if we acknowledge that the boundaries of the field remain unsettled, it is still probably accurate to argue that the foundations of legal aesthetics do, for the most part, draw on American scholarship. As one way into this complexity, we will contrast two pieces of work that represent opposing positions; different visions about the composition of legal aesthetics. One particular line is orientated towards a reading of what could be described as constitutional law.[7] This work's motivation is to produce a legal hermeneutics based on a sophisticated model of the understanding of literary texts and a humanistic ethics. It is rooted in

being or human community. Certainly the trajectory through Heidegger offered by Jean-Luc Nancy considered in this paper suggests that this understanding might be possible. The notion of poetics could also be built upon Heidegger's foundation. For an alternative account of aesthetics, without a Heideggerian underpinning, see P. Schlag, 'The Aesthetics of American Law' (2000) 115 *Harvard Law Rev.* 1049–117. See, also, A. Gearey, *Law and Aesthetics* (2001).

4 See, also, W. Le Roux 'From acropolis to metropolis: the new Constitutional Court building and South African street democracy' (2001) 16 *South African Public Law* 139–68.

5 P. Goodrich, *Working Friendships* (forthcoming).

6 See R. Sherwin, *When Law Goes Pop* (2000) 107.

7 See J. Boyd White, *Justice as Translation* (1990).

40

American legal and political culture. Indeed, one might think of it as legal aesthetics in the form of a 'democratic conversation', a pluralistic approach to a political reality that has always been mediated by a fundamental constitutional document. Although influential, recent work has departed from the concerns of this approach.[8] Acknowledging an inheritance from critical legal studies (CLS), it is perhaps sceptical of sweeping claims about democratic conversations, and attempts to deploy aesthetics to both map American jurisprudence, and to suggest a new direction in legal argumentation. This 'dis-associative' approach is not so much concerned with a model of democratic culture, as the mechanics of lawyering, and the legacy of critical legal studies for both practical and philosophical accounts of American law.

Another important theme that needs to be touched upon is the issue of race. Legal aesthetics in America either came late to this topic, or dealt with it in an implicit, or largely untheorized manner.[9] To deal with this point properly would require an extended consideration of CLS and the emergence of critical race theory (CRT); again, space prevents such an engagement, but we can make a couple of essential points that touch upon the possibilities that this thought offers to others working within related areas. In its American beginnings, critical race theory can be understood as a response to the failure of the anti-discrimination law to achieve any real sense of social advantage for the black community. In a more extended sense, CRT provokes a way of thinking about the law that is not limited to a historical time and place, but is an engagement with law's complicity in the violent perpetuation of an economic and social order. Building on both these elements, the second generation of CRT scholars are at present turning to aesthetic theory to elaborate a more sophisticated model of such themes as ideology, and the way that the 'colour line' is lived.[10] One would expect that this kind of thinking would be more central to legal aesthetics, but perhaps there is still a sense in which it remains somewhat ghettoized within American legal theory as a whole. Indeed, when we turn to the South African scholarship, it would appear that rather than draw on this body of work, the thematics of race, humanity, and community tend to take their reference points from continental philosophy.

So, our first observation would be that aesthetics has been an engagement with the specifics of American law and culture. Although American culture is certainly marked by social conflict, this scholarship does not emerge from a context where a war of liberation has changed the political order. In other words, legal aesthetics has worked within a conceptual universe that takes a

---

8 Schlag, op. cit., n. 3.
9 See K. Crenshaw et al. (eds.), *Critical Race Theory* (1995).
10 A. Farley, 'The Black Body as Fetish Object' (1997) 76 *Oregon Law Rev.* 480. See, also, J.A. Farley, 'Thirteeen Stories' (1999) 15 *Tuoro Law Rev.* 2. For a different treatment of anti-Semitism, see R. Weisberg, *The Failure of the Word* (1984).

41

democratic culture and the contestations within it, as its essential context. This is not to argue, however, that there are no influences from American scholarship, but, when legal aesthetics has to address a radically different political situation, the field should be rethought, and must open itself to transformation and reception in a different jurisdiction.

To return to our concern with the transformation of the field, we must look for a theme that has been taken and reworked, and adapted for a different context. This would put us back in touch with a certain legacy of CLS, but, as we will presently see, this is a mutated form, one that would see the American movement as only one of its reference points. Our concern is with Cornell's notion of recollective imagination.[11] This thesis can be read as both a continuation of CLS, and a work in aesthetics. Recollective imagination takes as its starting point the key CLS problematic; the indeterminacy thesis.[12] Indeterminacy must not be conflated with what now passes as 'postmodernism'. The thesis must be understood as an insistence that the questions one can ask of an institution are not made from a transcendental or external viewpoint; they come from within the context itself. Indeterminacy cannot be associated with a collapse into subjectivism, or a banal anti-foundationalism. In its most elaborate form, Cornell's development of indeterminacy suggests that there is no schema that can comprehend 'the real'. The truth of any given reality cannot be found in an account of its totality. There is something that resists reduction into an ideal schema. Recollective imagination, though, presents itself as a way of imagining a future, a future that might be different from the past. In this sense it carries forward the radical edge of CLS, but recasts it in aesthetic terms.

Aesthetics, then, is about situatedness. It is concerned with the complexities of embodied existence that cannot be reduced to ideal or interpretative schemata. Perhaps Cornell's work does represent a kind of terminal point in the CLS legacy; perhaps it indicates that the radical project is now only imaginable as an aesthetics. However, the suggestion that Cornell's work has been influential in the development of an aesthetics of truth and reconciliation needs to be taken with a number of caveats. Firstly, although there is perhaps a direct influence in some cases, it is not suggested that Cornell represents a reference point for all South African scholars working within this problematic. It is also worth noting that her work is itself mutated in its 'application' to South African political realities. This essay also risks a certain distortion of Cornell's own concerns. Whilst there is a hope that the present work is sensitive to a feminist perspective, it is clearly not an explicitly feminist engagement. There has been a rich and varied feminist response to the Truth and Reconciliation Commission, but

11 D. Cornell, *Transformations* (1993).
12 See D. Kennedy, 'The Structure of Blackstone's Commentaries' (1979) 28 *Buffalo Law Rev.* 7.

42

integrating this perspective more thoroughly within the present work would be difficult; it may be necessary, at least for the moment, to listen to the quiet voice of Emily Dickinson as a way of negotiating these concerns. But this is to run ahead of the argument. To some extent, the genealogy that has been presented thus far stresses the input of American scholarship into South African legal theory; arguably, there is also an influence that derives from a different, but related source: 'British' critical legal studies.

The appellation 'British' has to appear in quotation marks, as it is more properly described as work done by a diverse body of scholars in British institutions, who are themselves of different nationalities, or might even refuse to identify with something as reductive as nationality. It can also be read, again with certain caveats, as the transmission and transformation of traditions of continental philosophy. We can perhaps think of it as an ongoing negotiation of elements of Marxist, Heideggarian, and deconstructive themes, committed to a re-imagination of the possibilities of legal thought. Moreover, it remains a form of aesthetic thinking, taking seriously the centrality of texts such as *Antigone* for any authentic engagement with the law.[13] It poses the essential questions: 'how is my life to be lived; how do I create myself; how do I create a world of meaning?'

Although perhaps not explicitly an aesthetics or even critical legal studies, there is also work that draws on autopoesis and postmodern thought that has influenced thinking about truth and reconciliation.[14] It represents a certain style of thought; a particular way of setting up an argumentative approach. The pressing issue is to understand how the past continues its grip on the present; and whether it is possible to carry forward memory in such a way that we are not held by the dead hand of the past. Most importantly, this forces a thinking of institutional memory and, specifically, law's relationship with memory. One could deploy a more deconstructive register that sees memory as carrying a certain excess, something that escapes representation. This could be thought of as a problematic indicator of a path not taken, a past that could still be brought to be, there is a certain 'irrecoverable'[15] quality of the past, a remainder that ghosts those events that are remembered. Is it possible to imagine a future?

Approaching South African scholarship through this genealogy suggests that it is somehow derivative, or parasitic on 'modes' of though drawn from elsewhere. Unfortunately, this problem must remain as it is not possible to explain the other influences, the other intellectual trajectories that converge and diverge. Such a project will have to await another occasion. The central argument here, however, is that even if South African scholarship does draw

---

13 See C. Douzinas, *The End of Human Rights; Critical Thought at the Turn of the Century* (2000) and C. Douzinas and R. Warrington, *Justice Miscarried* (1994).
14 See E. Christodoulidis, 'Law's Immemorial' in *Lethe's Law; Justice, Law and Ethics in Reconciliation*, eds. E. Christodoulidis and S. Veitch (2001).
15 id., at p. 211.

43

on these resources, it claims them as its own, and transforms them into a new problematic. So, the next part of the argument will be to address the South African scholarship that has taken aesthetics as a way of approaching truth and reconciliation.

THE SLOWLY SPREADING LIGHT: A POETICS OF THE POLITICAL

Johan Van der Walt's work provides a poetics of the political that takes truth and reconciliation as a definitional moment. How can we understand it as a poetics? The poet is a maker; the poet puts together materials like a *bricoleur*, to suggest a new beginning, a new composition, to make the world anew. This returns, in part, to the indeterminacy thesis, but it is only one of its reference points. The poetic – or even the philosophical poetical – is a desire to posit the general account, to provide foundations, but it is not outside of the processes it observes; rather it occupies a 'reciprocal' relationship.[16] It is no more prior to the law or to politics that these terms are independent of the philosophical. This reciprocal constitution of these different discourses attests to our own situation or 'state', which, in a certain philosophical vocabulary, is the way in which our intellectual engagement with the moment is in part determined by an inheritance; a set of concepts and ways of thinking. Rather than separate out any of these strands of thinking, or 'moments', we perhaps need to appreciate their historical location: a history that is not necessarily one of a working through of a spirit or a determining logic, but an arrival at a particular conjugation that is enabled by its past. This demands a new approach. It cannot be thought on the basis of sociology, or a history of South African law and politics, which is not to say that it does not make use of these modes of thought. Perhaps, then, it is ultimately a poetics because it is concerned with a style of thought, a way of recomposing differently so that something new can appear.

What appears? This is the central question of a poetics of community. Returning to the issue of putting together the resource differently, we can focus this question most sharply if we return to the question of style. Certain discourses have always sought to speak for the community. Law, in this sense, has always been an account of the community under law through it articulation of sovereignty. Of course, law or jurisprudential reflections on sovereignty are not the exclusive articulations of community. One could equally find it in modernist sociology, where the consensual or conflictual underpinnings of human community provide an orientation to study. Likewise, political discourse seeks to talk of community in terms of power and authority. Hobbes' Leviathan, rethought in different ways in the liberal tradition; Rousseau's or Mandela's notions of the people; the notion of

16 See P. Lacoue-Labarthe and J.-L. Nancy, *Retreating the Political* (1997).

44

ujamaa in Nyerere and the different African traditions are all perhaps variations on this essential theme. Again, risking generality, and banality, a poetics would follow a certain line or a disturbance within these fields. Once again, this is not to say that poetics opposes itself to either law, politics, or any other discourse of the social. It is to suggest that it takes a different inflection, a different way of saying: but it also says something different. Community cannot be thought on the basis of the inclusion into a collectivity that is then spoken for by party, president, or spirit. Poetics would seek to de-link the movement from community to sovereignty, or, at least to see what gets left out, what is lost, in an easy movement between the two. It would prefer to speak in terms of a sharing, a relationship of specifics that cannot be turned into a generality.

Could this provide a thinking of truth and reconciliation?[17] There are many difficult registers here, not least the problem of truth, and its relationship to the very notions of community and poetry. The briefest of sketches will have to suffice, to suggest no more than the outline of a complex and necessary space of thinking. As it may be possible to sense from the above, what is at stake here is the mutation of a certain Heideggerian discourse; it is as if Heidegger is being rethought to privilege the notion of being together (*mitsein*), as the primordial human condition. There are many difficulties. Being in the world, as a structure, is already a given: an original and indivisible whole, a total system, which determines or conditions how we consider the elements that compose its totality: it 'always comes first'.[18] Does this totality of being suggest that it has to be encompassed by an equally totalitarian theory of truth? Even if we were to depart at once from models of truth as adequation and to deploy a notion of truth as uncovering or revealing, would this help us? Do we need a theory that sets everything and everyone in its right place? The theoretical orientation suggested above would demand a subtler account of the truth.

If one accepts that Heidegger represents only a beginning, then this way of thinking does not have to lead to a grand theory of truth as the unveiling of being, a philosophical discourse that creates itself as an ambitious and exclusive monument to a way of speaking the truth. How could this discourse be interrupted, without losing its essential and important insight, the notion of

---

17 See *After the TRC: Reflections on Truth and Reconciliation in South Africa*, eds. W. James and L. Van de Vijver (2000). Colin Bundy's essay in this collection (pp. 9–21) examines the location of the TRC within a 'broader' understanding of South African history; this is, in particular, an attempt to make sense of the Commission in 'fairly conventional social science terms'; an endeavour that would relate it to 'legislation', 'political and social processes'. It is a discourse that would 'distance' itself from the 'TRC as political drama or morality play, and eschew rhetorical celebration or denunciation of the Commission'. It would seem, then, that there is an idea of history that can be aligned with social science, against the misunderstandings of the aesthetic and the rhetorical.

18 M. Heidegger, *Being and Time* (1962) introduction, part 1, division 1.

45

our being in a world that makes sense for us? What would this make for in terms of a notion of truth: how could one talk about the truth of community? If, as Heidegger tells us, this returns to 'Being in the World'[19] then it must also return to the notion of *mitsein*, and what is shared in community as the form of being in the world. A thorough reworking would take us towards the notion of care.

Care is always a kind of disposition to the world, to projects in the world. Care, and hence a notion of truth that may relate to it, could indicate the way that life is always thrown up ahead of itself, enabling projection. But, might this projection be related to a truth that does not seek an essential revelation, or a return to a truth of being as that which is unvealed or revealed? Truth might be 'something' that must be shared amongst us, 'something' ongoing.

It is precisely this thematics of the truth and reconciliation that Van der Walt's work suggests. Truth and reconciliation becomes an 'event'; it does not posit a substance, a new sovereignty, a way of gathering together the 'being' of the new South Africa. As an event it is, in the sense to be elaborated, a telling, a sublime marker: it aims to undo three centuries of oppression and violence in two years, to save the law from the filth into which it had fallen.

There are at least two separate but related aspects of this account; they could be described as an idea of a non-totalizable 'we' and a future directedness. Given sufficient space, these concerns could be related back to the problematic of truth outlined too briefly above. Risking schematism, we shall develop these two themes in such a way as to appreciate their specificity, and their relationship. The 'we' that is to be addressed here is the 'we' of a *nomos*, and hence a law, yet not a 'we' that can be spoken for by the law. Perhaps, then, there is a *nomos* that may coordinate with the law, but is not identical with the law. This difficult relationship can be put in less normative terms, by thinking of a certain temporality, which is not necessarily historical time:

> The time or timing of reconciliation can therefore not be thought in terms of presence. Nor can it be thought in terms of a future not yet present, a future that will become present ... it must be conceived in terms of the non time or negative time between present and future ... It occurs as the time or timing that holds past, present and future in play.[20]

A time of being together, a time of a pure sovereignty that could found the law is not available. We must think the Commission's task as one of radical incompletion; a paradoxical openness and irresolution that must nevertheless provide a mark, a foundation, and a boundary between what was, and what can come to be. In words stolen from Jean-Luc Nancy, it is 'what happens when we risk saying "we are inaugurating history" instead

19 id., at p. 261.
20 J. Van der Walt; unpublished manuscript in the author's possession.

46

of simply saying "this has been history".'[21] Anticipating the way that we will speak of this problem, we could say that the paradoxical task that we need to think could be expressed in a poetic register: to redeem time from time in time; or rather, in a more political mode, to represent a break in a history.

However, we need to turn to another central issue, and to the work of a second scholar who shares, but cannot be reduced to, Van der Walt's problematic. We need to make this turn to think about the voice; a notion essential to poetics, and to a poetics of law. Such a thinking might build on the work of Karin van Marle. For van Marle, the voice is to disassociated from any sense that it summons into a presence of recollection. In this sense, we can trace a line of 'inheritance' back to the aesthetics of recollective imagination suggested above. But, this is now firmly related to the politics of truth and reconciliation:

> She is sitting behind a microphone, dressed in her beret or kopdoek and her Sundaybest. Everybody recognises her. Truth has become Woman. Her voice distorted behind her rough hand, her undermined Man as the source of truth. *And yet nobody knows her.*[22]

She, the truth, sits behind the microphone: she addresses us from a long way off (we might not hear her at all). A great deal could be said about the conjunction between the voice, truth, and memory, but we will take as our essential problematic that of van Marle's: how is it possible to talk about TRC now, from our present? This is a question that clearly raises issues somewhat different from the need to respond to the TRC in the moments of its operation. Any discourse about the TRC is problematic, as it can never respond to the pain of those who spoke before the Commission. Van Marle's essential theme is: how is a public discourse on the TRC possible?[23] This sense of van Marle's work also takes us back to the very notion of the poetic as a saying, but now to a wider set of questions about the audience and rhetoric.

Indeed, criticisms of the TRC have been made by other scholars that draw attention to these issues. The TRC is accused of failing to find a correct level of address and discourse. The report did not balance 'disclosure' with 'amnesty'.[24] For van Marle's work moves towards a concept of literature as the only form capable of carrying both a respect and a criticism of the TRC, but also a notion of the ongoing nature of reconciliation as a work in progress. Drawing on notions of narrative as 'patchwork' or 'jigsaw puzzle', her concern is with a thinking-of process that is not necessarily end-directed,

---

21 J.-L. Nancy, 'Finite History' in *The Birth to Presence* (1993) 144.
22 A. Krog, *Country of My Skull* (1998), cited in K. van Marle, 'Law's Time, Particularity and Slowness (2003) 19(2) *South African J. on Human Rights* 239–55.
23 K. van Marle, 'The Literary Imagination, Recollective Imagination and Justice' (2000) 15 *South African Public Law* 137.
24 Bundy, op. cit., n. 17, p. 14.

that can compose and recompose pieces differently.[25] Of course, this is motivated by the need is to push forward the legacy of the TRC, but not to this or that certain end. The key term is, perhaps, a thinking of open-ness, or in a slightly different metaphor, an ability to think in terms of uncertainty and doubt.

How can we develop these concerns? We need to turn to the report of the Truth and Reconciliation Commission.

THE VOICE OF RECONCILIATION

We need to focus on the foreword to the report of the Truth and Reconciliation Commission; we need to try to read the voice, the voice of Archbishop Desmond Tutu that is speaking – one might even say ventriloquizing – the other voices of the text.

But why a concern with a voice? Surely this ignores the fact that this voice is already a text. However, it is this very way in which the voice has become the text, the official account, that is the problem. It will be suggested that the sublime voice does not so easily become archived,[26] does not so easily speak on the basis of its founding legal authority (although one of its registers is that of the law).

Why the sublime voice? Without, at least at this stage, entering into a rigorous analysis of the sublime,[27] it will be suggested that it might lend itself to a reading of the report of the TRC.

In *On the Sublime*, Longinus writes:

> ... what transports us with wonder is more telling than what merely persuades or gratifies us. The extent to which we can be persuaded is usually under our control, but these sublime passages exert an irresistible force and mastery ... the proper order and disposition of material are not manifested in a good touch here and there, but reveal themselves by slow degrees as they run through the

25 Van Marle, op. cit., n. 23, at 149.
26 Bundy, op. cit., n. 17, provides a definition of the Derridean notion of the archive:

> at the heart of Derrida's critique ... [is] that it exercises power over knowledge. Archives confer authority on certain aspects of the past; they identify, classify and consign certain forms of knowledge into an apparent unity, and into a fixed, closed, artificially stabilised system.

At the same time, the archive is the repository of memory, and the site of a certain forgetting. This theme has been prevalent in critiques of TRC.

27 A starting point would be Jean-Luc Nancy's essay, 'The Sublime Offering' in his *Finite Thinking* (2003). Nancy draws attention to a distinction made by Boileau, Longinus's translator, between sublime style, a category of rhetoric, and the sublime in 'an absolute sense', namely, a way of speaking of subjects of 'great elevation'. The sublime as a rhetorical style is the sense primarily deployed in the present essay, although this, of course, shades into any way in which momentous events are themselves thematised.

whole texture of the composition; on the other hand a well timed stroke of sublimity scatters everything before it like a thunderbolt, and in a flash reveals the full power of the speaker.[28]

The sublime, then, is a way of speaking; it is a rhetoric known in its effects. It relates to 'the proper order and disposition' of material, that is revealed slowly; but also can flash before you like lightning. This account of the sublime is very close to the Emily Dickinson poem cited by Archbishop Desmond Tutu in the foreword to the *Truth and Reconciliation Report*:[29]

> Tell all the Truth but tell it slant –
> Success in Circuit lies
> Too bright for our infirm Delight
> The Truth's superb surprise
>
> As Lightning to the Children eased
> With explanation kind
> The Truth must dazzle gradually
> Or every man be blind – [30]

We will return to this poem in much greater detail but, for the moment, it is possible to hint that it concerns a sublime poetics of truth that might be one way of 'understanding' the event of truth and reconciliation, one way of listening to the sublime voice.

In some ways, though, the voice that will concern us is an institutional voice, a voice that has chosen to speak for other voices, a voice with a mandate. This voice cannot ultimately speak for those who suffered, and for those who have no voice. To the extent that it can be distinguished, then, the concern is not so much with the voice of the victim, or even the voice of the perpetrator, but with an official voice: the institutional voice of Archbishop Desmond Tutu. Perhaps critics of the TRC have not looked, or listened to a quality of voice, a voice that speaks against itself, opposes itself, finds its own mandate problematic. Despite the fact that this is the official voice, the archiving voice, the voice speaking the official version of history, it is a voice that speaks against itself; perhaps it even speaks against the very task that it has been given.

THE TRUTH OF THE TRUTH AND RECONCILIATION COMMISSION

The concern, then, is with how this voice gives itself a mandate to speak the truth, and how it problematizes its own mandate. We will focus on the foreword to the report of the TRC, because it is this very liminal space where the voice can best be heard; however, it will also be necessary to read

---

28 Longinus, *On the Sublime in Classical Literary Criticism* (1965).
29 TRC, op. cit., n. 1.
30 E. Dickinson, *The Complete Poems of Emily Dickinson*, ed. T. H. Thompson (1961) 506–7.

49

other parts of the first volume of the report to connect essential themes. There is one point to be stressed. The foreword is a peculiar space. It represents the last passage to be written, and yet the first confronting the reader; a kind of epilogue but at the same time a prologue. We could push this point. The foreword is both part of the report and strangely separate; both part and apart. Might it suggest possibilities by virtue of its positioning? If we speak of the success or failure of the TRC, the success or failure of the law, how does this relate to a voice speaking from a place that is both of and not of the report, a voice of the law, but of more or less than the law?

The truth to which the TRC was committed was, from the beginning, double and difficult. Criticisms have been made about the way in which the Commission resolved these difficulties, but our starting point is that there was a sophisticated understanding of the truth within the Commission. However, it is as if the TRC was hobbled from the very beginning. Its modus operandi severely restricted the 'truth' of the statements that it was charged to bring to light. The Commission was itself well aware of its founding dilemma. It is as if the need to record the narratives of human rights abuses changes their nature:

> On the one hand, the Commission was a legal institution with the responsibility of making defensible findings according to established legal principles. This was particularly important, both to safeguard the credibility of the Commission's final report and to ensure that those who received reparations were genuinely victims as defined in the Act. On the other hand, the Commission embodied a moral and therapeutic process that aimed at acknowledging suffering and giving victims an opportunity to tell their stories.[31]

One way in which the Commission hoped that it would resist a legal logic was in the public nature of its hearings, where victims were given the chance to tell their stories without cross-examination. This procedure, though, did mean that corroboration became more difficult, and the therapeutic was raised above the legal. How could this be resolved? Methodological protocols were developed. Consider, for the moment, the way in which the Commission operated. Statements were taken from victims that identified the abuses that had taken place. It was important that these statements could be considered in a 'systematic' manner [32] so that the juristic or quasi-juristic mandate of the commission could be fulfilled. The minimum requirement was that there should be some conformity and 'consistency'[33] in the material. In other words, it was necessary to place some grid over the 'raw' material of remembrance, in its confusions, in its many languages.

31 References to the TRC report, op. cit., n. 1, will give volume, chapter, and paragraph: 1, 6, 27.
32 id., 1, 6, 9.
33 id.

50

As the Commission notes, the narratives themselves were in a form that was unsuitable to a legal or perhaps even quasi-legal presentation of the truth: chronology and the names of those involved became jumbled and obscured, especially as some people were recalling events that happened two to three decades ago.[34] Eyewitnesses had vanished or were unavailable, records had been destroyed, as part of the general erasure of apartheid's official memory. How could this be reduced to an institutional logic?

If there was a need to 'fine tune' the accounts of the victims,[35] then one could imagine how a lawyer would be able to demolish the 'truth' value of such documents in court. Protocols developed that show an increasing need to move beyond mere consistency of statement, to impose further forensic structures on the victim's narratives. In particular, the Human Rights Violations Committee and the Reparation and Rehabilitation Committee[36] made use of 'corroborative pointers' that would allow a more precise evidential structuring of information. Other requirements that determined the shape of narrative were perhaps more institutional or practical than directly legal: these were the impositions of an information management system, with its own archiving and organizing logic that coordinated the regional and the local, that allow cross reference and capture of data flows. Please do not misunderstand. These comments are not meant as a valorization of 'raw' narrative, as opposed to a kind of institutional memorialization or archiving. For instance, the very collection and corroboration of materials did allow the Commission to move from perhaps incorrectly remembered events to a more coherent representation of an abuse

So, the Commission was well aware of the difficulties of the truth with which it was dealing. There was, indeed, a certain reflexivity in the Commission's understanding of the truth. The Commission's report is careful to provide a social-scientific defence of its methodology. Its foundation is a belief in the possibility of 'objective knowledge' of the social world. Objective knowledge is understood in a special sense, that of an intersubjectively agreed truth, a truth held in common between social actors. A footnote states that this may be 'weaker' than objective knowledge, but 'it has the same practical effect.'[37] This question of effect is not developed. The main text returns to criticisms of the 'decontextualised' nature of the forensic record of human rights abuses, and the equally decontextualized nature of 'quantitative analysis'. One criticism argues that violence is understood in contingent social ways, by reference to social meanings that are accessible in the world of the person recounting the abuse. Such a criticism is not fatal to the work of the Commission, as it suggests that a quantitative method must be supplemented by approaches sensitive to the culturally specific

34 id., 1, 6, 23.
35 id., 1, 6, 11.
36 id., 1, 6, 21.
37 id., 1, 6, appendix to para. 10

51

construction of meaning. Indeed, the Promotion of National Unity and Reconciliation Act 1995 that set up the TRC demanded a methodological pluralism that made use of both quantitative and context-sensitive analysis.

There is a Weberian underpinning for this approach. Weber's sociological method requires that 'uniqueness' results from the 'combination of general factors' that can in themselves be isolated and subjected to analysis. Classical sociological method thus shows the same concern as the Commission with a sensitivity to individual cases and the need for general reflection. Generalities are to be made analysable through the imposition of 'ideal types', which are defined as 'controlled and unambiguous conceptions'[38] which allow the specific cases to emerge in their uniqueness. The language of ideal types is used to conceptualize the 'coding frame' employed by the Commission. The standard form analysis thus becomes the 'controlled and unambiguous concepts' that are employed to order the data. The main function of ideal types is to act as an organizer of comparison. Or, in the words of the report:

> the aggregation of examples of a particular ideal type with one set of characteristics provides a basis for evaluation of a second aggregation of examples of a similar but distinct ideal type with a different set of characteristics.[39]

Ideal types thus allow a creation of categories of abuse, all with their own specific features, which can then be used to create general categories, that can form the basis of distinction from other general categories.

The concept of truth deployed by the Commission was based on a fourfold division, thus resisting the more usual distinction of subjective and objective truth. Truth can be divided into: factual or forensic truth; personal or narrative truth; social or 'dialogue' truth; and healing and restorative truth.[40] Different truths operated at different levels in the Commission's work. Factual or forensic truth was primarily a way of thinking about the way in which the Commission approached the organization of information, and the forensic requirements that impacted on the Commission's work. Its source is the Act itself and the task that the Commission is charged with, namely to:

> prepare a comprehensive report which sets out its activities and findings, based on factual and objective information and evidence collected or received by it or placed at its disposal.

In some ways this is a rather modest definition of factual or forensic truth. We will see that it is backed up by social scientific theory, and, at a more general level, by a theory of truth expounded by Ignatieff: 'All that a truth commission can achieve is to reduce the number of lies that can be circulated

38 id., 1, 6, appendix to para. 13.
39 id., appendix to para. 15.
40 id., 1, 5, 29.

unchallenged in public discourse.'[41] It is a version of the truth that allows a number of negative claims to be made; it allows the clearing up of disinformation.

Personal and narrative truth is somewhat different. In Desmond Tutu's words, it is the truth as perceived by an individual. It is perhaps easier to say what this truth is not. It is not legal or forensic truth, as tested in a court of law. Personal and narrative truth allows an approach to the past, a particular expression of memory, an oral tradition. It is the truth of subjective experience, recounted in a personal language. Personal truth, though, is not just the truth of individuals; it is an account of the past that builds into a national narrative: 'the Commission sought to recover parts of the national memory that had hitherto been officially ignored.' It is the undoing of silence, and the recognition of voices that have not been given a chance to enter into the archive and the record. It is, by its very nature, complex and messy: 'transcripts of the hearings, individual statements, a mountain of press clippings and video material'. Personal and narrative truth thus appears to exist in these excessive forms, resisting reduction to a simple thematic.

Social truth is the conjunction between the Commission's 'process' and 'goal'. The definition that the TRC employed presents this form of the truth as that which emerges through dialogue and contestation.[42] This theory provides the foundation for the central notion of the Commission's transparency, and the requirement that as many people as possible participate in its deliberations. It stresses a kind of due process, but not in strictly legal terms:

> [T]he process whereby the truth was reached was itself important because it was through this process that the essential norms of social relations between people were reflected.[43]

Healing or restorative truth sounds a religious note. It is truth in the context of 'human relationships';[44] borrowing a legal idiom, it could be said that it has both vertical and horizontal effect, describing relationships between fellow citizens, and between citizens and the state. Perhaps it is the most controversial form of truth; it is future-orientated, and performative:

> truth as factual, objective information cannot be divorced from the way in which this information is acquired; nor can such information be separated from the purposes it is required to serve.[45]

It is a truth that denies the objectivity of truth; it is truth in the services of a particular project. It is a kind of unveiling, or a placing in permanent record

---

41 id., para. 33.
42 id., para. 40.
43 id., para. 42.
44 id., para. 43.
45 id., para. 44.

53

of facts that were not considered worthy of public articulation. In this way it underlies reconciliation, as it is a public acknowledgement of the pain of the victims of apartheid, and a recognition that the future has to be different from the past.

To found; to justify the truth through philosophy or social science. A guarantee of the truth of the report through references to protocols, to different levels of the truth; perhaps ultimately to a complex, polyvocal truth, but, still something that can guarantee the truth of many voices. Is this the only way that the truth could be deployed?

Can we oppose another way in which the truth might be indicated, might appear? Might appear to disappear?

THE TRUTH MUST DAZZLE GRADUALLY

In the foreword to the report of the TRC, Archbishop Desmond Tutu alludes to a poem by Emily Dickinson: 'the Truth must dazzle gradually/ Or every man be blind –':

1129
Tell all the Truth but tell it slant –
Success in Circuit lies
Too bright for our infirm Delight
The Truth's superb surprise

As Lightning to the Children eased
With explanation kind
The Truth must dazzle gradually
Or every man be blind –

If there was a poetics of truth here, how would it announce itself? A starting point may be to speak in terms of the metaphors of visibility that the poem creates. We might say that this poem is about the modes of truth's revelation, or rather, truth as process, as a working through of something that resists revelation, of truth as resistance itself, perhaps. Can the truth announced by this poem be thematized?

Tell all the Truth but tell it slant – /Success in Circuit lies

Truth has to be a totality; its mode is to be entire, but it is precisely this entirety that demands a particular mode of announcement, a 'slant', an indirection. This is the meaning of 'circuit', that which is curved or slanted, but, and this is the sense of the metaphor, is closed in on itself. Circuit, then, picks up on the notion of truth's totality. The poem is concerned with an order whose totality can only be told all at once, but all at once through indirection. We need to pursue this conundrum. Indirection suggests that something is left out, indicated rather than stated; totality suggests the total self-presence of presence itself. Perhaps the circuit is even the world; the possibility of a world or – to borrow Nancy's word – a world that makes sense, and whose sense is connected with truth. At this most general level, then, it seems necessary that we engage with a certain ontology of both sense and truth, as indicated by the work of Van der Walt. But, for the moment, we need to remain with the words of this poem.

From where is the voice that announces this truth speaking? The poem is surprising in its modesty: the sublime theme of truth's revelation is expressed in two short stanzas, as if there is a virtue in a kind of indirectness, of allowing the sublime theme to announce itself by its absence. There is a register of voice that indicates by not speaking, or by saying very little, a voice that works through indirectness. If we are convinced by the poem, if we find it compelling, then its authority must be related to a similar gesture towards what is not said, or even what cannot be said. For this poem about the truth is perhaps a poem that avoids speaking about the truth at all. In the end the truth is something that must be surprising: 'The Truth's superb surprise' is a strange expression that promises everything and nothing. We know it is a surprise; a surprise whose nature is to be superlative, but this still begs the question of what is the object of the surprise. We are left with the sense of a superlative of which we can say very little. Is this the lightning? Or the explanation of the lightning that makes it less frightening; that explains it as an event less awesome than it is? There is a kindness, a care, which conceals the truth. The truth, it seems, must hurt, must leave its mark. We will return to the latter concern in a moment, for we need to pursue the relationship between truth and language. It is as if the truth's presentation must detract from the event itself, something must escape, must remain unsayable about the truth, for such is the very possibility of being able to talk about it. Does this take us towards the sense of the last strophe?

The Truth must dazzle gradually/ Or every man be blind -

If the truth is like lightning, then it must come of its own accord. Truth would appear, to shift the metaphor, to have its own agency; the place of the commentary, of the articulation of truth, is entirely secondary. But, at the same time, it is the commentary, the explanation, the poem as commentary on the truth, where truth appears – or appears to disappear. The resistance to truth could be language itself; or language that can form the only – but the flawed – record of truth's event.

But, it is not just language. Truth has a relationship with the body, with its gaze and hearing. Perhaps the truth is its effects. The peculiarity of the truth is that it appears to mark the body, and to leave its mark thereupon. If the truth has dawned, the subject who knows the truth would be dazzled, unable to see for the truth. The sense of the closing metaphor is strange. We are left with a choice between being dazzled and being blind – or a choice between blindness and blindness. To know the truth is to be crippled.

But what does the final mark of the poem indicate? A hyphen, a dash, indicates that something has been broken off, or discontinued but may be

55

picked up, developed. This is at least the conventional syntactical meaning. In the poem, the concluding hyphen might indicate that the poem itself is incomplete; it concludes with a pause, a pause that, in a sense, is its relationship to the world. It is the point at which the poem ends, and thus the point at which the reader stops; her gaze is drawn from the poem to the page, from the page to the book, and everything that lies outside of these two quatrains. At the same time, though, it echoes the hyphen that concludes the first couplet. The hyphen interrupts the movement from the slant nature of the telling, to the 'success' that lies in indirectness, in the circuit, or the totality. Perhaps, then, this hyphen marks the tone of a voice, that seeks to indicate the world as the interruption of the totality of the text; or rather, prepare the place where the world surprises the text, and the text surprises the world. A mark that indicates both openness and closure at the same time, by indicating what must disrupt the poem.

Could we hear this voice speaking in the report? Is there a quality in Emily Dickinson's poem, a tone of voice, a thematic that one can also hear in Archbishop Desmond Tutu's words?

Reading the foreword to the report, one might sense that Archbishop Tutu is describing the radical incompletion of the Commission's task. The report provides a paradoxical irresolution that must nevertheless mark a foundation, a boundary between what was, and what can come to be.

The task of the Commission is expressed, first of all, as an orientation to history; a history that is in some ways arbitrarily defined as a period that exists between the Sharpeville massacre, and inauguration of Nelson Mandela as President. This raises the question of how one defines and understands a history of violence and colonialism: how does one orientate to a historical violence? Could it be defined by the founding of the Boer state? Or the coming of the British colonialist? The Dutch Trading Companies? There is, of course, an institutional determinant. The Commission was charged with investigating abuses within a certain period. But this does not alter the fact that any date must be somewhat arbitrarily imposed. This point can be joined to the way history and violence are presented in the foreword. Violence is ongoing; the Commission is located within a history that is ongoing. Its paradoxical task could be expressed, first of all, in a poetic register: to redeem time from time in time or rather, in a more political mode, to represent a break in a history, and hence, the sublime task, to create a moment through which history can be judged.

These are terrifying themes. How can they be approached? Consider the narrative that opens Archbishop Tutu's account:

> All South Africans know that our recent history is littered with some horrendous occurrences – the Sharpville and Langa killings, the Soweto uprising, the Church Street bombing, Magoo's Bar, the Amanzimtoti Wimpy Bar bombing, the St James' Church killings, Boipatong and Sebokeng. We also knew about the deaths in detention of people such as Steve Biko, Neil Aggett, and others; necklacings, and the so-called 'black on black' violence on

56

the East Rand and in KwaZulu Natal which arose from the rivalries between IFP and first the UDF and later the ANC. Our country is soaked in the blood of her children of all races and of all political persuasions.

As in epic poetry, the narrative makes use of the form of the list: a catalogue of death and injury; a violence that explodes into the mundanity of the everyday; the dead littering the Wimpy bar, laid out on Church Street, in the ruins of a pub. The list does not discriminate. It suspends the debate about the legitimacy of a violence that opposes the apartheid state. It presents. History is a pile of corpses. These are the indiscriminate killings of the 'terrorist' bomb – but they must be seen as existing in a series, alongside those deaths in custody, alongside the abuses of the power of the state. Furthermore, this is not a violence that can be neatly divided between the actions of the state, and those of the liberation movement. Violence turns inwards, becomes 'black on black'. Note that this violence becomes the mark of being a South African. 'All South Africans know' or, later:

> Violence has been the single most determining factor in South African political history. The reference, however, is not simply to physical or overt violence – the violence of the gun – but also to the violence of the law or what is often referred to as institutional or structural violence.[46]

This is an appeal to a universal: to be South African is to have been implicated in this history of blood, to be 'soaked in the blood of her children of all races and political persuasions'. If a universal of suffering can be invoked, this might allow some movement towards that possibility of judgement, that im/possible division between a past and a future:
    There is always the possibility that this division could be marked by a forgetting; that 'bygones' could be left as 'bygones'.[47] The distinction between the past and the present is thus a certain amnesia. The present emerges from an erasure; and, of course, perhaps this could allow a certain point from which to start again. Why must be the past be confronted?
    This question is answered in different ways. A literary model is employed, Dorfmann's *Death and the Maiden* is cited, to suggest that the past needs to be confronted for the restoration of the human dignity of those who have suffered abuse. Dorfmann's play presents the torturer who takes responsibility for his acts, and, in so doing, allows the person who he has tortured to recover a sense of self. In this sense, then, the settling of accounts with the past is to restore to selfhood those who have been denied basic human dignity. Given the racist construction of the apartheid state, this can be conjoined to a second theme that we will examine separately, racism. The theme of the individual coming to selfhood cannot be separated from the effects of a racist political, legal and social order. If we were to take this particular theme at its most general level, we could see this confrontation with the past as the very dividing line between a Western racism, and an

46 id., 2, 68, 44.
47 id., 1, 1, 26.

57

order that might come after. Of course, the risk with this generalization is that we miss the specificity of the South African situation, but, by the same token, the sublime nature of the Commission is that it does make a demand for a total reassessment of a much broader history.

The question can be answered in a somewhat different way. This focuses on the problem of repetition. If the problems of South Africa's past are not resolved, they will repeat themselves, and revisit the problems of the past on the future. At the risk of imposing a broader theme, what we are reading here is a theory of historical time. Against repetition is a time that remains open to future possibility. Repetition is a time of no movement, of a poisonous stasis. Against repetition there must be some form of affirmation that is simultaneously a breaking with the past, and an inauguration of the future as that which is properly to come. Again, let us consider another modest statement. Archbishop Tutu is dealing with an attitude towards the past:

> It is to take care that the past is properly dealt with for the sake of the future.

Another paradox: care of the past is in fact an attitude towards the future. It is a phrase that invokes a notion of human finitude, of a life in time. We can thus see the coming together of themes that relate both to the political situation in South Africa, and a more general, perhaps the most general of questions: what does it mean to be human? In other words, facing the past is not just an essential South African political reality; it is as if this reality manifests the most pressing of questions that could be asked of a contemporary politics. To elaborate this theme, to allow the future is to allow the appearance of a genuinely human ontology. This, of course, relates back to the first way in which the question has been answered. Racism is what blocks this possibility of the human, and condemns to repetition, to a circular time. To relate this back to the earlier point, it takes us to the very inauguration of the Commission itself, and the possibility of creating the break in time, the judgment of the past. Presently we will relate this to the other central themes of the Commission's task: the nature of truth and the quality of reconciliation.

Perhaps this question is left open. It is as if the Commission cannot itself resolve the need to confront the past, at the same time that its legal and political duty is to do so; the modesty of the last sentence attests to a process that is itself a passage of time, an ongoing attempt to understand a history. It might also be possible to say that this is an evasion that concludes this section of Archbishop Tutu's argument; indeed, the foreword goes on to consider the composition and operation of the Commission. Should this point have been more thoroughly discussed, given the importance of this opening statement? Or, is there not a textual strategy in operation at this point in the discourse?

One could read it in two ways. In the moment of composition, there is clearly no way in which the Commission can offer any assurance that the legacy will be faced, that a democracy will emerge from the ruins of the apartheid state. All it can perhaps offer is an account of itself; of its own functioning and brief. It is as if in this innocuous statement, 'And I imagine we can assume ...', we again encounter a kind of sublime. In this deft movement from an 'I' to a 'we', there is an embodiment of the very task of the Commission, the creation of a space where the I and the we correspond; here is a kind of imagined universal, existing for this moment only in the terms of this address, in this spoken or written text, in the very imagination that it is possible to make a distinction between the past, the present, and the future, a distinction that cannot be guaranteed, but has to be made.

CONCLUSION: THE SUBLIME, SLOW VOICE

Perhaps there is a need for an aesthetics of truth and reconciliation. Karin van Marle has written:

> [L]aw in its relation to time, to the past, the future and the particularity of the event, fails to follow an approach other than that which its own institutional form necessitates. The TRC is one example of an event that exposed these limits and failures. The example of art and its relation to and interaction with time, memory and imagination show a more open and fluid way of contemplating time and show the significance of slowness as a way of interaction with daily life, past, present and future.'[48]

This is clearly a powerful claim that art must enter into and disrupt law's institutional logic. But how would this thematics of slowness and of temporality relate to the voice: what is the relation between the voice and time? Could we speak of a time of the voice, the moment of utterance, and the time of history (without borrowing T.S. Eliot's voice)? But, to return to one last theme, if the voice speaks from the foreword, which is both within and outside of the law, what possibilities existing within the law might it whisper?

48 Van Marle, op. cit., n. 22.

JOURNAL OF LAW AND SOCIETY
VOLUME 31, NUMBER 1, MARCH 2004
ISSN: 0263-323X, pp. 60–86

Then and Now: The Natural/Positivist Nexus at War: Auden's 'September 1, 1939'[1]

MELANIE L. WILLIAMS*

This article returns to a little examined moment in the history of jurisprudence. A moment fleetingly considered, it has been ascribed, nevertheless, an iconic status in that history,[2] and it is meet to return to it now, at the war-shadowed dawn of the twenty-first century to consider how the juxtaposition of war with the positivist-Natural Law debate compares with the outbreak of an earlier war. The consideration of poetry alongside philosophy and jurisprudence permits reflection upon the history of ideas permeating many strands of thought and allows tentative conclusions to be drawn concerning implications for 'local' theory – especially 'Anglo-American' debate and the influence of discrete aspects of theory as they impinge one upon the other. The history also holds lessons for the very notion of theory itself – in the need to consider the 'tensile' properties of legal and political theory, any putative interactions between the formerly separate worlds of the analytic and normative, the 'natural' and 'positive' – particularly tested in the contingent event.

INTRODUCTION

The locus for this study is Auden's 'September 1, 1939' – written in New York on the day war broke out. The poem clearly resonates with recent

* Department of Law, University of Wales, Swansea, Swansea SA2 8PP, Wales

1 'September 1, 1939' was published in *The New Republic* 18 October 1939. It can currently be found in an anthology of poetry, *Staying Alive*, ed. N. Astley (2002) 357.
2 Most famously in the Hart-Fuller debate, with especial reference to law under Nazism. Whilst clearly galvanized by the work of Hart and Fuller, the broad question of the Natural Law and Positivist nexus was in another sense somewhat distilled by the *perversion* of law their debate examined – see, for example, the discussion in R. Cotterell, *The Politics of Jurisprudence* (1989) especially at 131, which emphasizes the focus placed by Fuller upon *irregularities* of form (nevertheless begging the question whether positive law would be law provided formally regular, though substantively doubtful).

events and this resonance has not escaped the notice of the popular and official polity (of which more anon). For the moment however, let us concentrate on those elements of particular relevance to the jurisprudence.

It is a commonplace of jurisprudential historiography that the events and horrors of the Second World War induced a revival of Natural Law theory.[3] Though there is some recognition that the failures of law in the first half of the twentieth century were multi-factorial,[4] two concerns remain dominant and to some extent interconnected – a 'failing' Protestant rationalism and a return to Natural Law theory: both are reflected in the poem. Firstly the poem refers to the concern that the horrors of Nazi Germany could be attributable in some way to Protestantism, specifically Lutheran Protestantism: 'Accurate scholarship can/Unearth the whole offence/From Luther until now/That has driven a culture mad/Find what occurred at Linz/What huge imago made/A psychopathic god'. Though the reference to a 'huge imago' making 'a psychopathic god' bears some faith in the Jungian imagery of a damaging culture creating a damaged individual, there is a note of scepticism extending to sarcastic disbelief in the invitation to scholars to successfully locate 'what' made the locus: the several pressures elude the precision of scholarship ('go on then – I defy you to show us this time *what* made it all happen').[5] This scepticism is further underscored by these rather offhand reference points – the improbable gumshoe image of 'unearthing' the 'whole offence', the lazy provocation to '*find* what occurred at Linz'.

Scholarship, rationality, analysis – the flowering of enlightenment skills in politics, creativity, intellectual life altogether – has failed: 'I and the public know/what all schoolchildren learn/Those to whom evil is done/Do evil in return'. The analysis provided by the political theory of Western liberalism, its claim to be able to trace a link between a crazed Germanic culture and Hitler's Nazism and thus safely 'locate' the enemy vis-à-vis ourselves, can be undone by the public, even by schoolchildren. The lesson of the playground is played out in international politics: the stringent and punitive terms of the Versailles Treaty were bound to return evil to its makers. Positivism as rationalism fails – fails to deliver a convincing account or remedy, and the positivism of an allegedly liberal international politics and law fails – in perpetrating a failed ethics under the guise of a 'reparatory' and corrective agenda. For Auden, and for many of his generation, and thus for the collective intellectual mind, this presaged a retreat into the classical notions of 'fundamentalist' values, either as religious, or as metaphysical elementals. The 'challenge' of positivism to adhere to the rationalist project 'through thick and thin', to adhere to it even when the physical world

3 W. Morrison, *Jurisprudence: From the Greeks to Postmodernism* (1997) 312–21; M. Freeman, *Lloyd's Introduction to Jurisprudence* (2001) 367.
4 Freeman, id., p. 123.
5 A. Hecht, *The Hidden Law* (1993) 156–7, seems to hold that this line reveals a sincere faith in scholarship, though picks up a similarly 'gumshoe' flavour to the enterprise.

threatens imminent death and chaos – proves too great a challenge to the human psyche when positivism can only offer the tentative steps of the logician, without any accompanying promise of spiritual security or redemption.[6]

The fifth verse concentrates upon the hopeless vulnerability of mankind and its tendency to seek security and stasis in an illusory world of material comforts: 'Lest we should see where we are/Lost in a haunted wood/ Children afraid of the night/Who have never been happy or good'. Auden's view of human nature is essentially compassionate but not particularly hopeful: persons, citizens are 'children', never 'happy' or 'good'. This is followed, in the sixth verse, with a reminder that these citizens suffer from a particular flaw: susceptibility to 'The windiest militant trash', which is 'not so crude as our wish/... the error bred in the bone/Of each woman and each man/Craves what it cannot have/Not universal love/But to be loved alone'. This confirms the trajectory begun with an 'enlightenment driven away': any collective project, any 'strength of Collective Man', is liable to be dessicated by the needy insatiable vulnerability of each of its constituent parts. As verse seven reflects, individuals *do* apprehend the 'pull' of community ethics, of an ethical polity, and they make attempts to respond to it. But such attempts are inevitably driven by small local and personal imperatives and by the pressures of daily existence, none of which are sufficiently responsive to a reflective ethical transformation:

> From the conservative dark/Into the ethical life/The dense commuters come/ Repeating their morning vow/ 'I *will* be true to the wife/I'll concentrate more on my work'.

And now that large scale ideologies have failed, who can provide a workable template for salvation from such treadmill mediocrity? – 'Who can release them now/Who can reach the deaf/Who can speak for the dumb?'

In verse eight, Auden's response to his own question recognizes its essential hopelessness. As poet, any 'release' he can offer is merely an

6 The third verse reflects not only the historical lessons of the battle fought between claims to democracy and those of dictatorship, but heightens the sense that the cycle is possibly unavoidable, *not* susceptible to reason – that the 'habit forming pain' of contingent disaster is always liable to predominate, to conquer attempts to nurture rational progress. In times of crisis we cannot rely upon the salvation of reason, but return to our primitive selves. To a logician, this might simply provide a stimulus to rationalizing how to overcome the failure, perhaps a central challenge to analytical positivists; to Auden, it seems to have presaged a retreat to religion as the only 'logical' outcome – an acceptance of our inability to control events.

The fourth verse again emphasizes the failure of rationalism and liberal politics: differing explanations are, in the end, simply vain (useless) and also vain in the sense of ego-driven, as is emphasized with the immediate juxtaposition of 'competitive'. Intellectual debate cannot explain away the images which stare back at it: imperialism, with its full history of justification, and 'the international wrong', the complicity which has led to a crisis which should be understood as a result of complex historical forces, rather than the easy depiction of 'us' and 'them'.

incantation, a 'voice', ending with an imperative. The material conditions of existence, social and physical – 'There is no such thing as the State/And no one exists alone/Hunger allows no choice/To the citizen or the police/' – predicate one conclusion: 'We must love one another or die'. In this conclusion we see the seeds of both utilitarian pragmatic positivism – that we must have ascertainable rules and a willingness to abide by them – and of an appeal to naturalist metaphysics, and in a sense the trajectory of arguments leading to this anti-climactic climax encapsulates the history, the currency of the debate, the intransigent dilemma *and* its relevance to modern philosophical discourse in the face of similar crises. Yet, though for Auden the poem was a prelude to his rationalized journey to religion,[7] the conclusion does not herald a sentimental journey. Of all the poems, this was one Auden was to repudiate most strongly, and his repudiation lay in his identification of the hopeless collapse of rationality, the dangerous emotivism of 'We must love one another or die'.

Accounts of the poem, and of Auden's rejection of the poem, produce a fascinating insight into political and philosophical cultures. The poem in its entirety has been colonized and metabolized for a huge range of purposes, and indeed so lends itself to propagandist claims as to form a further insult emanating from the poem in the mind of Auden. A reflection upon the poem's resonance with the events surrounding '9/11' would be an 'easy' essay indeed. The poem chimes strangely with our time in many ways – most dramatically for some, perhaps, in its location in a New York of 'blind skyscrapers' which 'use/Their full height to proclaim/The strength of Collective Man' where 'The unmentionable odour of death/Offends the September night' and marking the beginning of war. But a more interesting story can be retrieved from consideration, simply, of the conflict and collapse of ideas which almost certainly formed the core of Auden's own repudiation of the poem and the possible links to fields of conflict across theory in general. The title 'The Natural/Positivist Nexus at War' is a reference to the link between the time of the poem and of ideological change in the teeth of war: jurisprudential historiography marks the event as a point of reference, as a time when, so it is argued, the alleged 'vacuum' created by positivism permitted the amorality, in Hannah Arendt's term, the 'banality' of evil.

---

7 In fact, a fascinating journey can be tracked through his poetry. Many scholars, for example, A. Hecht, E. Mendelson, J. Replogle, A. Rodway, and S. Smith, have produced careful accounts of the developments, with varying emphases. Hecht, for example, concentrates upon the religious journey. Perhaps the most consciously political analysis is however provided by S. Smith in *W.H. Auden: Re-reading Literature*, ed. T. Eagleton (1985).

PROTESTANTISM, IDEOLOGY, AND THE 'WRONG KIND' OF AUTONOMY

Broadly, the poem appears to corroborate – or at very least, not to contradict – that key folk tale of jurisprudence, the link between Nazism and the Natural Law revival. Though Auden expresses scepticism as to the ability of scholarship to provide a convincing account of 'the whole offence', though *one* ultimate answer is the simple, playground answer that evil returns evil, the poem, by its very location of argument, gives some credence to the hypothesis concerning 'a' journey from Luther to Linz. In one sense, this feeds into contemporary theorizing concerning the seductive capability of National Socialism and Nazism to metabolize those aspects of indigent culture and belief which will create the best composite ideology for popular German consumption: let the people hang on to some of their old icons, parade this as an *ethical* and yet *spiritual* ideology, attach it to their own Lutheran Protestantism.[8] But in another sense, Auden is perhaps playing out his own concerns about the trajectory created by Protestantism: the link between Protestantism and intellectual independence, its proto-political contribution not only to rationalism, individualism, liberalism, positivism (all creatures of an antic enlightenment period reaching full maturity in the modern period of his day) but thereby to a ludic, anarchic intellectual stage guilty of *complicity* in the assemblage of dubious ideologies from scavenged remnants.[9] Though perhaps no more than retrospective and impotent posturing, the 'low dishonest decade' of the 1930s, with its personal and collective ideological wars – via socialism, communism, fascism – and claim to be able to *reason* solutions, could be characterized as part of the offence

---

8 The impact of Protestantism, and of Lutherism was widely discussed in the early twentieth century. Reinhold Niebuhr, who became a friend of Auden and stimulated (though did not necessarily profoundly influence) his thinking (see E. Mendelson, *Later Auden* (1999)), wrote prolifically in the 1930s and 40s. R. Niebuhr, *The Nature and Destiny of Man* (1943) 198 bears a searching discussion of the difficulty for Lutheran Protestantism in the conception of law. A more recent, comprehensive critique is that of J. Witte, *Law and Protestantism* (2002).

9 The possible links to Luther, Protestantism, and Nazism are numerous. They include the Lutheran contribution of the separation of Church and State; the specific creed that individuals are responsible for their own moral decisions; Protestantism as anarchy leading to a vacuum; the anti-Semitism of the later Luther; Protestantism as human intellectual vanity leading to the misleading 'pretensions' of positivism; that rejection of Catholicism by Protestantism provides the 'latitude' or 'vacuum' for pseudo-ideologies such as Nazism specifically or the general collapse of values less specificially. For Auden, the Luther-Linz journey has personal implications, given his dalliance with aesthetic Germany; also on a personal level, this stage of Auden's life marked an incipient return to High Anglicanism (and the preceding failure of political ideologies – yet note Auden and Isherwood's later agreement that they might just as easily have 'fallen for' Fascism as a favoured ideology under slightly different circumstances).

compounded by Luther and exploited by Hitler. Ultimately, *this* reading of the link between Protestantism and positivism – the link between Protestantism as independent thought and rationalism as an empirical ethic – provided an essentialist retreat for Western intellectuals recoiling from Nazi atrocities, the 'return' to Natural Law. The verse identifying a journey 'from Luther to Linz', invokes the preamble, so to speak, to the mechanics of the Hart-Fuller debate, where Hart and Fuller discuss the boundaries and meaning of the separation thesis in relation to dystopic legal systems such as that subsisting under Nazism. This quotation reminds us that in the 1930s and 40s two debates raged which impinged more broadly upon any such separation. One was the impact upon epistemology created by the sciences of society, by 'accurate scholarship' and by science itself.[10] The other related question was how the separation of Church and State has assisted in the inception of such dystopic law. As Auden appreciated well, the challenge reaches beyond the realm of 'accurate scholarship' alone. The separation of 'fact' systems from 'value' systems – of 'physical' worlds from 'metaphysical' worlds – is characteristic in both developments, the consequent impact upon notions of individual and collective responsibility more than merely incidental, for each, and both together, create variants upon the notion of autonomy. A key factor in current debates upon how we model 'rights' and also in the way normative and analytical forms of jurisprudence are positioned in relation one to the other, 'autonomy' may be understood as the particle at the heart of competing theories of law. For Auden, it presaged something very similar, turning to God via a rationale provided by Kierkegaard and closely mirroring Auden's personal experience: a journey from aesthetics (art and the Bacchanalian) to ethics (an engagement with politics) to God.

Auden's identification of the contribution of Luther, of a particular form of Protestantism to the inception of an aberrant order, keys into a still debated fragment in the history of ideas concerning Protestantism more generally. Simmonds[11] traces the roots of the separation thesis via a recovery of the strands linking Aristotle to Grotius, Hobbes, and Kant, demonstrating how early scholarship understood its own contribution to notions of the natural and the physical, the individual and the collective, and how this contribution has been misunderstood by subsequent transcription. Simmonds models the form of Protestantism which shaped a particular embodiment of autonomy:[12]

> Retaining the Aristotelian view of humanity as essentially social, such late scholastics and early Protestants as Grotius found it natural to regard our moral nature as articulated in the form of our institutions. Such assumptions were fundamental to the Grotian origins of systematic doctrinal scholarship. The

10 Especially relativity – considering the range of works from J.B.S. Haldane to A.N. Whitehead.
11 N.E. Simmonds, 'Protestant Jurisprudence and Modern Doctrinal Scholarship' (2001) 2 *Camb. Law J.* 271–300.
12 id., p. 286.

65

inwardness of Protestantism, however, was to undercut this position and encourage a perspective that regarded actual institutions as potential threats to autonomy, rather than as anchors of moral reflection ...

Simmonds demonstrates how this process is exacerbated by the distorting influence of the notion of the Categorical Imperative which fostered the locus of that particular notion of autonomy within the separation thesis[13] and shows how this trajectory of 'misunderstood' or unworkable Protestant autonomy leads directly to Dworkin.[14]

Returning to the writing of the 1930s and 40s, we can retrieve the immanence of such concerns. Neibuhr, a Christian political theorist writing in the 1930s and 40s asserts that the fault lies with Protestantism itself. A friend of Auden, Neibuhr, like Auden, found himself considering the historical developments in Europe from the vantage point of New York. Neibuhr's analysis bears some relation to that offered by Simmonds, and contributes an additional strand in the possibilities posed for the 'Anglo-American' political and jurisprudential debate:[15]

> Modern Protestantism frequently betrays greater indifference to, and ignorance of, the ultimate problems for which the doctrine of justification by faith was the answer than either Catholic Christianity or secular culture. The former may have solved the problem too easily; but it has never ceased to be aware of it. Secular spirituality, on the other hand, is frequently prompted by a wholesome commonsense to recognize the inevitable relativities and frustrations of history more generously than the perfectionist presuppositions of many modern Protestants permit them to do. Sometimes it develops a secularized version of the doctrine of justification to meet the problem of historical frustration; while liberal Protestantism remains enmeshed in sentimental and illusory historical hopes ...

Moreover, Neibuhr appends a gloss to this assertion which holds a bearing upon present-day discussion, both in relation to Simmonds's fine-tuned analysis of how a particular history of ideas can be tracked to a Dworkinian mindset, and to a broad, less tangible, but nevertheless immanent link to this mindset in terms of Dworkin's location in Anglo-American politics and law.[16] Though on the one hand, Neibuhr's comment could be regarded as more

---

13 id., pp. 285–7.
14 id., pp. 293–4.
15 Neibuhr, op. cit., n. 8, p. 164.
16 Neibuhr's comment could be regarded as so removed from a firm analytical tracery as to be purely speculative. Nevertheless, attempts to produce a 'global' account of links in the history of ideas were, and continue to be, timely. Neibuhr's footnote reads (id):
> This judgment is more applicable to the spiritual situation in America than in Europe. European Protestantism has, generally speaking, remained in closer contact with its own Reformation roots. American Protestantism is predominantly sectarian in origin and has therefore inherited the perfectionism of the sects of Reformation. This perfectionism belongs spiritually to the Renaissance rather than the Reformation. In America it is frequently compounded with the secular perfection, derived from the French enlightenment. Liberal Protestantism belongs, on the whole, to the Renaissance rather than the Reformation side of the debate on human destiny...

66

predominantly speculative than analytical, it bears intriguing implications for the role of such cross-currents of thought in the history of ideas and specifically in the production of the combination of Protestant, puritan, and constitutional ideology apparent in Dworkin and in present-day domestic and international Anglo-American, and particularly, American, politics and law.

With reference to the particular strand of Protestantism forged by Luther, Neibuhr demonstrates that this too contributes to the modelling of 'inner' and 'outer' selves fostering skewed notions of autonomy and of the state, creating a strand which underscores the 'inward' focus of Protestantism identified by Simmonds.[17] Moreover, Neibuhr apparently echoes that linkage, from Lutheran Protestantism to National Socialism and Nazism, traced by Auden in his poem of 1939, noting that:[18]

> The weakness of the Lutheran position in the field of social ethics is accentuated to a further degree by its inability to define consistent criteria for the achievement of relative justice ... Since it rightly has less confidence than Catholicism in the untainted character of reason, it relegates the 'natural law', that is, the rational analysis of social obligations, to the background, as an inadequate guide. But it has only odds and ends of systems of order to put in the place of 'natural law' ...[19]

Consideration by *current* scholarship of the impact of Lutheran influence upon the development of law tends to take on a somewhat defensive position, overshadowed as it is by a retrospective knowledge of the full extent of Nazi corruption and atrocities not available to Auden and Neibuhr. Thus Witte, writing in 2002, proffers an even-handed assessment[20] which nevertheless underplays the role played by Protestantism in championing an alternative, 'human' source for law and jurisprudence, though he warns against 'modern' readings of Luther as a progenitor of Hitler.

Auden himself however *did* pay close attention to this more positive ambit of Lutheran Protestantism. As early as 1933, his extensive reading had produced an appreciation of the role played by Luther in the history of intellectual independence.[21] This ties in to the fundamental contribution of

17 And oddly presages the abstracted inner self which Simmonds notes can be traced more firmly to Kant's Categorical Imperative (id., p. 202).
18 id., p. 204.
19 Somewhat oddly to Anglican ears, however, Neibuhr continues his thesis with a suggestion that Hobbes is a legitimate target for blame in the search for the origin of a skewed political and legal mindset. He speaks (pp. 249–50) of a 'sceptical and irresponsible attitude towards the religious problem ... In the thought of both Hobbes and Bodin, [the] demand for unconditional loyalty to the state is implicitly rather than explicitly religious ...'. Neither Auden, nor Simmonds would subscribe to such a view, which derives from locating religion as the focal point in this history of ideas.
20 Witte, op. cit., n. 8, p. 297.
21 'Luther and Calvin put in a word/the god of your priests, they said, is absurd/His laws are inscrutable and depend upon grace/So laissez-faire please for the human race' – W.H. Auden, from his verse-drama, *The Dance of Death* (1933) quoted in Hecht, op. cit., n. 5, p. 32.

Lutheran Protestantism to the development of positivist law – in the affirmation of individual judgement within a contextual rationale for a separation of Church from state law – a separation which Luther championed for essentially *moral* reasons.[22] Moreover, it is easy to see how a pragmatically selective and omnivorous collation of social and political needs and prejudices may well have tapped into the proud German history of Lutherism in the production of the ideologically piecemeal body of National Socialism. Auden himself was aware of the complex philosophical strands connecting such diverse belief systems.

Clearly, that aspect of Protestantism which lauded individualism would *not* have suited the call to collective faith that marked aspects of socialism exploited by 'National' Socialism. Though in his verse of 1933 Auden had circled the significance of Luther and Protestantism in the evolution of state law as a move *away* from arbitrary divine law, by 1949[23] Auden contrasts:

> The popular notion of the Renaissance as something that began promptly in 1450, and whose beginning consisted in the complete eclipse of what was known as mediaeval man, with a more accurate description, consisting of what he terms 'the real revolutionary events':

> 'The publication of Luther's ninety-five Theses in 1517, of Machiavelli's *Prince* in 1513, and of Descartes' *Discours de la Methode* in 1637. With these end five centuries of uninterrupted humanism, during which the energies of European civilisation were directed towards making the whole of reality universally visible to the physical eye or to the eye of reason, on the assumption that there was no truth, however mysterious, that could not be objectified in an image or a syllogism. This humanistic period begins with Anselm's ontological proof of the existence of God; it receives a temporary check with the condemnation of Abelard through the efforts of St. Bernard; it is seriously challenged by the Cathar Movement with its doctrine that matter was incapable of salvation. But after the crusade against the Albigenses in 1226, the orthodoxy of Christian humanism remains secure until Luther.'[24]

Hecht concludes this quotation from Auden with the observation that

> Luther, of course, split Christianity irrevocably, but he did more than that. The Thirty Years War was a secular conflict as well as a religious one, and society was divided against itself in ways that were both novel and terrible. That war, and the doctrinal, political, and philosophical disputes from which it began, was the first flowering of the 'offence'. It is an offense that, the poet claims, 'has driven a culture mad' ...

---

22 Witte, op. cit., n. 8, p. 296.
23 See Mendelson, op. cit., n. 8, p. 307 for discussion of the genesis of the book edited by Auden, *Poets of the English Language* (1949), from which the quotation used by Hecht is taken.
24 Quoted by Hecht, op. cit., n. 5, p. 157.

Hecht's juxtaposition of the quotation from Auden's comment on Luther written ten years *after* the poem of 1939, with the poem itself *as if* the comment can be read as an unproblematic gloss *upon* the poem of 1939, is clearly questionable. Whilst Auden's review of humanist history clearly flags an ideological divergence, it does not necessarily maintain the view of Luther's contribution as one of purely offensive schism, but is expressed in more measured terms, in an attempt to produce a balanced history of the humanist *ouvre*, specifically the commitment to rationalist enquiry and of a 'workable' notion of autonomy.

Whilst Hecht builds a thesis concerning Auden's journey towards religion *simpliciter*, Auden here marks the Protestant focus on the individual alongside the Catholic focus on community, as part of a broad intellectual debate with himself upon sustainable and rational models for social organization, whether nominally religious or political. In a later essay on Erik Erikson's biography of Martin Luther, Auden wrote:

> in terms of religious history, Newman's conversion to the Roman Church in 1845 marks the beginning of our era. The Christian doctrine which Protestantism emphasizes is that every human being, irrespective of family, class, or occupation, is unique before God; the complementary and equally Christian doctrine emphasized by Catholicism is that we are all members, one with another, both in the Earthly and the Heavenly city ...[25]

Considering specifically the notional link between Luther and Nazism, Protestantism and law, it is meet to review the summary produced by Witte.[26] Witte's critique is deliberate, recognizing the ease with which the epistemology of Protestantism and law can become entwined with a cultural schema which in a sense corroborates Auden's account 'from Luther to Linz' (almost certainly sharpened in Auden's mind via his own former intimacy with German culture) and the broad linkage between Protestantism and Positivism which allegedly produces Nazism, and the discussions between Hart and Fuller in the 1950s and 60s.[27] Furthermore, Auden traced the fracture created by Luther in contributing to the world of representations, decrying:

> The loss of belief in the significance and reality of sensory phenomena. This loss has been progressive since Luther, who denied any intelligible relation between subjective Faith and objective Works, and Descartes, with his doctrine of primary and secondary qualities ...[28]

25 Quoted by Hecht, id., p. 245, in the context of a discussion dealing predominantly with the late 1930s and early 1940s period of Auden's writing. Erikson's book, *Young Man Luther: A Study in Psychoanalysis and History,* was however written in 1958 thus Auden's review must have appeared at some date after that.
26 Witte, op. cit, n. 8, p. 297.
27 Morrison, op. cit., n. 3, pp. 312–21.
28 In 'The Poet and the City' in Auden's collection of essays, *The Dyer's Hand* (1963) at 78.

For Auden, the interference with the 'synthetic' fact and value enquiry has a particular impact upon the rational enquiry and of the viability of the autonomous judging self. Noting the importance of 'sensory' phenomena reveals Auden's appreciation of the physical world underpinning the metaphysical. As well as identifying the 'Protestant' origins of the 'offence', Auden's poem also appears to corroborate the intellectual debate heralding the 'return' to Natural Law theory. Mankind, despite its apparent 'collective' strength, its rationalist claims, is essentially frail, in a truly Biblical sense: 'For the error bred in the bone/of each woman and each man/Craves what it cannot have/Not universal love/But to be loved alone.' Moreover, this *moral* frailty is exacerbated by the perennial dictates of *physical and material* existence – 'Into the ethical life/The dense commuters come/Repeating their morning vow/"I *will* be true to the wife/I'll concentrate more on my work"' – so that ethical life is choked off by such imperatives and threatened by bare pragmatism: 'Hunger allows no choice/To the citizen or the police/We must love one another or die'. The trajectory from 'the error bred in the bone' to 'we must love one another or die' appears to subscribe to a view of the human condition, of human *nature* as frail and contradictory allied to the Natural Law jurisprudential canon, rather than the attempt to *resist* an overweening view of human nature which is part of the positivist project. The poem, then, at the very least, is at the nexus of ideological debate and would seem to presage Auden's own return to the Church and the return of jurisprudence to Natural Law. It also marks the divide in theory, as Auden grapples with a *sense* of an irreconcilable human nature, alongside scepticism of over-developed and prescriptive socio-political structures. Modern jurisprudence traces the divide and increasingly examines points of contact. Simmonds traces the historical misunderstanding of the implications of Protestant jurisprudence, which led to the bifurcation of positive law from its Natural Law roots. One aspect of this misunderstanding derives from piecemeal transplantations from political to legal theory.[29]

The poem was rejected by Auden and this may in part have been because of the paradox produced in the lines: 'The error bred in the bone/Of each woman and each man/Craves what it cannot have/Not universal love/But to be loved alone' leading directly to the assertion that 'We must love one another or die'. This in part expresses the paradox for jurisprudence in any attempts to encompass the natural within the positive, the deontic within logic, the normative within the analytical. Simmonds's historiographical account provides a compelling explanation of how that paradox becomes currently expressed in the work of Dworkin.[30] Furthermore, Simmonds argues that, in believing 'a shared sense of danger might protect us from the centrifugal forces of "protestant" interpretation', Dworkin simply ignores the fact:

29 As Simmonds explains, op. cit., n. 11, p. 288 (and see, also, Simmond's footnote to this summary).
30 id., pp. 293–5.

70

... that the situation he is discussing resembles in its structure the classic 'tragedy of the commons' beloved of economists and Hobbesian philosophers. Individual agents would have a strong incentive to proffer interpretations of law that favoured their own position and preferences (this is so whether we conceive of these individuals as having egoistic or altruistic preferences).[31]

In other words, the 'error bred in the bone': a fatal disability in the call to 'love one another or die'.

LOVE ONE ANOTHER *AND* DIE

Alongside this history and critique, lies a complementary, though more broadly based cultural account of relevant intellectual strands. Simmonds himself traces some radical attempts to approach the uncertain boundary between the positive and normative which is so much bound up with questions of linguistic practices and semantic rules. The 'interpretative' ground, described in 'core' and 'penumbra' terms by Hart, and in terms of 'integrity' by Dworkin was, Simmonds reminds us, traversed by Kelsen. Simmonds's caution[32] regarding the absolute separation of analytical from normative questions is an assertion which itself holds an extended and complex epistemology centring upon the collapse of the fact-value distinction.[33] Simmonds provides a workable dynamic for the potential impasse created by such collapse by reminding us that, rather than search for a 'purified core' of law or meaning either in terms of broad interpretive practice or strict semantic classification, we should recognize that broad juridical structures create a framework within which a variety of questions and positions may be addressed. The framework does not supply all-encompassing answers; rather, it provides a structured context for asking questions, for approaching each issue as a problem-solving exercise which should ideally be so framed as to be sensitive to broad contextual and narrow semantic shifts:[34]

> Once we see that the core of settled meaning of a concept is constituted by nothing beyond the fact of agreement in application, we see that such agreement may or may not result from adoption of a shared criterion. In some cases we may agree in our usage of a word across a range of instances because we share criteria for its use; but in other cases we may agree in our usage across a range of instances because we hold different criteria that happen to overlap in specific situations. Such criterial divergence would be compatible

31 id., p. 294.
32 id., p. 299.
33 The impact of this collapse has been fuelled of late by the writings of Hilary Putnam, reviewing the fact-value dichotomy in the realm of science and affirming that *scientific* questions of fact will be tainted by the value-loading of the questions being asked by the frail human agent. This further confirms apprehensions impacting upon the fields of legal theory and legal science, and upon analytical and normative jurisprudence. For an evaluation of Putnam, see R. Scruton, *Modern Philosophy* (1994).
34 Simmonds, op. cit., n. 11, p. 296.

71

with agreement on a number of abstract precepts, in addition to agreement upon a range of applications; but ... such abstract precepts would be provisional guides only, taken as settled relative to an envisaged range of applications but tending to fragment in the face of unexpected circumstances.

Arguably, one of the benefits of a more positivist-orientated approach[35] is that it can more readily accommodate this problem-centred, or purpose-centred enquiry without imposing a preordained notion of essences, both for contingent doctrinal purposes, and for any attempt to create a broad rationale of the identity of law itself. There is here a striking resemblance to the early scientific writings of Russell and more particularly Whitehead.[36] In so far as law lays claim to a systemic model analogous to science, such conceptions could serve as a useful summary of the parameters of legal science.

But the vision of the natural-positivist divide, and of blurred philosophical and semantic links at least partially reconciled via recognition of the problem- or purpose-driven nature of the exercise (of the inherent flux, not only between questions of fact and value, but between those of the universal and the particular, the concrete and contingent – key points of legitimacy for legal theory) places emphasis upon the *dynamics* of the enquiry.[37] This relationship between process and rationality – and its implications for dealing with contingent, material events as uncontrolled and uncontrollable aspects of our physical existence – was as much challenged, and sharpened by events in 1939 as it is today.

Auden, a worldly and sceptical intellectual, turned most naturally to rationalist and political texts as the world of events unfolded around him. Somewhat fatefully, the rationalist he lighted upon at this time was A.N. Whitehead, whose *Process and Reality*[38] attempted to bring about a synthesis of mathematics, logic and metaphysics. Potentially most far-reaching perhaps, are the impacts, for logic, of 'process' – that neither space or time 'exist' simply as concrete entities[39] but can only be identified *as* entities, within a process. The implications for logical positivists became scattered across different cognate fields[40] and anyway threaten such a world of intangibles that they surfaced in the politically loaded discourse of postmodernism with greater ease than evolving through the structures of

---

35 As implied by Simmonds, id.
36 See Emmet on this earlier period in Whitehead's writing, D.M. Emmet, *Whitehead's Philosophy of Organizm* (1932, 1966 edn.) at 110.
37 In modern theory the dynamic has been expressed variously, from Dworkin to Unger.
38 A.N. Whitehead, *Process and Reality* (1929).
39 Of course Wittgenstein as well as Russell contributed to such debates. For a modern summary, see 'Realism and Anti-Realism' in *The Internet Encyclopaedia of Philosophy* at <http://www.utm/edu/research/rep/w/wittgens.htm>.
40 Tracing the impact of the Logical Positivists as they scattered at the end of the 1930s is a complex task. From their intellectual 'cradle' in the Vienna Circle of the 1930s they influenced many disparate groups. For a broad context, see G. Iggers, *Historiography in the Twentieth Century* (1997) 120.

positivist logic. The implications for legal science and legal theory remain no less tantalizing. Mendelson[41] traces Auden's unwillingness:

> to give a personal name to the absolute, and as he tried to describe a basis for values that was more secure than liberalism, his prose became ever more polysyllabic and opaque ... In an essay for *The Nation*, arguing that 'In a civilized society ... orthodoxy can only be secured by a cooperation of which free controversy is an essential part', Auden again built his argument on a foundation given by Collingwood, but he seems to have sensed that the structure was dangerously shaky ... He now propped it up with new arguments that he took from Alfred North Whitehead's *Process and Reality* (1929), a philosophical account of (among many other metaphysical and scientific matters) a society's need for an order that is inevitably mutable and imperfect. Whitehead's vocabulary – with such negatives as 'triviality' and 'vagueness' and such positives as 'actuality' and 'order' – saturated Auden's work for the next few months, and never entirely disappeared from it. Whitehead, more subtly and convincingly than Collingwood, found a common language for social order and personal order. He emphasized that both are inherently dynamic[42] and that the same principles apply to each; in arguing this, he called attention to the intellectual trap in which one kind of order is treated as the subordinate or image of the other, as in the myth of the 'body politic', where society has a single ruler because the body has one. Whitehead's double focus, and the explicit theological basis of his thought, gave Auden hope that he could at last integrate private and public matters in ways that he had not been able to learn from Marx or Freud. But his argument in 'A Note on Order,' with its numbered propositions and proliferating qualifications ('every orthodoxy, in fact, is, in an absolute sense, heretical'), [Auden] rose to a level of abstraction and imprecision in which the psychological and political dilemmas that had first prompted it seemed to disappear. Generalising about a Christian doctrine it refused to identify, the essay collapsed into empty exhortations that few readers were likely to understand and none likely to follow.

Reading Whitehead for a *logician's* solution alienated Auden; it was too abstract, too ridden with qualifications, despite the attractions of an intellectual account promising a marriage of theory and practice, public and private. Indeed, Whitehead's philosophical position, as a mathematician and Idealist philosopher is difficult to embrace, taking Humean empiricism to a realm of transcendentalism.[43] Auden's intellectual instinct was ever sceptical and attracted to pure rationality, yet he could observe and justify his instinct to recoil from this. In his essay 'Hic et Ille' in *The Dyer's Hand*, he wrote:

> [as a child] I spent many hours imagining in the minutest detail the Platonic Idea of all lead mines. In planning its concentrating mill, I ran into difficulty: I had to choose between two types of a certain machine for separating the slimes. One I found more 'beautiful' but the other was, I knew from my

41 Mendelson, op. cit., n. 8, pp. 157–8.
42 A dynamic of central importance to the poem under discussion herein.
43 The extent to which other British Idealists, Bradley, Green, Bosanquet, later developed different versions of idealism within their own philosophical systems more in keeping with a concrete empiricism and logic forms an additional strand.

73

reading, the more efficient. My feeling at the time, I remember very clearly, was that I was confronted by a moral choice and that it was my duty to choose the second.[44]

Auden's subsequent adoption of the more accessible, linear approach of Kierkegaard expressed his turning from a rationalism which attempted to absorb the divine as an adjunct, when rationalism itself was clearly staggering forward on shaky foundations. A barometer of his time, such recoil was unfolding in the more general philosophical return to Natural Law theories.

After writing the poem, Auden was particularly shocked into the arms of religious explanations by his realization of human weakness and his loss of faith in rationality as an *adequate* source of solutions. Yet his subsequent insistence that we must 'love one another *and* die',[45] that we keep justice alive through *ironic* points of light, relies upon a plea to rationality independent of essences. The admission that even a successful polity – 'love' – will *still die* marks a refusal to pour the balm of a falsely Utopian *worldly* resolution or divine immortality, upon the political wound. Given that law could be described as a system designed to contain the impact of the immanent and contingent, war – as we have recently observed – becomes its most rigorous test. Just as Auden's poem reveals this moment of ideological fracture – what might be described as the collapse of the natural-positivist *engagement* in human perception – with the loss of a credible secular rationality becoming overwhelmed by a tide of metaphysical neediness, so Whitehead's discussion of uniformity and contingency seems more relevant. In the endless recalibration of factors that forms the discourse between analytical and normative jurisprudence, the unpredictable nature of the contingent world is poorly debated.

Attempts to formulate points of contact between analytic and normative models of philosophy and law may with good reason appear more sophisticated than those of the early twentieth century. Identification of Dworkin's theoretical weakness as traceable to autonomy culture and decontextualization (both of individual and semantic operations) is *part* of the story of current legal theory. The weakness is also a predictable outcome of the truncations in theory generally. Part of this may be traced to a mistaken Protestant inheritance, partly to the symbolic magnitude of war in relation to an overweening ego-driven mechanistic Positivism. But less visible contingencies may also have been co-incidents.

---

44 Auden, op. cit., n. 28, at p. 102. This statement directly precedes the observation, 'Like all polemical movements, existentialism is one-sided' – regretting the spiritually unsatisfactory aspects of the existential movement.

45 Altering the line in the poem from the original injunction to 'love one another *or* die'.

74

REJECTION OF THE POEM, METABOLIZATION, AND THE LESSON OF 'THE WINDIEST MILITANT TRASH'

Perhaps one of the most profound lessons for any analysis of unfolding processes of theory is not just the poem itself, but its subsequent rejection by Auden, alongside its unending metabolization for varying purposes, by others. In spite of its being a poem most frequently referred to, adopted by popular causes, and endlessly prescient of contingent events, Auden was quick to distance himself from it and attempted to excise it from the corpus of his work. Appearing at a crucial point in his own ideological crisis, the poem inhabits a space of transition, where adoption of a compelling but inauthentic synthesis is immanent. Two expressions in the poem were altered by Auden. The first related to the call to collective unity to 'love one another or die'. The second alteration related to the notion of justice preserved through the dark days: the initial impotence of the agents of justice signalling their 'little' points of light were later modified to 'ironic' points – arguably a more potent vehicle for the preservation of justice, despite temporary suspension. He knew that the momentary zeal producing 'we must love one another or die' was logically, and ideologically thin – altering it to 'we must love one another *and* die' before abandoning it altogether – and his apprehension was borne out by the successive generations of popular zealots, political spinners, and desperate myth makers to whom such sentiments so readily lent themselves. Accounts of the significance of the poem, and of Auden's recoil vary, and this variation too is a point of caution to analysis. Carpenter notes that:[46]

> The poem's closing words were echoed in a book review Auden wrote about two weeks later ... 'There is one way to the true knowledge and only one,' he wrote, 'a praxis which, if defined in terms of human relations, we should call love'. But there was still no question in his mind of this view becoming anything that could be called religious belief ... he suggested that belief in God as a conscious agent outside Man was 'dualist' and therefore wrong ...

Nevertheless, within weeks, the inexorable attraction back to a metaphysics which would provide divine support was completed when:[47]

> Two months after the outbreak of war, in November 1939, he went to a cinema in Yorkville, the district of Manhattan where he and Isherwood had lived for a few weeks in the spring. It was largely a German-speaking area, and the film he saw was *Sieg im Poland*, an account by the Nazis of their conquest of Poland. When Poles appeared on the screen he was startled to hear a number of people in the audience scream 'Kill them!' He later said of this: 'I wondered then, why I reacted as I did against this denial of every humanistic value. The answer brought me back to the church.' He had been through many changes of heart since reaching adulthood, but all the dogmas he had adopted or played with – post-Freudian psychology, Marxism, and the liberal-socialist-

46 H. Carpenter, *W.H. Auden, A Biography* (1992) 274.
47 id., p. 282.

democratic outlook ... had one thing in common: they were all based on a belief in the natural goodness of man. They all claimed that if one specific evil were removed ... sexual repression ... the domination ... by the bourgeoisie, or Fascism, then humanity would be happy ... [even his viewpoint in] the summer of 1939 ... which might be called liberal humanism with religious and pacifist overtones, was still based on a belief in man's natural goodness. Its message was, in the words of the poem which summed it up, 'We must love one another or die': that is, only the exercise of love between human being would save humanity from self-destruction ... Auden's experience in the Yorkville cinema in November 1939 radically shook this belief. He now became convinced that human nature was not and never could be good ... 'The whole trend of liberal thought', he wrote during 1940, 'has been to undermine faith in the absolute ... It has tried to make reason the judge ... But since life is a changing process ... the attempt to find a humanistic basis for keeping a promise, works logically with the conclusion, "I can break it whenever I feel it convenient".'

This view was confirmed by Auden's reading of Kierkegaard, for whom the 'ethical' stage of experience (which followed upon the 'aesthetic' – note the similarities to Comte)[48] with its clear identity with politics and ideology:

> would soon in its turn prove inadequate, because it made no claims on any transcendent notion of eternity, and because its foundation, a belief in the individual's (or humanity's) basic righteousness would soon prove false – which was precisely what Auden had just realised.[49]

In a letter written to Stephen Spender in April 1940,[50] Auden writes:

> Just been reading Neville Henderson's book. What emerges most strongly I feel is that the basic weakness of the democracies is the failure to realise that if you give up Catholicism – and I think we must – one has to discover one's base again and that is a very long and very exhausting job. Henderson is the typical lazy Protestant living off the fat of his Catholic past and imagining that metaphysics and mysticism are unnecessary – the virtues will be kept alive by good form ...

Yet retracing a workable lineage for a new belief system – trying to 'discover one's base again' – clearly proved too great a challenge for Auden himself. In a sense, the poem quite clearly flags this *moment* of ideological crisis, a moment quite visible in the chronology of reading and thoughts in Auden's personal accounts. And the symptom, the visible stigmata of this crisis, lies in the failure of thought at the heart of the poem. If Neville Henderson was a 'lazy Protestant', Auden was a hazy metaphysician. As Smith comments of the poem:[51]

48 Comte, a leading Positivist, devised a linear philosophy which posited the development of human intellectual understanding in terms of a movement from a theological, to a metaphysical towards a final positive, *scientific* phase. Kierkegaard similarly posited a linear development but beginning with the aesthetic, or sensory, moving on to the ethical, and concluding with the religious.
49 Carpenter, op. cit., n. 46, p. 285.
50 Quoted in K. Bucknell and N. Jenkins (eds.), *The Map of All My Youth* (1990) 73.
51 Smith, op. cit., n. 7, pp. 30–1.

The only way to elude this power of positive lying, in which every text is subverted by its negation, is to speak with the irony and indirection that is linked to justice in the last stanza. But even here the lie suborns affirmative speech ... What the poem affirms, in effect, is its own desperate sense of failure, its yearning for a community and a succession, at the moment that it realizes this is no more than one grand rhetorical gesture before falling on the floor ... One can understand Auden's embarrassment in the grey light of dawn. But it is precisely its honesty in catching the duplicity and bad faith that makes it a fine and powerful poem ... The poem undoes the folded lie of the ideologically composed subject ...

Hungry for a *comprehensive* – transcendent – ideological pathway, a religious, or at any rate, metaphysically rich 'solution' was perhaps incipient for Auden, as it was for many thinkers of the time. Yet he continued to grapple with the political implications of semantics, howsoever resolved his divine contract. In the 1950s Auden further crystallized and objectified the problem of the thin ideological seam. By this time, as Smith makes clear, Auden recognized the corruption of the word:[52]

... the song from the resonant heart in the grand old manner no longer work[s]. These forms have been hopelessly compromised by a mass society, where 'All words like peace and love,/All sane affirmative speech,/Had been soiled, profaned, debased/To a horrid mechanical screech.' In 1950–1, for veteran socialists like Auden ... such a profane language was not confined to the Eastern bloc, but was embodied in the United States by the horrid mechanical screech of McCarthyism, in a language 'Concocted by editors/Into spells to befuddle the crowd', 'pawed-at and gossiped over', leaving the only surviving civil style that of a marginalized 'suburb of dissent', wry, ironic, *sotto voce*. It is the quietness of Auden's dissenting style, in the fifties, which misleads the critic into believing he has renounced politics ...

Scholarly 'threads' on the internet indicate the extent to which Auden's poem has been adapted to political rhetoric, notably by a speech-writer for George Bush Senior and for Ronald Reagan.[53] Most dramatically however, Mendelson records:[54]

... in 1964 ... the advertising consultant who prepared television spots for Lyndon Johnson's presidential campaign – a campaign that accurately portrayed Johnson's opponent as eager to use nuclear weapons while inaccurately portraying Johnson as a committed peacemaker – produced a thirty-second film in which a young girl counted the petals she was picking from a daisy while a male voice-over counted from ten to zero. When the countdown ended, the image of the girl disappeared and a nuclear explosion filled the screen. Over the expanding mushroom cloud was heard Johnson's voice: 'These are the stakes: to make a world in which all of God's children can live, or go into the dark. We must love each other or we must die.' The dark, the children, and the night, together with the resonant misquoted line, were all lifted from Auden's poem.

52 id., p. 169.
53 See D. Lupher, internet thread 'Auden, 'Sept. 1, 1939' (was: Re. 9/11) at <http://omega.cohums.ohio-state.edu/hyper-lists/classics-1/01-99-99/0011.htm>.
54 Mendelson, op. cit, n. 8, p. 478.

77

An internet search for 'September 1, 1939' reveals a mass identification of 1/9/1939 with 9/11/2001:[55]

> Auden's words are everywhere ... the Times Literary Supplement ... It was read on National Public Radio ... the Chicago area ... four blocks from ground zero in Manhattan ... newspaper cited one of the poem's most familiar lines, 'We must love one another or die'.

The thin ideological seam, its tensile weakness, continues to fracture with this benighted line, providing a muster station of collective emotivism.

CONCLUSION: THEORY THEN AND NOW – ANGLO-AMERICAN ALLOYS

The points of fracture in Auden's poem – and responses to them – reveal the network of ideological and historical factors besetting the development of functional notions of autonomy in a destabilized world. As in the world of pragmatic decision, so also in the world of theory, the claim to rational neutrality bound to the myth of the individual unfettered by prejudicial interests holds great sway. Yet, whether in his juristic, political or philosophical mode, this 'creature' of autonomy is subject to poorly reconciled tensions, between the inhibitions of mortal life and of personal, local, and global polity. The pragmatic message that we must love one another *and* die, remains submerged by competing claims to deliver an integrity of immortal magnitude.

It was Auden's fate – and that of developing theory itself – to encounter the fulcrum of ideas at a time when, to quote W B Yeats, 'the centre cannot hold':[56] at a time of war. The excesses of visible collective human weakness drove Auden, like Wordsworth before him,[57] away from the pursuit of politics and rationality back into the private and, for him, the religious. And it is likely that not only the intellectual uncertainty of this encounter with *logic itself* proved too great. For Whitehead's *presentation* of the arguments may also have fuelled the failure.[58] Nevertheless, Whitehead's discussion of

---

55 Sites continue to proliferate, but see for example *The Boston Globe* at <http://www.boston.com/news/packages/sept11/anniversary/globe-stories/lyrics/9-1-1939.htm>.

56 W.B. Yeats, 'The Second Coming' was written in the wake of the First, 'Great' World War.

57 Wordsworth famously returned from witnessing the appalling excesses of the French Revolution and, despairing of his erstwhile hope of witnessing the birth of a new humanist polity, his poetry became markedly committed to the private, individual, and domestic life.

58 On the one hand, his writing is so impenetrable as to obscure the rational appeal held out by his position. In addition, he claims to achieve a further, macroscopic synthesis, an 'organic' process, encompassing not only the time-space problematic, but also God – the 'vertigo' of freefalling space and time invites a compensatory organic

78

our engagement with the contingent world around us provides a conception of the appalling range of factors to be apprehended in the understanding of any moment, or cluster of moments. War is the result of a tension between a collective prehension and apprehension, in a world of distant 'perceptual objects' and unpredictable 'ingressions'.[59] Add to this the elements of human nature contributing to the inception of war – aggression, territoriality, passionate ideological identities, greed, anxiety (all identified as competing claims in Auden's poem) – and the challenge facing the philosopher and jurist is significant indeed.[60] The 'vertigo' of this incredible metaphysics of physics steered Auden away from faith in rationalism towards a more tenable rationalism of faith, which he soon found in the more comfortably *linear* approach of Kierkegaard. The poetic, moral, and rational failure embodied in the line 'We must love one another or die' is symptomatic of the crisis. Arguably it exemplifies a collapse of reason into a sea of sentiment. More profoundly, it heralds the further separation of belief in systems and systems of belief that characterized intellectual thought in many fields from that time on. The process-driven argument was overshadowed by that forerunner of postmodernity, the threat of relativity – in science and philosophy – and then, as now, seemed therefore to presage a loss of all values. In jurisprudence as in philosophy, the new insights derived from the human capacity for war and atrocity had their own antecedents, not least in terms of cultural flux on each side of the Atlantic.

The contingent event of war – and the ideological strains leading up to war – drove theorists back to 'Natural Law' models, in part because of the altered picture of human nature and the associated need to review the credibility of man-made laws. This 'trauma' also drove individuals like Auden, and possibly the unconscious trends within the greater intellectual community, back to the Natural Law view, sometimes amounting to a reliance upon the divine as the only 'bearable' way to deal with the vertiginous reality of war and human suffering. Alongside Simmonds's historical account of the natural-positivist divide as unnecessary bifurcation, we can still observe an unexplored parallel line. Auden's poem betrays a personal turning away from the philosophical journey of

metaphysics. It is likely that at the very least, this undermined his claim to scientific objectivity and thus his credibility. For Davidson, it confirmed a psychologically sceptical positivism, though Davidson adapted Whitehead's notion of the event as moment (Scruton, op. cit., n. 33, p. 374). The impact of this analysis reminds one of Philip Larkin's observation (in *Deceptions*) that 'suffering is exact/but where desire takes charge/readings can grow erratic'.

59 To borrow directly from Whitehead's terms, which at times bear some resemblance to those of Gerard Manley Hopkins.

60 Whitehead's rationale would seem to point up the ethical challenge of incipient events; his view of a dynamic universe in which both man and God are implicated in the realms of possibility nevertheless places great focus upon the percipient intervention, the *action*. Though there is a kind of optimism inherent in the idea of 'process', it bears an uncertainty not present in conventional notions of teleology.

79

positivism (and indeed his attraction to Kierkegaard places him in almost exact opposition to Comte) and it reflects the 'popular' account – quite apart from the exchanges undertaken by scholars such as Fuller and Hart – of why the natural/positivist divide became crystallized by war, as atrocity and human frailty drove theory 'back' towards 'Natural Law' certainties and humilities.[61] Yet the continuing influence of positivism as an offshoot of an enlightenment project which sought to explore intellectual possibility as an expression of human capability and potential[62] – as a quest for an ethical legitimacy born of reason – remains vast. The links between logical positivism and linguistics, as well as logical positivism and legal positivism, are more than merely historical. They reflect a deliberate resistance to emotivism and are sustained by a separability thesis of which a *sense* arguably should be sustained, despite the caution voiced by the collapse of the fact/value distinction.[63] The alteration to the actual course of theory is more difficult to chart, with its strands of cross-fertilization, but despite the small shockwave of the war/Natural Law tremor, British positivism is still predominant because of an 'incremental', sceptical intellectual tradition (a characteristic which Whitehead deplored for obvious reasons). Yet we cannot resist the iconic power accorded to war in the minds of men as a locus of *ideological* reaction, even if we understand it intellectually and physically as just another contingent event, or just another collision of historical forces, as opposed to a predominantly *engineered* act of aggression, of a controlled embodiment of 'evil'.[64] The event itself provides a testing ground for possible conflicts between – and the credibility of natural and positivist models of – notions of legality, *and* for arguments about whether and to what extent each *contains* elements of the other, given the potential of 'the event' in posing an opportunity for theory to be tested against a problem-centred moment. Certainly, the 'contest' between positivist and Natural Law theories seems writ large in the political rhetoric surrounding accounts of legality, and the

---

61 Indeed, as has been noted, the event of war itself contributed to the fragmentation of the Vienna Circle as an unfolding centre of Logical Positivism.

62 In contradistinction to the infantilizing mindset forced upon humanity by an overweening metaphysical shadow. The position emerging here would tend therefore to 'lean' towards a positivist 'emphasis' *as an ethic*, in contrast to the analysis posed by Stephen Hall: see S. Hall, 'The Persistent Spectre: Natural Law, International Order and the Limits of Legal Positivism' (2001) 12 *European J. of International Law* 269–307.

63 Albeit a collapse with more ancient roots than are often admitted, with Humean restoration and with an added potency in current scientific and humanities theory.

64 The European split over whether military action in Iraq was legitimate, with a failure to comply with a multitude of resolutions on the one hand and a lack of consensus on the final resolution on the other, has certainly been an interesting lesson in international law and politics. The division of international lawyers regarding action on the status of Resolution 1441 is summarized by P. Gould, 'War with Iraq "could be illegal"' *BBC News Online*, <http://news.bbc.co.uk/1/hi/uk/2826331.stm>.

embarrassment of religious faith *behind* the machine of secular law and politics an interesting entity[65] threatening a potential collapse of the claimed distinctive ideological integrity vis-à-vis the 'fundamentalism' of Eastern positions. On the one hand, we may say that philosophy is now more fit to raise an analytical account of potentially synthetic conceptual strands. On the other hand, any such highly evolved positivism capable of rising from the ashes of a fragmented international legal and political order is threatened, not just by that fragmentation, but by the clear seduction power of alternative principles which offer to *salve* as well as *assuage* the brute conditions of material existence – a real battleground between natural and positivist views of legality.

How then does this affect how we envision the Natural Law/positivist divide, or future models of law? How do currents of theory presently unfolding compare with those of the 1930s and 40s, remembering that, in so far as the disputes about relativity and its possible/probable impact on metaphysics were concerned, they were anyway in place long before the war, and that the argument that positivism can be a more conscientious, because conscious, basis for ethics remains compelling. Legal Positivism in the 'macrocosmic', 'structural' sense may be 'about' the source of law, but its adumbration of analytical positivism is a direct descendant of empirical method. The most difficult question is still the relation of sense data – including our articulation of it via semantic logic – to constructions of 'reality'. Looking back at Auden's crisis, his turning, like many of his generation, from positivist polity to fundamental faith can be characterized as a failure of rationalism, an inability to stem the tide of atavistic instinct in the face of ideological crisis. Specifically for Auden, A.N. Whitehead proved a poor propagandist for rationalism compared to Kierkegaard, partly because of Whitehead's obscurity but also, arguably, the *sentimentality* behind Whitehead's drive for an *organic* account of rationality and science – a Process and Reality which seems very much like an act of bad faith – a forced synthesis. Whilst noting the patent danger that *positivism's* own logical resistance to the annexation of a moving popular ideology may leave it vulnerable to being 'overrun' by mass ideological appetite, the failure of an 'organic' account linked to logical positivism at *that* time may provide a warning to us now. Though the collapse of the fact-value distinction is further verified in the scientific as in the philosophical realm, with implications for logical and legal positivism which may herald a necessary and natural flowering of synthetic theories such as consideration of deontic logic, the need for a fundamental *sense* of a neutral positivist ethic should hold the centre together in time of crisis. Similarly, in Auden's poem, the 'leap' of 'we must love one another *or* die' looks very like a metaphysical knee-jerk, a 'thin' theory of the good, a Natural Lawyer's assertion of faith,

---

65 For a discussion of perceptions of the religious 'war', see 'Atlantic Storms' *Time*, <http://www.time.com/europe/magazine/2003/0120/cover/story-4.htm>.

81

with its promise, behind the apparent stake in utility ('if we don't create a workable polity, a workable international relations, we will kill ourselves') of immortality ('if we achieve universal love, we achieve a kind of immortality, a defeat of mortality itself'). The alteration to 'we must love one another *and* die' at least gives proper place to the knowable physics of our mortal imprimatur. The final verse acts both as a warning, and as a reclamation of this need for a centre. The collapse of rationality preceding it (which Auden himself could not control, yet subsequently found intellectual and artistically untenable) the insoluble paradox of 'the error bred in the bone' wishing not for 'universal love', but 'to be loved alone', so improbably juxtaposed with 'we must love one another or die' implies a centre that cannot hold. The final verse reminds us that the focus of this debate lies not with attempts to produce rationalizations of compromise, but to concentrate on notions of justice. The institution of 'ironic' points of light in the approach to justice (in the final verse of Auden's poem) reasserts the sense of the sceptical, whilst the erasure of the 'little' points of light with irony in place of littleness is a rejection of the vision of an impotent human agent and concomitant fatalism that tends to underlie the 'Natural Law' model, secular or otherwise, in the thrall to a static rather than dynamic metaphysics.

At the time of writing the poem, Auden was sceptical of political and philosophical discourse – he had witnessed their corruption in Europe and their contribution in the journey to war. Auden's poem bears witness to the contention that the complete fracture of individual and collective views of the polity, alongside the separation of 'positivist' from 'naturalist' accounts of philosophy, is a historically *and* logically questionable phenomenon. The section tracing a direct line 'from Luther to Linz', whilst daring scholars to produce an 'accurate' account of the pathway, is admirably met by Simmonds's analysis of the misunderstood journey from Protestantism to Positivism. Furthermore, Dworkin's work is symptomatic of this mistaken history and, in utilizing a cathected form of Protestant autonomy, runs the risk of suffering the selfsame tensile weakness exhibited in the irreconcilable aspects of Auden's poem. Auden was also at that time infused with a faith in American claims to philosophical and political neutrality and this may well have imbued the poem with its sense of the masses sincerely hurrying towards their ethical life. His later rejection of the poem hints at his more characteristic intellectual scepticism and at his recognition of the tensile 'fracture' or 'seam' in the poem. As time went by, his realization that the United States offered simply another flawed promise of a noble dream was corroborated by the political and popular colonizations endured by the poem itself. His reservation could reflect the reservation we should maintain regarding the roots of American jurisprudence which claim a foothold in *both* natural and positivist traditions.[66]

66 The maintenance of ongoing parallel strands is intriguing and complex, clearly linking to genuine influences in the American Realist tradition.

The poem's tensile weakness, its conception and colonization in the context of political cultures claiming neutrality, exemplifies the ease with which theoretical fracture is metabolized for sundry purposes. It also points up the need to consider the complex interaction between ideological rhetoric and intellectual cultures. In this regard, Dworkin may be seen against the backdrop of an American history of belief in the *possibility* of neutrality, in individual integrity quite divorced from the taint of the subjective. Hart clearly identifies the particularly American locus of this phenomenon – naming Dworkin, Posner, and Pound as particular examples.[67] Yet Hart does *not* fully explore the political culture which gives rise to this illusory path.[68] Is not this same rhetoric of neutrality, coupled with the culture of a Constitutional rights 'shield', detectable in recent American political theory and international policy? Auden's initial poetic weakness may reflect a moment of seduction by this puritan political voice, with its apparent resolution of individual and collective – in a local politics of global aspirations – heralding intimations of immortality of a kind. The noble aspiration of neutrality and integrity had long characterized American jurisprudence and tended to colour the presentation, at least the rhetorical stance, of international political policy.[69] But the conclusion that:[70]

> ... rights theory has a long and honourable ancestry in the Natural Law tradition in America ... and has long been closely associated with less formal and more substantive modes of legal reasoning

betrays an innate fealty to a particular metaphysical framework, 'natural', pervasive, and sometimes febrile in its expression. Though Fuller forwards a hypothesis concerning the source of law which draws upon the American model,[71] in the words of Atiyah and Summers, he 'fails to develop, as has American legal theory generally, a synthesis reconciling Natural Law and positivism'.[72]

---

67 H.L.A. Hart, 'American Jurisprudence through English Eyes: The Nightmare and the Noble Dream' (1977) 11 *Georgia Law Rev.* 969, reproduced in Hart, *Essays in Jurisprudence and Philosophy* (1983) 123–44.

68 Indeed, Hart, id., p. 127 identifies the decision in *Roe* v. *Wade* as an example of judicial partiality *simpliciter*. Yet the decision may be characterized altogether differently. For 'finding' a constitutional source through the indirect route of 'privacy' (as was the case in *Roe*) whilst fettering the freedom with inbuilt constraints might be seen as a persuasive sop which, whilst appearing to bear the force of constitutional right, is nevertheless vulnerable to assault. On this same point, Dworkin himself is persuaded that the decision really does bestow a 'right', see R. Dworkin, *Life's Dominion* (1994). Thus, Hart and Dworkin are oddly in agreement in their understanding of the *significance* of the judgment, though differing in their accounts of the antecedents.

69 Though not, of course, domestic politics: see P. Atiyah and R. Summers, *Form and Substance in Anglo-American Law* (1991) at 248.

70 id., p. 266.

71 id., p. 261.

72 id., p. 262.

A more general conclusion may also be derived from these attempted conciliations. Whilst remembering the false footing of the 'separation thesis', there is a need to ensure that engagement between analytical and normative, natural and positivist theories foster *meaningful* encounters which serve the semantic and conceptual possibilities whilst remaining alive to their own logical limits, resisting the attractions of a wish-driven synthesis, as exemplified by Whitehead and Auden, amongst others. Auden divined that, though eccentric, Whitehead made some attempt to sustain the link with 'sensory phenomena'[73] and thus his odd conjunction of physics and metaphysics holds both a caution and a lesson to current theorists.[74] Though collisions of space-time in terms of 'natural' disasters may be closer to the kind of examples Whitehead had in mind, the contribution of human cognition to the concatenation of events not always entirely derived from human activity, and ending in war, is an especially meaningful testing-ground for the contest of the 'then and now' in the juristic evaluation of the natural/positivist nexus. A theory of how we apprehend the contingent world seems intimately bound to how we perceive the jurisprudential model of law.[75] And it is our inability to reconstitute destroyed matter, or the irrevocable alteration in or world that is 'history' (whether as death, murder, war, pre-event ignorance, pre-discovery innocence) which makes the linear view of time and space *appear* the only tenable vision of reality: in other words, mortality, and the *permanent* effects of contingent events force us to order our world, both practically and morally, in a particular way. If we could grasp – howsoever it may be an illusion – that we are all obliged to share our physical condition as laws which appear to operate as linear event sequences with teleological implications, what impact would or could this have on our collective understanding of individual moral responsibility, and therefore of the shape of our institutional structures, such as law? Would our envisioning of the entire framework be altered, as well as that of the

73 See quotation linking to n. 41 above..
74 The vision of an 'absent' space and time, with a dynamic model of human and divine existence 'in process' may render his theory fundamentally frail, if not in terms of vulnerability to logical attack, then in terms of intellectual reception of the model. In addition, his ability to *transmit* his ideas may in part have suffered from his own transition across epistemologies at a time when the attendant vocabularies were not particularly receptive. Nevertheless – and this is a lesson – Whitehead's discussions of spatio-temporal co-incidence had become more intelligible by the 1940s, when Auden was undergoing his war-induced crisis. War could be described as the ultimate historical example of ideological fracture becoming 'visible' in a space-time collision as contingent event.
75 The focus of early twentieth-century physics and philosophy became the problem of relativity, and Whitehead's attempt to explain this in terms of the relationship between a non-linear space and time and the 'fixation' of space and time in the moment of the contingent event may provide the root of a contrasting ethical position to that posed by the concept of relativity.

normative significance of the individual act, of individual agency?[76] Are we then better able to see the legal system, model the source of law, as a pragmatic response to a vertiginous situation, rather than the 'inevitable' outcome of an unfolding though disputed empirical narrative – are we better able to see or justify the 'multi-positional' nature of the contingent event, of legal and political discourse? In short, could such a view of the physical world affect our 'necessary' metaphysics?

If the 'error bred in the bone' of all humanity is our need 'to be loved alone'; if this habitual self-concern is not only dominant, but normal, which form of legitimation for the legal order *logically* will have *imperium*? A vigorous qualification of purist assertions of Natural Law might recognize that a 'return' to Natural Law provoked by contingent crisis is a predictable return to the atavistic, or shamanistic intellectual device at a time of peril – as seems to have been the case with Auden himself. Certainly account should be taken of the metaphysics of morals which, though in one sense questionable as so much incommensurable ephemera of the sentimental mind, nevertheless reflects an enduring and universal 'meta' or 'supra'-physical reality for mankind. Modern scholars such as Simmonds and Coyle, for example, are revisiting the intellectual and historical reasons for such synthesis, from the epistemological and conceptual bifurcations traced by Simmonds to the growing scepticism of the fact/value distinction.[77] But account should be taken on the *other* hand of the history, and intellectual locus standi, the intellectual robustness of the *logical* positivism which contributes to legal positivism.[78] Though some 'truce' may be desirable, though it may even be logically, rationally inevitable or incontrovertible, it is nevertheless the case that the natural/positivist nexus is itself a battlefield. This may be a natural[79] as well as accidental or contrived site of difference, more or less intellectually tenable than the 'opposition' theory might

---

76 This nods towards the original empirical concerns of the Logical Positivists. See, also, M. Williams, *Empty Justice: One Hundred Years of Law, Literature and Philosophy* (2002), 'Conclusion'.

77 Synthetic enquiries form an influential current in contemporary jurisprudence: see S. Coyle, 'The Possibility of Deontic Logic' (2002) 15 *Ratio Juris* 294–318.

78 There is no escape from an element of subjectivism, yet the inherent location of positivism as an attempt to approach a value-neutral enquiry itself amounts to an ideological position. Resistance to asserting a locus on the ideological register, provided it adheres to a declared political integrity *through* resistance, is a potential ethical strength, and to some extent a precondition, of the positivist mode of reasoning. On either side of the 'divide' however, a loss of consciousness of such constraints renders theory vulnerable to the *visceral* attractions of an all-encompassing metaphysics.

79 There may even be a neurological, as well as historical and cultural, reason for the tendency to polarize belief, to adopt either a predominantly religious or metaphysical world view, or a more physical and empirically-driven account. V.S. Ramachandran at the University of California, San Diego, 'has found evidence of brain circuitry in the temporal lobe that has given rise to religious experience', see <http://www.internet-encyclopedia.org/wiki.phtml?title=Religion>.

suggest: as with the atomistic world of physical positivism, and grafting of any supra-physical 'natural' theory, so also with the 'molecular' structures of global politics. Just as the overt fundamentalism of some 'non-liberal' ideologies clearly pose the threat of primitivism, so too will the covert threat – disguised as an allegedly flexible, secular heterogenous polity – of undeclared fundamentalism posed by liberalism.[80] In the 'contest' between 'natural' and 'positivist' models of international law recently invoked, experts were divided as to which model prevailed in the analysis of international pacts and breaches leading to war, but political characterization appeared to rely upon a prioritization of naturalist arguments, with positivist justifications supplied in a rearguard, retrospective, and defensive campaign.[81] Both Natural and Positive law theories are attempts to erect justifications for legitimacy and authority of law as system of control and order: the tendency to be oppositional and essentialist is likely to be driven by this, by an underlying caution that authority will dissipate if either appear to compromise inherent claims to a coherent belief system – the one based on internal/Biblical 'moral' code, the other on a dispassionate rational code, neutral as to content. Auden's poem marks the crisis of ideas that such tension represents. In a collection of Auden's essays we are told:[82]

> Towards the end of the 1930's Auden began to question ... whether natural community ... could still be deemed to exist. At the root of this questioning was the rise of Fascism with its dependence on identity of feeling as a substitute for the quest for truth. Auden found it impossible to deny Fascism's socialist roots. At the same time he was unwilling to reject socialism simply because it had, like any political philosophy, a potential for distortion. Instead he laid the blame firmly on something he had always mistrusted – the imprecision of romanticism. He traced this back to Rousseau's desire for a return to nature and original community. While he recognized the earlier value of community, Auden now believed that society was progressing from Catholic community to Protestant individualism ... 'it will be only when they fully realize their "aloneness" and accept it, that men will be able to achieve a real unity through a common recognition of their diversity ...'.

80 Dworkin's Protestantism might be characterized as the atomistic corollary of this.
81 See n. 64 above.
82 Bucknell and Jenkins, op. cit., n. 50, p. 99.

86

JOURNAL OF LAW AND SOCIETY
VOLUME 31, NUMBER 1, MARCH 2004
ISSN: 0263-323X, pp. 87–112

The Jurisprudence of Travel Literature: Despotism, Excess, and the Common Law

^{PIYEL HALDAR*}

PIYEL HALDAR*

This article is an attempt to gauge the influence of Orientalism upon western ideals of judgment. More specifically, it focuses on descriptions of despotism in early travel literature as a measure of what the emerging rationality of western legality was attempting to disavow.

INTRODUCTION

The men who grow angry with corruption, and impatient at injustice, and through those sentiments favour the abettor of revolution, have an obvious apology to palliate their error; theirs is the excess of a virtuous feeling. At the same time, however amiable may be the source of their error, the error itself is probably fraught with consequences pernicious to mankind.
W. Godwin, *Enquiry Concerning Political Justice* (1793)

There certainly however, some may say, are some advantages peculiar to despotic governments: they have fewer lawyers, and fewer law-suits, and those few are more speedily decided.
F. Bernier, *Travels in the Mughal Empire* (1671)

This article is an attempt to gauge the influence of Orientalism upon western ideals of judgment. More specifically, it focuses on descriptions of

* *School of Law, Birkbeck College, University of London, Malet St., London WC1E 7HX, England*

Thanks to Peter Goodrich and Elena Loizidou for all their suggestions. This article is part of a longer project on legal Orientalism that was undertaken after numerous chats in London's East End with the late Michael Caswell and the ghost of Marmaduke Stalkhart. The actual research for this particular article was conducted even further East. I would like to acknowledge the assistance of Dipan Das and Raithin Bishnu for facilitating my stay in Calcutta during a research trip in January 2000. Yet further, a version of this paper was read out at a staff seminar while I was a visiting fellow at the Faculty of Law, Griffith University, Brisbane (April 2000). Comments made by Rosemary Hunter, Bill Macneill, Shaun McVeigh, Graham Orr, and Brad Sherman are much appreciated. Any remaining causes of disorientation remain my own.

despotism in early travel literature as a measure of what the emerging rationality of western legality was attempting to disavow. It is no longer novel to claim that the methodological criteria that informs the just decision-making process emerge historically during a crisis of sovereignty that sees western European monarchies break free from feudal social structures. That is to say, a theoretical schism opens up between modernity and those pre-modern social structures that failed to conform to consciously theorized logical principles.

What remains to be charted, however, is the manner in which Orientalism managed to crystallize legal rationality. But the non-despotic model of authority and decision making that emerges from the early accounts of travellers to the Mughal Empire is unexpectedly complex. For this reason, they manage to reflect a different set of jurisprudential concerns than those accounts of despotism given by later philosophers such as Montesquieu, Rousseau, and even Bentham.

What we find in the pages of these early travel accounts is an attempt to situate despotism within an environment in which everything is excessive. Indeed, what will be argued here is that excess enjoyment becomes the common law of the East. The despot was not a one-off. Indeed, the whole machinery of interdiction, east of the Sublime Porte, had to be manifestly corrupt in order to explain the ubiquity of the despot. The despot and his subjects, his court and his countryside all show symptoms of pathological excess enjoyment. The idea of excess enjoyment is used in a strictly Lacanian sense. That is to say that such excess (*jouissance*) lies beyond mere pleasure (those pleasures permitted by all western states). In this sense, excess enjoyment does not restrict itself to the orgiastic. It includes other forms of monstrous aberrancies and ecstasies such as death, the pain of castration, and the expenditure of all that is deemed essential to the fabric of western civility. If excessive enjoyment refers to ecstasy, it is because ecstasy itself refers to that which is beyond life, or beyond *stasis*. This being so, excess enjoyment cannot be experienced in any other manner than as fantasy. Descriptions of such excess by the early travellers are rooted in nothing other than suspicion and fantasy and betray more about the mind of these travellers than about the figure of the despot. This article will thus conclude by examining the pathology of the literature that forms the basis of my analysis and what this might reveal as the other face of European legality.

IDENTIFYING THE FORMS OF ORIENTAL CORRUPTION: NATURE

From the jungle to the seraglio, the whole of the east, or so it was imagined, was absorbed in the sort of behaviour which transgressed European codes of civility. Early narratives of journeys to India uncovered a land of excess linked to experiences of corruption. Before turning to the Imperial seraglio,

88

it is important to note the significance of nature as the backdrop, emblem, and cause of wasteful expenditure. Early descriptions were fond of describing the oriental jungle in which vegetation spreads occupying all available space. The accounts of Marco Polo, Vasco da Gama, and John Mandeville not only described the seductive profusion of exotic fauna, flora, and precious commodities that were to be found throughout the east, but they also reported diabolical aberrations of nature. Descriptions of rhinos, pythons, ostriches, and giraffes were exaggerated and metamorphosed into colossal beasts. Elephants were so large that locals were able to 'fix castles on their backs, from which eight or ten men fight with javelins, bows, and those weapons which we call cross bows'.[1] Every aspect of nature was reported as being in excess of normality. Nicolo di Conti, for instance, asserts that he saw among the men of India 'one who was three hundred years old'. These accounts of the aberrations of oriental nature have a long history. Megasthenes reports that:

> They [Indians] get the gold from ants. These creatures are larger than foxes, but are in other respects like the ants of our own country. They dig holes in the earth like other ants. The heap which they throw up consists of gold the purest and brightest in all the world. The mounds are piled up close to each other in regular order like hillocks of gold dust. The people who are next neighbours to the ants, with a view to plunder these heaps, cross the intervening dessert, which is of no great extent, mounted on wagons to which they have yoked the swiftest horses. They arrive at noon, a time when the ants have gone underground, and at once seizing the booty make of at full speed. The ants on learning what has been done, pursue the natives, and overtaking them fight with them till they conquer or die, for of all the animals they are the most courageous. It hence appears that they understand the worth of gold, and that they will sacrifice their lives rather than part with it.[2]

Of course, it was not only the profusion and size of species, but also the unpredictability of their behaviour that was regarded as aberrant and transgressive. The land, described as being populated by people 'eating carrion, wearing the guts of sheep about their necks for health and rubbing their heads with dung of beasts and dirt',[3] was also a hunting ground for animals that killed for a pleasure beyond utility. In the eighteenth century, James Forbes, based in India for sixteen years as a clerk to the East India Company, comments of the tiger that 'he will eat nothing but what he destroys himself'.[4] His description of a man killed by an animal during a hunting party turns from simple report to horrific narrative in order to emphasize the unnecessary nature of the murder:

1 N. di Conti, *The Travels of Nicolo Conti in India in the 15th century being a collection of narratives of voyages to India*, ed. R. Major (1858).
3 Megasthenes in J.W. McCrindle, *Ancient India as described by Ktesias the Knidian, Megasthenes and Arrian* (1877) 70, 217.
3 T. Roe, in S. Purchas, *Hakluyut Posthumus or Purchas his Pilgrims*, vol. IV (1625) 320.
4 J. Forbes, *Oriental Memoirs, Selected from a Series of Familiar Letters Written During Seventeen Years Residence in India*, vol. II (1988) 285.

his hands and feet sucked, and chewed to a perfect pulp, the teguments of the limb in general drawn from under the skin, and the skull mostly laid bare; the skin of it hanging down in strips, obviously effected by the talons.[5]

Forbes's writing employs the narrative device of adding more detail than absolutely necessary not only to depict horror, but to suggest that this was no simple efficient killing for the sake of hunger. Gratuitous detail mirrors a gratuitous motive and the addition of extra detail attempts to recreate a sense of the tiger's frenzy.

While the passage conveys the unfathomable pointlessness of the animal's behaviour, there was more to the danger inherent in nature than the immediate threat of physical harm. The external image of Indian nature, often regarded as luxurious, was all the more evil for being deceptive:

> Aromatic gales and spicy groves; trees adorned by flora and Pomona; pellucid lakes and murmuring fountains; charm in poetical descriptions; we wish to dwell in such delightful scenes; a residence in the torrid zone *convinces us of their fallacy*; hot winds and arid plains, unrefreshed by a cooling breeze or living spring annoy the Asiatic traveller; and admitting the existence of such pleasures in the temperate climate and fertile provinces of Hindustan, we know from experience, that a constant possession of the loveliest objects, often renders them insipid; the revolving seasons and variety of Europe seem more congenial to an Englishman than the luxurious monotony of India, even in its most pleasing form.[6]

The venality of 'pleasing forms' and 'delightful scenes' which disguised the monotony of oriental life is a theme repeated again and again in order to link together the paradisaic setting of rural India to a post-lapsarian state of sin and corruption. It is a point made by Forbes in the following description of the dangers of bathing in oriental gardens:

> One morning [a] young lady in the state of Musidora, was alarmed by a rustling among the palmyra leaves which covered her bath; and looking up, beheld one of the garden genii, with brilliant eyes under the expanded hood of a large *cobra de capello*, pushing through the thatch, and ready to dart on the fountain.

As if the allusion were not already obvious, Forbes continues the biblical reference in more explicit terms: 'Pure and unadorned as Eve when her reflected beauties first met her eyes, the lady and her handmaids made a precipitate retreat through the grove.'[7] At one level, the moral of the tale may simply be to abstain from bathing in dangerous places. But it is obviously more than this. The scene in which the drama is set – the paradisaic garden, and the proto-diabolical figure of the serpent – institutes an immediate relationship between the fertility of nature and its allure into the ways of death or sin. The princess never stood a chance. Faced with the choice of certain death, or dishonour, she chooses the latter and runs naked

5 id., p. 288.
6 id., vol. I, p. 234.
7 id., vol. II, p. 245.

90

through the garden before 'gazers, whether in the form of gardeners, snakes or monkeys.' No fatal act of disobedience needed to be committed, no choice needed to be made between good and evil, for nature had already immersed everything (everyone) in death or shame.

Paradise was always-already linked to the corrupt pleasures (*jouissance*) of nature which writhed beneath each leaf.[8] The idea of a land of fabulous wealth, (this 'earthly paradise') was destroyed by an endless profusion and abundance of diabolical aberrations and natural dangers. The function of describing the peculiarities of oriental nature was not simply to tabulate, name, and colonize that which needed to be tamed. These descriptions of nature set the backdrop against which ideas of oriental despotism could emerge as natural disposition. For, what these descriptions of nature allow travellers to do is to characterize despotism as being something more than the product of individual corruption, so that despotism is seen to be fixed as part of an overall structure of life and behaviour peculiar to the East. Excess, cruelty, and deception were instituted as intrinsic both to the nature of the orient and to the oriental character. The passion with which the Sultan exercises justice is of the same dangerous and frenzied order of behaviour to be found in nature.

Consequently, there are many examples related by these travellers of the manner in which the exercise of the Sultan's powers of punishment reflect the unfathomable evil of oriental nature. It is during the infliction of pain that the despot appears as an insane animal, a 'mad dog', or a cunning serpent who takes pleasure in the suffering of others. Hawkins relates the incident of an official whose duty it was to guard and protect the wardrobe of the Great Moghul. Once, having accidentally broken a 'faire china dish', the keeper of the King's wardrobe sent a trusted servant to 'China-Machina over land' to find a replacement dish. When the servant failed to return after two years, news of the damaged dish eventually reached the King. The wardrobe keeper was ordered to be whipped by two men. After a hundred and twenty lashes, the King commanded his porters to beat the man with small cudgels: 'at the least twenty men were beating of him, till the poore man was thought to bee dead, and then he was haled out by his heels ... and carried unto perpetual prison.'[9] A particular pleasure accompanies these descriptions of cruelty which, like the descriptions of animal behaviour, goes beyond comprehension and the utility of punishment. One ventures into the inner sanctum of the harem as if entering into the jungle. Servants live in fear of the Sultan who, very often titled himself after a particular animal. Much was

---

8 See G. Pommier, 'From the Gods to Monotheism, from Demons to the Devil; An Examination of Biblical Texts concerning the Singularization of the devil, in the light of Freudian Metapsychology' in *Jouvert* <http://social.chass.ncsu.edu> 1–19. On the more political thematic of *jouissance* and fantasies of despotism. see A. Grosrichard, *The Sultan's Court; European Fantasies of the East* (1998).

9 W. Hawkins, in Purchas, op. cit., n. 3, vol. IV, p. 39.

made of the fact that Tipoo Sultan had decided to call himself the 'Tiger of Mysore', and that his bed chambers were guarded by four Royal Tigers. Even daily meals are turned into bloody rituals in which the Sultan enjoys to excess the product of his cruelty: 'Hyder Ali and his son Tipoo were *regaled* at breakfast with a vesselful of the ears and noses of our poor sepoys who fell into their hands.'[10] Where the descriptions of despotism reach maximum intensity is in the frenzied and remorseless behaviour of the Sultan which mimics the dangers and force of oriental nature. It is little wonder that those such as Locke and Montesquieu, in their own different ways, relate despotism to a state of nature and in opposition, therefore, to the goals and ambitions of human nature.

RELIGION

The very existence of earlier travel narratives may well be sufficient evidence that travellers had discovered not only a land of commodities, but had entered the dark territories of sin. These journals, richly informative though they are, may be read as a form of confession through which the author attempted to purge himself of any moral infection he may have caught during his time abroad. The case of Nicolo di Conti, a Venetian nobleman and merchant explorer who set out in 1419 with his wife to travel east, is instructive. Joining a caravan of six hundred other merchants in Arabia, and learning Persian on the way, di Conti arrived in India at the port of Cambay from where he began his exploration of the subcontinent. There is nothing to render di Conti's account of his journey any more remarkable than those of other explorers of the time. Descriptions of the oriental forms of nature are as detailed and as exaggerated as any other account from this period. On his return journey, however, he and his family happened to be captured by 'a band of infidels', and, in order to save his wife and children from certain execution, Conti was forced by his captors to renounce Christianity. Five years after he had returned home, the Venetian decided to seek absolution from Pope Eugene IV, whose proscribed penance was to make Conti recount his adventures to the Papal secretary and scribe, Pasggio Bracchiolini. The *Travels of Nicolo di Conti*, was a result not of a desire to describe mere observations, however exotic, but of a desire to atone.[11]

There are many images which present the Indian religions in a violent and obscene light and it is sufficient to take one example of sacrifices made to an idol of Juggernaut. What was designed to impress the reader was the sheer colossal scale of the ritual. The throne of 'this lascivious God' is described as having been at least sixty feet high and placed on a 'stupendous car'. Attached were six long cables by which the crowd drew the chariot along.

10 Forbes, op. cit., n. 4, vol. II, p. 458.
11 di Conti, op. cit., n. 1.

The idol itself is described in details which bear semiotic association with Christian depictions of the devil. The impropriety and deformity of Asian images of angels who almost always fitted the description of the Christian devil was a persistent and relevant theme in Elizabethan and Jacobean travel literature. Take, for example, the description given by the merchant explorer, William Finch (1608–11), who describes the Hindu deities as 'divells, intermixte in most ugly shape, with long hornes, staring eyes, shagge hair, ugly pawes, long tailes, with such deformity and difformity, that I wonder the poore women are not frightened therewith.'[12] These descriptions alerted the reader, during the post-reformation, to the idolatrous zest for images.

Once we have a sense of the magnitude of the idolatrous ceremony at Juggernaut, Forbes introduces to his account dramatic images of perversity and violence. A high priest having pronounced 'his obscene stanzas' made way for 'an aged minister of the idol who then stood up, with a long rod in his hand, which he moved with indecent action, and completed the variety of this disgusting exhibition.' More disturbing are the vivid descriptions of those pilgrims who would offer themselves in sacrifice to the idol by lying down before the wheels of the moving tower. These victims of their own sacrifice 'were left to view a considerable time, and were then carried by the hurries to the Golgotha, the place of skulls.'[13]

What was denigrated was not simply another faith, but the hostile forces of uncontrollable excess and the manner in which the ceremony undercut the Christian code of manners and civilization. The self-immolation of the followers of Juggernaut indicated the barely fathomable idea of a type of enjoyment reached only at the point of death, the point at which the individual abandons himself to annihilation.[14] The profusion of gods and cults, the mingled confusion, and the group ecstasy in which individuality was submerged became cause for antagonism. All that which exceeded the civilized norms of monotheism was to be found in India attached to the different forms of heathen worship.

Observations of religious excess, and the fatal lure of its excitement, were inevitably made in the first journal to be written by an ecclesiastic in India. Edward Terry, chaplain to the first English embassy in Agra in 1619, compares the Mohammedans at the court of Jahangir to the 'priests of Baal' and to 'mis-led Papists, who seeme to regard the number rather than the weight of prayers'.[15] The attack was levelled both at a religious attitude which mistook form for content and at one in which multiplicity and duplicity could only be regarded as symptoms of evil. Continuing the mathematical bent of his observation that Hinduism in particular was divided

---

12 W. Finch, in Purchas, op. cit., n. 3, vol. III, p. 54.
13 Forbes, op. cit., n. 4, vol. II, p. 10.
14 On the proximity between enjoyment and the point of death, see G. Bataille, *Eroticism* (1962).
15 E. Terry, in Purchas, op. cit. n. 3, vol. IX, pp. 316–7.

into a number of different sects, Terry declares 'but I know Satan (the father of division) to be the seducer of them all'.[16] The difference between Christianity and Hinduism was based simply on the opposition of monotheism to an unlimited polytheism but this divergence was felt in the stark contrast made between order and excess. Poly-dissemination was a common enough cause of Christian anxiety which warned against the incarnation of the devil in the multiplicity of forms. Where Christianity had only the one devil, paganism bred an infinite hoard of demons, and where Christian authority was unlimited, paternal (despotic), and contained in the single figure of God, a religion such as Hinduism vested its authority among any number of mothers and fathers. Where the theocratic legal order of western legal institutions relied on a singular cause of causes, the polytheocracy of Hinduism suggested the anarchy of cause. The paradoxical conclusion which escaped the notice of these travel writers was that the Christian God, with his unlimited and jealously guarded power, must surely have been a more despotic God than one who had to share power with others.

Evidence of diabolical forces was not restricted to these religious displays. The devil infiltrated the whole of the Moghul government. The point was made by Thomas Roe, the ambassador of James I at the court of the Moghal Emperor Jahangir, who writes that: 'All cunning that the Divell can teach us is frequent eaven in the cort where is wanting noe arte nor wicked subtilty to bee or doe evil.'[17] The examples of such evil activity, during Roe's embassy, saturate life in the Imperial seraglio. Any capacity for rational judgement which the Emperor may have had is rendered impotent through the lure of superstition. Roe, for example, scorns the fact that the King should have taken advice from a beggar, 'a pooer silly olde man all asht, ragd, and patcht', or that once he entertained, in all seriousness, a Bengali juggler who had brought to the court an ape who, it was claimed, held the power to prophesy and conjure tricks.[18] A further incident which features in the account of Roe as well as those of William Hawkins and William Finch is more symbolic. Jahangir had publicly converted his nephews to Christianity. Roe, who describes the grand baptismal parade of the three boys through the streets of Agra, also records the general suspicion levelled at the Emperor: 'Others supposed he suffered this policie to reduce these Children into hate among the Moores for their conversion',[19] thereby prohibiting their claim to the sultanate. William Finch, described the incident as one of pure 'dissimulation', 'so to make the Christian Name not as an Ointment powred out, that the Virgin Soules may be converted, and love Christ, but as filthy matter running out of rotten hearts and poisoned lips.'[20]

16 id., p. 321.
17 Roe, in Purchas, op. cit., n. 4, vol. IV, p. 449.
18 id., p. 386.
19 id., p. 453.
20 Finch, in Purchas, op. cit., n. 4, vol. III, p. 39.

94

Behind the obvious implications of this episode, however, it is possible to detect a further shock to the Western scheme of things. The abuse of all potential male heirs to the throne was a common effect of the absence of any laws designed to secure heredity. The entire kingdom of the 'Great Moghul' was built by side-stepping genealogy. The orient destroys the concept of filiation, and by obvious implication, nullifies the principle of paternity (indeed, for the early merchants, the only discernable filial principle seemed to be the one which connected the despot to a barbaric deity). As Niccolao Manucci put it in the final paragraph of his *Memoirs of the Mogul Court*:

> [t]hus do matters go in the Mogul kingdom; sons, grandsons, and great-grandsons are making preparations for the terrible wars which must ensue upon the death of the old king. For, there are many aspirants to dominion, it being one of them a saying that in such a case a father should not trust a son, nor a son his father.[21]

The French physician Bernier illustrates this occidental anxiety in his *History of the States of the Great Moghul* with the following anecdote:

> Shariyar was the most beautiful of all the princes. Once when he was troubled with a severe pain in his eyes, he was cured by the Mukawab Khan. The Emperor (Jahangir) heard of this cure and cynically remarked that no doubt his eyes would remain entirely well until they were put out by his brother – as indeed came to pass.[22]

These observations of 'evil deeds' noted by the travellers emphasize the gravity attached to the principle of heredity. From a Western perspective, the sacred principle of heredity informs both religious and political thought. The importance of the laws of inheritance to Western statecraft is well stated by Burke for without these laws, the crown could not be settled, and the fabric of the ancient constitution dissolves, staining 'the throne of England with the blot of a continual userpation, and calling into question the whole line of our kings whose laws determine liberties.'[23] But the principle of heredity is rooted even more deeply. If genealogy may be regarded as the law of Law in the Christian West, it is because it establishes the relationship between 'the Law of the Father' and those who must obey. It is the principle through which the totemic father organizes desire, regulates pleasure, and manages enjoyment. Ignorance of genealogy only constitutes the loss of continuity and the anarchic evil of uncontrollable urges, dark pleasures, and illicit enjoyment.

21 N. Manucci, *Memoirs of the Mogul Court*, ed. M. Edwards (1978) 178.
22 F. Bernier, *History of the States of the Great Moghul* (1745) 211.
23 E. Burke, *Reflections on the Revolution in France* (1790, 1968 edn.) 97–107.

In one of the earliest accounts of commercial travel, written in 1470, the Russian merchant Athanasius Nikitin describes the women of India as 'harlots, or witches, or thieves, or cheats; and they destroy their masters with poison.'[24] The corrupt form of enjoyment as embodied in the figure of femininity is a classic feature of Western symbolic orders and the spirit of these invectives was resuscitated in the travellers' literary treatment of the women found in the Imperial seraglios. Oriental women were depicted as the quintessence of intellectual vacuity and spiritual emptiness, devoting their lives only to pleasure and luxury. Plato, for example, blamed the despotism of the Persian monarchy on the fact that the young princes had to suffer a 'womanish education conducted by the royal harem'.[25] This education, being one of extreme luxury, ignored the acquisition of traditional Persian skills of shepherding and soldiering. The same criticism is levelled at the women of the Moghul court whose life of luxury sets the backdrop to the court and by-passes the intellectual tools required for good government. According to Forbes:

> [w]hether confined within the secluded harem, or of more easy access in a voluptuous city, the oriental females, far from cultivating intellectual entertainment, pass their time either in listless apathy, or personal decoration.[26]

This indulgence in 'personal decoration' is a feature of harem life that absorbs the attention of many authors. Manucci, who lists the 'extraordinary' daily expenses of the court, comments on the clothes and jewellery provided for the women whose every inch of flesh were decorated with silk saris laced with gold, pearls, and other precious stones that were often brought in on great golden trays 'solely as an opening for a conversation',[27] while 'their amusement at night is generally to have large torches lighted on which they will spend more than one hundred and fifty thousand rupees.'[28]

The economy of these descriptions is that they signify simultaneously a number of different forms of corruption that are traditionally associated with femininity. First, the definition of enjoyment (*jouissance*) as unproductive expenditure is given full expression. This self-consuming and expensive form of enjoyment eclipses the meaning of value, particularly for the merchant travellers. Second, these expenses expose, for the reader, the vanity of oriental women:

> on their fingers are rich rings, and on the right thumb there is always a ring, where in place of a stone, there is mounted a little round mirror, having pearles

---

24 E.F Oaten, *European Travellers in India* (1902) at 41.
25 Plato, *The Laws*, iii. iv. 145
26 Forbes, op. cit., n. 4, vol. III, p. 419.
27 Manucci, op. cit, n. 21, p. 35.
28 id., p. 37.

around it. This mirror they use to look at themselves, an act of which they are very fond, at any and every moment.[29]

Third, the care which they lavished on themselves is considered part of the process of ensnaring men. Here, feminine narcisism threatens the fantasy that man becomes the object of desire. The jewels received from the Sultan debase what would otherwise have been regarded as respectable positions in the hierarchically organized seraglio, with the stigma of prostitution.

Everything in this fantasy about the Imperial harem consequently seemed to be directed toward pure enjoyment and unadulterated gratification. Women were thought to be regarded by the courtesans as part of a collection of rarities from around the world akin to trophies of war. The fantasy bestowed upon the Great Moghul the power to exploit resources and a boundless appetite for sexual satisfaction. This superabundant vitality is all the more transgressive for being debauched. The Reverend Terry writes that 'there lodge none in the Kings house but his women and eunuchs, and some little boyes which hee keepes about him for a wicked use.'[30] And Bernier describes the behaviour of Shah Jahan during the visits of common dancing girls (*kenchens*) to organised festivals as:

> transgressing the bounds of decency ... it was not enough for chah-jehan that the kenchens visited the fairs; when they came to him on the Wednesdays to pay their reverence at the Am-Kas he often detained them the whole night and amused himself with their antics and follies.'[31]

While life in the seraglio aimed towards the surplus accumulation of pleasure, the fate of the harem women was one which led only to purdah. This seeming paradox was partially resolved by a prevalent belief that, in spite of their confinement within the walls of the inner court, Indian women enjoyed life only in acquiescence. Forbes explains this in picturesque terms after being granted rare permission to enter the women's chambers (vacated):

> I had the opportunity of seeing the haram: all the windows look into the enclosed gardens, and have no prospect of anything beyond them. It seems calculated to furnish every pleasure that can be expected by the unfortunate females immured under the Argus-eyes of the duennas and eunuchs. Baths, fountains, fruits and flowers, the European fair ones would think a poor compensation for liberty; the Asiatic ladies, accostemed to this confinement, are not discontented with their lot.[32]

Women, according to this view, took pleasure in being forced to withdraw into a life of meaningless luxury. A direct relationship is established between confinement and 'every pleasure' against which even the enjoyment of liberty seems insignificant. The pseudo-erotic image of an oriental princess

29 Manucci, op. cit., n. 21, p. 36.
30 Terry, in Purchas, op. cit., n. 4, vol. IX, p. 311.
31 Bernier, op. cit., n. 22, pp. 273–4.
32 Forbes, op. cit., n. 4, vol. I, p. 250.

bathing in her private quarters surrounded by fountains, fruits, and flowers, while guarded by eunuchs has, of course, been a central stereotype in establishing the lazy pleasures of the East. In fact, what is found to be troubling about these images is not simply the indolent atmosphere of the harem but the presence of the watchful slave-guard. The whole business of confinement itself seems crucial to the notion of corrupt enjoyment.

Guarded and secluded from visitors, the harem signified a further dimension to the issue of oriental enjoyment. The physical location and dynamics of the women's quarters indicated that the Sultan's enjoyment was exclusive to himself and inaccessible to others. Internal administration placed the women under a complicated system of guardianship which enlisted the services of eunuchs, *duennas* (governesses), and *daroghas* (matrons). The 'entry of men inside the mahal was meticulously checked ... [the visitors] name, physiognomy and other details were carefully noted down and verified at many check points.'[33] Besides, it was not only men who were forbidden entry but 'whatever is brought in of virill shape, as instance in reddishes ... so frequent the wickedness of this people, that they are cut and jagged for feare of converting the same to some unnaturall abuse.'[34]

The prohibition of men and phallic objects contributed to the process of jealousy felt for the Sultan's exclusive enjoyment as well as to an anxiety over this form of symbolic castration. Enjoyment was not so much excluded as cut off (*coupure*, to use the Lacanian terminology), and the traveller was made to feel emasculated. In 'short', the traveller was made to feel like the figure of the eunuch. What 'arose' was a provocative overturning of the acceptable state of affairs, where the male traveller in fact enjoyed less freedom than the women.

Herein lies the most crucial paradox about the fantasy of harem life. While indolent and acquiescent, these women were thought to have enjoyed a great deal of power over the male traveller. What came to be noticed as a symptom of this threat to the Western scheme of things was that some of the women in the harem were armed with 'bows and arrows, a poynard and cimiter,' and that the King (who becomes both the Master and the guest of the women) was 'during his sleep, guarded by women slaves, very brave and highly skilled in the management of the bow and other arms.'[35]

In inverting the hierarchy of masculine reason over feminine sensuality, life in the harem also undercut the supposedly proper location and identity of political power. Descriptions contained in all of these oriental memoirs associate political power with plethoric enjoyment particularly since it was suspected that the women of the harem acted as the 'cabinet council of the Moghul'.

33 K.S. Lal, *The Mughal Harem* (1988) 58.
34 T. Coryate, in Purchas, op. cit., n. 3, vol. IV, p. 234.
35 Manucci, op. cit., n. 21, p. 34.

For just as the King has his officers outside, he has the same among the fair sex within the palace. Among these ladies are some who occupy the same offices that are held by grandees outside; and it is by mouth of these illustrious persons, when the King does not come forth, that the officials outside receive the orders sent them from within.[36]

The idea of the wrongful accumulation of power appears in the many invectives against the eunuch. Like oriental women, the eunuch is avaricious and accumulates wealth in excess of his needs. Manucci writes that:

among the other qualities of this sort of animal is their extreme covetousness in collecting gold, silver, diamonds, and pearles ... the tongue and hands of these baboons act together, being most licentious in examining everything, both goods and women coming into the palace.

Their position of power derives from their guardianship of the women. As Manucci goes on to note:

they hold themselves in estimation, for they are the favorites of princesses, who are very liberal to them, in order to win them, and from time to time get permission to enjoy that of which I cannot speak. They are useful for the introduction secretly of men into the harem.[37]

What was further cause for concern was that eunuchs, while considered to be mere attendants, often rose in ranks to command armies or govern provinces. As Grosrichard points out: 'Like the Roman pontiff, the eunuch renounces his own desire in order to command that of others.'[38]

The relationship between the vice of feminine enjoyment and power is only one aspect of a more general order of effeminacy that ripples through the seraglio. The energy of oriental power upsets because it emanates from women and eunuchs. It is also seen to be located within a physical architecture that is described as over-indulgent and effeminate in style. Take, for example, the description provided by Roe of the Sultan's throne room:

[A wooden pavillion] inlayed with mother of pearle, borne up with the fore pillers, and covered with clothe of gold. Above the edge overhead like a valence, was a net fringe of goode pearle, upon which hung downe Pomgranats, Apples, Peares, and such fruits of Gold, *but hollow*: within that the King sate on cushions, very rich in Pearles, in jewels, round about the court; before the throne the principall men had erected Tents which encompassed the court and lined them with velvet, damask and taffatae[39]

Roe, however, cannot concede that this luxury was appropriate to the Sultan's position; 'it was rather patched then glorious, as if it seemed to strive to shewe all, like a lady that with her plate, set out on a cupboard her imbroydered slippers.'[40] The imagery employed by Roe is, of course, curious.

36 id., p. 33.
37 id., p. 62.
38 Grosrichard, op. cit., n. 8, p. 155.
39 Roe, op. cit., n. 3, at p. 332.
40 id.

Its moral effect, however, comes not from deriding the random, promiscuous design of the throne room but from its association with femininity. Such are the qualities of femininity employed by Roe in order to turn simple description into political invective (as Roe elsewhere states, this is the 'basest place I ever saw ... and the Moguls are an effeminate people').[41] On one hand, these descriptions of ornament create of the court an impression of frivolity and immorality in comparison to the serious and sober business of treaty negotiation (the purpose of Roe's embassy). On the other hand, the idea that ornaments were considered feminine had been a feature of Protestant discourses against the image at the time of Roe's visit to India. Ornaments took on the feminized qualities of charm and seduction and came to be regarded as orgiastic sites of contemptible lust before which the rational capacity of the eyewitness turns fallow and helpless. The denigration of the cornucopia of Moghul forms, the baroque surfaces and gilded surfaces of imperial display, were thus complicated by the debates surrounding both religious and civil forms of ornament and image worship raging throughout Europe at the time. Unashamedly carnal and cosmic, the Oriental world of appearances came to be regarded as an effeminate space which privileged the sensual over the rational and the poet over the lawyer. Travellers such as Roe recognized the threat of free play and alternative possibilities in the boundary-less forms of the East. Everything about it seemed antithetical to a Western political order attempting to rid itself of the papal psychology of the imagination. Thus, where the Oriental court was an extravagant riot of colour, reformation England emphasized the simplicity of religious forms; where the Hindu obeyed images, the Protestant followed 'the inner light'; and where Eastern crowds celebrated with deliberate cacophonies, the lonely Western individual placed himself in a world of euphonious reasoned order.

EFFEMINACY AND PASSIVITY

These descriptions of effeminacy also allow travellers to develop the Aristotelian idea that the barbarian people were more inclined to slavery. They too are used to establish despotism as being more than the product of the Sultan's individual passions. The Protestant argument that the subject turns passive in front of the image is translated into the Orientalist idea that despotic regimes remain in power largely due to the effeminate and sedentary nature of the people:

> the inhabitants of the torrid zone are generally indolent and effeminate; the climate is equally inimical to bodily and mental exertion: physical causes produce these effects. History shews the fatal effects of arbitrary power and effeminate indulgence.[42]

41 id., at p. 319.
42 Forbes, op. cit., n. 4, vol. I, p. 234.

Time and again, the charge of effeminacy (coupled with a lack of air-conditioning) is used as the barrier which prevents the Asian subject from adopting, 'the noble sentiments which animate free-born souls'[43] and which would prevent the formation of despotic government. Oaten, in pointing out that fault of despotism did not lie exclusively at the feet of the ruler but, rather, with the subjects themselves, cites the opinion of Sebastian Manrique, who in 1612 arrived in Bengal as a friar of the order of St. Augustine in order to propagate Christianity. Manrique found the people of Bengal to be spiritless and: 'who understood nothing better than rough treatment, kindness was wasted on them. He who gives blows is a master; he who gives none is a dog.'[44]

But this effeminate and slavish nature is once again connected to an absurd sense of enjoyment:

> the languor occasioned by the hot climate of India, inclines the native to indolence and ease; and he thinks the evils of despotism less severe than the labour of being free.[45]

What the subject enjoys, in other words, is the satisfaction derived from a belief that an all powerful figure, an arbiter of destinies, is in command protecting against some abysmal uncertainty that might befall at any given moment. As Anton Schutz, in summarizing Zizek, puts it:

> all you need is to assume that the master, the despot, the collective receptacle or master of power, is simultaneously also the master of possibilities and ... in effective command of what happens, of history.[46]

Even when perceived to be in a state of servitude, the idea of oriental enjoyment is inextricably connected with corruption and excess in so far as such enjoyment is useless and justifies the excesses of despotism.

LUXURY/LEISURE

The reason why femininity and effeminacy were considered such a disturbing locus for political power was that, far from softening the effects of oriental leadership, they rendered it more extreme. The effeminate luxury of the court was inextricably linked to the barbarity of despotism. Describing his first interview with Jahangir, Roe says he:

---

43 id., p. 154.
44 Oaten, op. cit., n. 24, p. 99.
45 A. Dow, *The History of Hindostan* (1772) vii.
46 A. Shutz, 'Desiring Society: Autopoesis Beyond the Paradigm of Mastership' (1994) 5 *Law and Critique* 149–64. Or as Zizek puts it: 'Enjoyment is provided by an awareness that people were living in an universe absolved of uncertainty, since the system possessed an answer to everything, but above all the enjoyment of the very stupidity of the system – a relish in the emptiness of the official ritual.' (S. Zizek, *The Metastases of Enjoyment* (1994) 64.)

101

was brought in by the cutwall: at the outward court were about one hundred horsemen armed, being gentlemen that attend the Princes setting out to salute him. In the inner court hee sate high in a gallery that went round with a canopy over him, and a great carpet before him, in great *but barbarous state*. Coming toward him thorow a lane of people, an officer came and brought me word I must touch the ground with my head, and my hat off.[47]

The carpeted and canopied pavilion, as already noted, belongs to that stock set of orientalist images from these travel accounts. Yet, in this context, the carpet and canopy are not mere signs of indulgent splendour. Roe loads their significance in order to exaggerate the imperious figure of the King to the point of barbarity. At one level, the enjoyment of excessive luxury and effeminate diversions emphasizes the split between rich and poor, 'the one pampered by voluptuous indulgence, the other degraded below the monkeys which surround them.'[48] This theme is recorded in some of the earliest European narratives. Athanasius Nikitin (1486), for instance, notes the discrepancy between the wealth of the Great Moghul's palace (where every stone is carved or gilded) and the poverty of the people:

> The land is overstocked with people, but those in the country are very miserable, whilst the nobles are very opulent and delight in luxury. They are wont to be carried on their silver beds, preceded by some twenty chargers caparisoned in gold, and followed by three hundred men on horseback, and five hundred on foot, and by horn-men, ten torch bearers and ten musicians.[49]

Terry makes a similar point in comical fashion when describing the image of princes travelling through the streets:

> [they] ride on Elephants, or else are carried upon men's shoulders alone, in a slight thing they call a palankee, which is like a couch or standing pallat, but covered with a cannopie. This should seeme an effeminacie sometimes used in Rome, Juvenal thus describing a fat lawyer that fil'd one of them: *Causidici nova cum veniat lectica Mathonis plena ipso* [Matho the pleader comes in his new chaire, Fil'd with himself when he takes the air].[50]

The luxury of the Sultan's harem not only indicates a sedate form of sovereignty. It was seen to derive from greed, where every resource is devoted to the exclusive enjoyment of the Emperor and his court: 'If a land holder cannot pay his proper rent, the governor seizes not only his property, but even his wife and children.'[51] Luxury constitutes despotism, by taking everything in excess of requirement and giving nothing back: 'its principle is *coupure*, the cutting off all that circulates.'[52] Every European account of travels to the Moghul court in the seventeenth century devotes at least a chapter to the absurd

47 Roe, in Purchas, op. cit., n. 3, vol. IV, p. 324.
48 Forbes, op. cit., n. 4, vol. II, p. 514.
49 A. Nikiten, 'Travels of Athanasius Nikiten of Twer' in *India in the Fifteenth Century*, ed. R. Major (1858) 14–15.
50 Terry, in Purchas, op. cit., n. 3, vol. IX, p. 312.
51 D. Barbarosa, in Oaten, op. cit., n. 24, p. 99.
52 Grosrichard, op. cit., n. 8, p. 19.

accumulation of wealth. Hawkins's account, for example, revels in the Sultan's treasure-house. The following is one paragraph in a whole chapter devoted to an inventory of the Sultan's jewels, his clothes, armies, bestiary, and so on:

> swords of Almaine Blades, with the Hilts and Scabbards set with divers sorts of rich stones, of the richest sort, there are two thousand and two hundred. Of two sorts of Poniards there bee two thousand of Saddle Drummes, which they use in their Hawking, of these there are very rich ones of Gold, set with stones, five hundred. Of broaches for their heads, whereunto there Feathers be put, these be very rich, and of them there are two thousand. Of Saddles of Gold and Silver set with stones, there are one thousand. Of Teukes there be five hundred and twentie, this is a great Launce covered with gold and the Fluke set with stones, and these instead of their colours are carried when the King goeth to the warres, of these there are five hundred and twentie. Of Kittasoles of state, for to shaddow him, there bee twentie. None in his Empire dareth in any sort have any of these carried for his shadow but himselfe, of these I say there are twentie. Of Chaires of Estate, there be five, to say, three of Silver and two of Gold; and of other sorts of Chaires, there bee an hundred of Silver and Gold, in all a hundred and five. Of rich Glasses there bee two hundred. Of Vases for Wine very faire and rich set with Jewels there are an hundred. Of Drinking Cuppes, five hundred, but fiftie very rich, that is to say, made of one piece of Ballace Ruby, and also of Emerods of Eshmin, of Turkish stone, and of other sorts of stones. Of Chaines of Pearle, and Chaines of all sorts of precious stones and Ringes with Jewels of rich Diamants, Ballace Rubies, Rubies and old Emerods, there is an infinite number which only the Keeper therof knoweth. Of all sorts of plate, as Dishes, Cups, Basons, Pots, Beakers of Silver wrought there are two thousand Battmans. Of Gold wrought, there are one thousand Battmans.[53]

It should be added, however, that the despot is not simply one who can exploit resources greedily 'extracting oil out of sand,' or 'sunlight from cucumbers'.[54] In theory, the despot already owns everything. For the rest of the population, in the Moghul Empire, there existed no such notion as private property. It is this absurd enjoyment of all property that properly connects oriental leadership to despotism; 'take away the right of private property in land, and you introduce, as a sure and necessary consequence, tyranny, slavery, injustice, beggary and barbarism.'[55] Thus, 'in Asia, if justice be ever administered, it is among the lower classes, among persons who, being equally poor, have no means of corrupting the judges, and of buying false witnesses.'[56]

The exclusive enjoyment over land rights is only one aspect of an overall luxury that interferes in the exercise of justice. Access to justice itself required permission to tread on land owned by the sultan. It is important to note the significance of palace architecture and its exclusivity as a significant element in the overall derision of Oriental justice. It was already observed (mistakenly) from the use of overelaborate Imperial titles such as the

53 Hawkins, in Purchas, op. cit., n. 3, vol. IV, pp. 32–33.
54 Bernier, op. cit., n. 22, p. 236.
55 id., p. 238.
56 id., p. 237.

'Asylum of Pardon', the 'Shadow of God', or 'the Fountain of all Honours' that the Sultan placed himself well above the supervision of the courts. This was all the more disturbing since they indicated the exclusive power of the Sultan to dispense justice according to his will:

> The Emperour stiles himself: *the King of Justice, the Light of the Law of Mahomet, the Conquerer of the World.* Himselfe moderates in all matters of consequence which happen neere his court, for the most part judging *secundum allegata et probata.* Tryals are quick, and so are executions: hangings, beheading, impaling, killing with dogges, by elephants, serpents, and other like, according to the nature of the market place. The governours in cities and provinces proceed in like forme of justice. I could never heare of law written amongst them: the King and his substitutes will is law.[57]

Not only is authority exclusive to the Sultan but it is inaccessible to others. It is exercised in a private domain where he keeps matters for and to himself:

> In the silence which attends despotism everything is dark and solemn. Justice itself is executed with privacy, and sometimes a solitary gun fired at midnight from the palace of the despot, proclaims the work of death.[58]

The idea of the Sultan's private domain is one which is used as emblem of all that is contrary to the juridical values of the west. The private domain becomes signifier of a private mysterious will and the aesthetic structure of the Imperial palace is used to signify the difficulty of gaining access to the Emperor as dispenser of justice. While the overelaborate architecture of this structure is described in most journals, Tavernier's is the most detailed:

> When the King administers justice he comes, as I stated, into the balcony which overlooks the square, and all those who desire to be present stand below, opposite to where he is seated. Between the people and the wall of the palace three rows of sticks the length of a short-pike are planted in the ground, at the ends of which are attached cords which cross one another, and no one, whosoever he may be, is allowed to pass these limits without being summoned. This barrier, which is not put up except when the King administers justice, extends the whole length of the square, and opposite the balcony there is an opening to allow those who are summoned to pass. Then two men, who hold by the ends a cord stretched across this opening, have only to lower it to admit the person who is summoned. A Secretary of State remains in the square below the balcony to receive petitions, and when he has five or six in hand he places them in a bag, which a eunuch, who is on the balcony by the side of the King, lowers with a cord, draws up and presents them to his majesty.[59]

Much more keenly aware of western jurisprudence than other travellers, Bernier notes the effect of this inaccessibility on those who actually seek justice:

---

57 Terry, in Purchas, op. cit., n. 3, vol. IX, p. 326.
58 Dow, op. cit., n. 45, p. xvi.
59 J.-B. Tavernier, *Travels in India* vol. I (2001) 125–6.

how is a poor peasant or a ruined artisan to defray the expenses of a journey to the capital, and to seek justice at one hundred and fifty or two hundred leagues from home? He would be waylaid or murdered.[60]

Bernier subsequently notices that the intervention of the secretary of state, the eunuch or any other friend of the King would increase the chances of 'distorting the truth, and misrepresenting the whole affair.' The more complicated these rituals were, the more the palace was walled in or cordoned off through an elaborate architecture, the more despotic the system came to be regarded.

In all of these journal entries, it is the combination of luxury and the dispensation of justice which causes most concern. Luxury may imply the Sultan's inordinate wealth, exclusive ownership of property, or the closed walls of the royal palace. It also implies the indolent enjoyment of leisurely diversions. Not a day passes but there is not a curiosity to be noted, an event to be remembered, or an observance to be laughed at in the exercise of justice. These events, which usually take place during the daily durbars, are described as being more than examples of cruelty. They become examples of cruelty staged as spectacular events for the exclusive enjoyment of the Sultan. Roe, for example, describes the attendance of Jahangir at ritual executions 'once weekly where sometimes he sees the execution done by his elephants with too much delight in blood.'[61] Roe does not calculate how much delight in blood is permissible. Perhaps the most celebrated emblem of the spectacle of Eastern cruelty comes in the form of the Tippoo Sultan's mechanical toy tiger which shows a royal tiger (representing the triumph of the *khood a dand Sircar*, or God given) devouring a prostrate Englishman. For Forbes, this automaton, while not a spectacular piece of cruelty in itself, 'affords us great reason to suppose he would have enjoyed direful spectacle.'[62] In continuing his description, Forbes strengthens the charge of tyranny levelled against Tippoo by drawing parallels with Nero, yet even Nero 'had the grace to turn away his eyes from the horrors of his reign.' Tippoo, on the other hand, becomes the more tyrannical of the two because, as spectator, he keeps a 'register of our sighs and groans'. It is the participation in the rituals of torture and execution, in the aesthetics of display, which maintains the level of tyrannical power. That this level of enjoyment far exceeds that which is permissible is made all the more poignant on those occasions where the Sultan would, in a fit of excessive passion, execute men with his own hand, instead of leaving the work to the official executioners, where he takes over and presents himself as part of the spectacle:

> He put to death in my time his Secretary, onley upon suspicion; whereupon the King not having patience, arose from his seate, and with his sword gave him his deadly wound, and afterwards delivered him to be torne by Elephants.[63]

60 Bernier, op. cit., n. 22, pp. 235–6.
61 Roe, in Purchas, op. cit., n. 3, vol. IV, p. 440.
62 Forbes, op. cit., n. 5, vol. III, p. 185.
63 Hawkins, in Purchas, op. cit., n. 3, vol. IV, p. 38.

More disturbing is that to the spectator ignorant of the full meaning and symbolism of Mughal court ritual, which must surely be the position occupied by the authors of these travel journals, these incidents appear to be leisurely diversions with no discernible political ends. They are presented to the reader as occasions where the Sultan indulges in sport in order to satiate his whimsical desire to see cruelty done:

> The King not yet contented but desirous to see more sport, sent for ten men that were of his horsemen ... these men one after another were to buffet with the Lyon, who were all grevously wounded, and it cost three of them their lives. The King continued three months in this vaine, when he was in his humors, for whose pleasure sake, many men lost their lives untill some fifteen young Lyons were made tame, and played one with another before the King, frisking betweene mens legs, and no man hurt in a long time.[64]

Accounts of these indulgent events allow authors to establish, explore, and exploit one of the most persistent stereotypes of the Eastern potentate as an arch-schemer. First and foremost, the despotic character suggests cunning and an endless appetite for double-dealing. The following account, although having less of a game-like quality, demands a belief in the treachery and deceit of the jealous Sultan as if he were playing a game:

> It is said that Begum-Saheb (one of the Princesses in the harem of Shah Jahan) although confined in a Seraglio, and guarded like other women, received the visits of a young man ... Chah-Jehan was apprised of her guilt, and resolved to enter her apartments at an unusual and unexpected hour. The intimation of his approach was too sudden to allow her the choice of more than one place of concealment. The affrighted gallant sought refuge in the capacious cauldron used for the bath. The King's countenance denoted neither surprise nor displeasure; he discoursed with his daughter on ordinary topics, but finished the conversation by observing that the state of her skin indicated a neglect of her customary ablutions, and that it was proper she should bathe. He then commanded the Eunuchs to light a fire under the cauldron, and did not retire until they gave him to understand that his wretched victim was no more.[65]

Sly and witting, the oriental despot is characterized by his unwillingness to put what, in the West, would be regarded as his imperial wisdom to any other use than the illicit enjoyment of cruelty. It is through the descriptions of the Sultans' leisurely activities and their enjoyment of excess wealth, that these narratives manage to convey a sense of the injustices that attach to despotic rule.

ILLUSION

It has already been mentioned that, for these travellers, the Moghul court contradicts efficient order since power is held by women, by eunuchs, by the

64 Terry in id., vol. IX, p. 27.
65 Bernier, op. cit., n. 22, p. 13.

people who command his presence every day. And it has been noted, that examples of the Emperor's appetite are provided against the lavish backdrop of the court and emerge from a world apparently mad on ostentation. There is, nevertheless, more to this process of distinguishing Eastern from Western forms of government than simply focusing on courtly pretension. The key to despotism is not simply in the display and enjoyment of wealth and power. It is in the idea that the entire display is no more than a deception of power designed to manipulate those who are subject. The duplicity of the Sultan, which reflects the duplicity found in nature, and among the Eunuchs of the harem, has already been noted. On one level, the deception of power, which is probably no more than tactical warfare, had brutal consequences for the British. Forbes, for example, describes the fate of two British residents who were summoned to Tipoo's durbar, and:

> received with respectful politeness, which he knew how to assume. After being seated on the carpet they were each presented with a cup of coffee ... In a few minutes [they were] either carried out in the struggles of death, or expired at the tyrant's feet.[66]

On another level, the deception of Sultanate power indicated a more profound emptiness at the heart of Oriental government. This illusory insubstantiality of the court is hinted at by Roe having described the Sultan's daily routine of showing himself to the crowds:

> Hee comes every morning to a window called the jarrneo, looking into a plaine before his gate and shewes himself to the common people ... from whence hee retires to sleep among his women ... this course is unchangeable, except sicknesse or drink prevent it, which must be known: for as all his subjects are slaves, so is hee in a kind of reciprocall bondage, for hee is tyed to observe these houres and customs so precisely, that if hee were unseen one day, and no sufficient reason rendred, the people would mutinie; two days no reason can excuse, but that he must be seen by some to satisfie others.[67]

The public display of the Sultan's body, which is as regular, solemn, and as spectacular as astral phenomenon, introduces the whole suspicion of fakery and impotence. The daily spectacle disguises the dangers and intrigues of the court. Away from the window, Jahangir suffers the 'vice' of drink. A gloriously opiate-addled lethargy which infuses the sultanate court is hidden well away from public sight, a concern shared by Roe's predecessor William Hawkins. Each night Jahangir indulges by drinking and smoking opium:

> And then he ariseth, and being in the height of his drinks, he layeth him down to sleep, every man departing to his own home. And, after he hath slept two hours they awake him, and bring his supper to him, at which time he is not able to feed himself; but it is thrust into his mouth by others, and this is about one of the clock; and then he sleepeth the rest of the night.[68]

---

66 Forbes, in Purchas, op. cit., n. 3, vol. IV, p. 184.
67 Roe, in id., pp. 327–8.
68 Hawkins, in id., p. 46.

107

Elsewhere in his narrative, Roe becomes suspicious of the value of all this wealth. During Jahangir's birthday celebrations, the Emperor sits cross-legged on a pair of scales and his weight is measured against gold and jewels which Roe believes to be make believe: he describes sacks full of that which:

> they say was silver, gold and jewels and precious stones, but I saw none, it being in bagges might bee pibles. then [he is weighed] against cloth of Gold, Silke, Stuffes, Linnen, Spices and all sorts of goods, but I must believe, for they were in fardles. Lastly, against Meale, Butter, Corne, which is said to be given to the Beniani, and all the rerst of the Stuffe: but I saw it carefully carried in, and none disturbed.[69]

If Roe's descriptions of sultanate rituals and ornament are so detailed and so vivid, it is in order to validate the claim that there is no substance to despotism beyond frippery. It is all show: 'To describe it rightly, it was like a great stage, and the Prince sate above as the Mock Kings doe there.'[70] Or '[t]his sitting out had so much affinity with a theatre, the manner of the king in his gallery: the great men lifted on stage, as actors, the vulgar below gazing on.'[71]

For Roe, Oriental luxury exceeds the order of resemblance by masking the empty relations of power. Throughout Roe's account the world of luxury is a world of dissimulation; fruits of gold are in fact hollow, sacks of jewels may be full of pebbles, and the whole scene is staged to glorify a 'mock King'. Objects and persons are never what they seem. Borrowing directly from a favourite maxim of Protestant iconoclasm, Roe concludes his description of Jahangir's Imperial pavilion, by making scathing reference to the transitory nature of the oriental vanities: *sic transit gloria mundi*.[72] All of this theatrical display of Imperial power, for Roe, was based upon deceit rather than fact. Its extravagance hid an emptiness within the structure of power itself. Oriental government was more deceitful a form of power in that it managed to captivate, seduce and, ultimately, dupe those attendant subjects. The formal arrangement of Mughal rule, as stated much later by a company director, although 'beautiful in its simplicity upon paper, is apt to charm the imagination and mislead the judgment of men.'[73] The theory that the king is king only through appearances was well noted by travellers such as Roe, and with it the power of images to manipulate the affections of the 'vulgar' spectators. This deceitful manipulation through the arts of representation is what made the idea of despotism so abhorrent.

Yet, a paradox emerges. In terms of the fantasy, the more that emptiness is envisaged at the heart of despotic power, the more tyrannical it becomes. The more sedentary, drunk, effeminate the despot gets, the more despotic he becomes. Despotic power finds its paradigm in the image of the drunk, lazy,

69 Roe, in id., p. 405.
70 id., p. 325.
71 id., p. 328.
72 id., p. 333.
73 H. Verlest, *A View of the Rise, Progress and Present State of the English in Bengal* (1772) at 45.

108

and inefficient Sultan. The force of despotism lies in the dazzling display that is nothing more than dissimulation. Dissimulation, consequently, comes to be regarded as the origin of illegitimate force; it is what institutes despotic power. And in manipulating and manoeuvring the desires and behaviour of those who are subject to its display, this dissimulation is not without real effect.

What is more disconcerting is the suspicion that, beneath it all, the despot may not be enjoying himself, and that, in fact, no difference exists between Western and Eastern manners in so far as both are established on the non-existence of enjoyment.

CONCLUSION

It is the jurisprudential attitude towards enjoyment that condemns 'the oriental' to a fantastical space in which everything is a corrupt surplus. And, it is this fantasy of excess that institutes the Orient as an illegitimate site of despotic decision making.

Yet, this attitude also reveals the proximity between Eastern and Western subjectivity, for Western travellers and imperialists are clearly not immune to the strategic theatre of despotic enjoyment. The illusion that enjoyment has been denied to ourselves and is exclusive to some other person (who claims to have no need for analysis) gives rise to feelings of envy (what Lacan termed the *lebensneid*) and consequently, seduction. We covet what is forbidden. For Zizek:

> the aim of the prohibition is not to 'raise the price' of an object by rendering access to it more difficult, but to raise this object itself to the level of the thing around which desire is organised.[74]

We might also add, that this process of seduction is prompted by surfaces rather than depth, images rather than 'reality', and veils rather than flesh. Seduction takes place before or beyond any understanding, it is stimulated not by any inaccessible object, but by what masks the object. Consider, for example, Thomas Roe's description of having furtively glimpsed the private quarters of the Emperor's wives.[75] In spite of what he tries to repress, in the name of propriety, Roe acknowledges the exoticism and sensuality of the seraglio. Yet, he is unable to describe what he calls 'the full proportion' of the women in the harem. The eroticism of the scene is channelled through the tangle of matter that obstructs access, and a fuller vision of the women's bodies. Bernier's visit to attend to a sick patient in the seraglio is even more extraordinary in betraying that sense of seduction: 'a Kachemire shawl covered my head, hanging like a scarf down to my feet, and an eunuch led me by the hand, as if I had been a blind man.'[76] What maintains the frisson

74 Zizek, op. cit., n. 46, at p. 94.
75 Roe, in Purchas, op. cit., n. 3, vol. IV, pp. 375–6.
76 Bernier, op. cit., n. 22, p. 267.

of delight in these descriptions of the seraglio, are the veils, the clothes, and the screen. The importance of cloth in the seduction of westerner travellers, was not lost on these authors. Forbes, for example, deliberately quotes Ezekiel's portrait of an oriental lady:

> I clothe thee with broidered work, I girded thee with fine linen and covered thee with silk: I decked thee with ornaments ... Thus was thou decked with gold and silver; and thy raiment was of fine linen, and silk and thou wast exceedingly beautiful.[77]

Seduction operates at exactly the same level as denigration. It cannot be said, therefore, that the effect that the illusion of despotic enjoyment was meant to have on the Sultan's own subjects did not have a similar effect on the western traveller. As soon as the Sultan becomes an object of derision, his escapades begin to fascinate. This is made clear in a number of instances and certainly so in the case of Hawkins. In dancing attendance on the Mughal Emperor, Hawkins's primary objective was to secure a treaty. In so doing, he listens attentively to the Sultan's every word and watches his every signal. Each gesture, each whimsy, becomes a clue as to the imperial decision. Just as every lover becomes a detective in the early stages of courtship and tries to decipher the desires of another, so Hawkins seems desperate to place the chaos of these signs within an understandable lexical framework. Such is the inflaming power of all things enigmatic; it is inevitable that the Englishman will be seduced into the ways of the Moghul court. In his early years, Hawkins ('a typsy-swiller of the most pronounced type')[78] had established himself as a favourite drinking companion to Jahangir. He eventually began dressing as a muslim of the court and married a Christian Armenian wife chosen for him by Jahangir. He decided to remain in India on the Sultan's promise that:

> If I would remayne with him, he would grant me Articles for our factorie to my hearts desire ... and he would allow me by the yeare, three thousand and two hundred pounds sterling for my first, and so yearely, hee promised to augment my Living, till I came to a thousand Horse. For the Nobilitie of India have their Titles by the number of their Horse.[79]

In spite of the denigration of oriental ritual, it is clear from many accounts that the Western traveller sought to share in the enjoyment held by the Eastern courts. Orientalism maniacally dances to the discordant yet amorous strains of courtly music. Portraits of Westerners dressed in muslin and silk twisted into scarlet and gold turbans, belong to a cult of exoticism in which the West is held in thrall by the dress and rituals of eastern nobility. Different and select aspects of courtly rituals thus formed part of the perception of the East as a veiled yet sensual and dangerously carnal world. They were as much part of its exotica as were 'spices and drugges, silke, sandales and

77 Forbes, op. cit., n. 4, vol. II, p. 258.
78 Oaten, op. cit., n. 24, p. 142.
79 Hawkins, in Purchas, op. cit., n. 3, vol. IV, p. 14.

110

Elephants teeth'.[80] They were as much part of its fearful collection of fabula as were the legends of colossal beasts, and deities all of which seduced and captured the Western imagination.

On the one hand, throughout the colonial period Indian styles of government were mocked for their corrupt excess. Yet, on the other hand, the inaccessibility of what was perceived to be the abundant vitality of the sultanate became a cause of seduction and envy. The British were enthralled, captured, and enticed by what was paraded before their eyes. It seems more in the nature of a ritual itself than a moment in life, that one is tempted by the object of denigration or fear. So deeply did the British come to be seduced by the lavish trappings of Indian imperialism that all the irrational mechanics of superficial display and pageant became the indispensable condition of the juridical and political structure of colonial administration.

More pertinently, the English nabobs and factors attempted to mimic the living conditions of the Emperor himself. Punishments such as public whippings handed down by the English courts provided 'free entertainment', whereas:

> The head of the factory lived in almost as great a state as the Mogul Governor. Outside the door of his bedchamber stood servants with silver staves and when he appeared they followed him from room to room. If he went downstairs a picket of liveried guardsmen sprang to attention in the hall, and if he left the factory Bandarines and Moors under two standards marched before him. He was provided with well filled stables for pleasure or services and he had his own chaplain, physician, surgeon, linguist and mint-master. At his entry into the dining room trumpets blew and while he sat at table violins played softly.[81]

What is interesting about the above passage is that the President does not quite reach the excessive luxury of the Emperor. Presidential life is lived only in *almost* as great a state as the Mogul Governor. While numerous reports, particularly around the time of Hastings impeachment, criticized the opulent living conditions of the English in India, a difference of degree was always maintained between the English nabob and the oriental despot. For those such as Burke, the threat of nabob corruption was that it approached but never quite reached the 'dread majesty' of oriental despotism. However, this form of distancing may be explained otherwise. It was precisely because excessive enjoyment does not exist other than as a set of fantastical presumptions that there was/is a radical failure to steal the enjoyment of the other. It was by no means accurate, for example, to locate sex at the centre of despotic politics.[82] Again, a mystical theory of reciprocity subsisted beneath the surplus of gifts (*nazar*) which western travellers thought were bribes

---

80 Ralph Fitch, cited in R. Masani, *Britain in India; An Account of British Rule in the Indian Subcontinent* (1960) 5.
81 D. Kincaid, *British Social Life in India, 1608-1937* (1973) 41.
82 '. . . sex . . . was only one of several forces [within the Imperial Harem] and one of relatively little importance.' L.P. Pierce, *The Imperial Harem: Women and Sovereignty in the Ottoman Empire* (1993) 3.

111

which accrued to a greedy Sultan. In mimicking the imaginary structures of Indian government and, yet, in marking out their difference, colonial authority could not therefore indulge in the copious excesses, the superabundant vitality, or the fun which they wrongly perceived had been enjoyed by the Nawabs, Sultans, and Maharajahs. These poor melancholic, upright, yet impotent Englishmen, seduced by what they believed to be the passion of oriental government were unable properly to participate in the enjoyment they simultaneously denigrated and envied.

Put differently, there was little difference in manners between the East and West. As Zizek puts it: 'The unbearable is not the difference. The difference is the fact that in a sense there is no difference.'[83] Or, the difference exists only by way of a suspicious fantasy about how others might live their lives. Despotic judgment contains no greater madness, no greater excess, in the moment of decision making than judgment in Western legal systems.

83 Zizek, op. cit., n. 46, p. 2.

JOURNAL OF LAW AND SOCIETY
VOLUME 31, NUMBER 1, MARCH 2004
ISSN: 0263-323X, pp. 113–30

Literature in the Dock: The Trials of Oscar Wilde

MORRIS B. KAPLAN*

This essay uses the recently published expanded record of the Queensberry libel trial to revisit the relationship between the 'literary' and 'sexual' dimensions of the Wilde scandal. The defence was guided by an integrated conception of the links between the two that shaped both the public responses and the legal proceedings, including the criminal prosecution. The conflict between moral literalism and aesthetic indeterminacy not only informed the legal determination of sexual guilt but also was inflected by social class in ways that contributed to the construction of male homosexuality and of the 'literary'.

It is well known that the trials of Oscar Wilde included contested evidence concerning both his literary work and his sexual behaviour. Frequently these have been treated as two independent tracks with commentators emphasizing either the aesthetic movement that Wilde championed or the extension of criminalized homosexual conduct from sodomy to 'gross indecency' between men. However, the defence in the Queensberry libel trial established intimate links between the two facets of the case. Given the proliferation of recent work on the history of sexuality, one scholar has commented that: 'There is a tendency in some recent scholarship to forget that Wilde was by profession a literary man, and that it was his writing as much as his conduct that got him into trouble.'[1] William A. Cohen goes on to propose that 'the way in which literature – both specific literary works and the notion of the literary in general – also went to court in his trials has often gone unnoticed.'[2] Cohen describes the conflict between Wilde's insistence

* Purchase College, State University of New York, 735 Anderson Hill Road, Purchase, NY 10577, United States of America

Many thanks to Dr. Leslie Moran and the staff of the Birbeck College Law School for their hospitality and engagement during my stay as a Visiting Fellow and to Prof. Michael Levenson for urging me to write about Wilde. This essay is dedicated to the memory of my colleague and friend Prof. Michael O'Loughlin.

1 W.A. Cohen, *Sex Scandal: The Private Parts of Victorian Fiction* (1996) 213, fn. 22.
2 id., p. 213.

on the inherent indeterminacy of literary meaning and his legal adversary's contention that his writing comprised a coded expression of 'sodomitical' tendencies. He argues the writer's aesthetic commitment to open-ended interpretive possibilities left him vulnerable to the accusation that some among his readers, including those most impressionable, might well take him to advocate prohibited desires and conduct. In this essay, I build upon Cohen's interpretation to demonstrate how profoundly the 'literary' and the 'sexual' were imbricated with social class in the Wilde trials and their attendant publicity. The recent publication by Merlin Holland of a more extensive record of the Queensberry libel trial allows us to see how these juxtapositions resulted from deliberate strategy on the part of Queensberry's attorneys that influenced press coverage and was perpetuated by the prosecution in Wilde's two criminal trials.[3]

One aspect of this strategy was to inscribe Wilde within a prior history of criminal sexuality. A hostile reviewer in 1890 already had sex scandal in mind when he suggested that *The Picture of Dorian Gray* was fit only for 'outlawed noblemen and perverted delivery boys'.[4] Readers would hardly miss the reference to the Cleveland Street affair, which had filled the newspapers from fall of 1889 into the spring of 1890. Police investigating petty thefts in the central Post Office had discovered telegraph delivery boys to be employed part-time as prostitutes in a male brothel at 19 Cleveland Street. Further investigation revealed that the clientele had included highly-placed figures with connections to the court and the government. The radical press was filled with accusations of cover-up, naming names that led one son of a Duke and equerry to the Prince of Wales to flee the country to avoid arrest. Widespread rumour implicated Prince Albert Victor, Queen Victoria's grandson and heir-presumptive.[5] By linking Wilde to Cleveland Street, the reviewer conjured images of aristocratic decadence and sexual exploitation of working-class youth. When Wilde was finally driven to take legal action against the Marquess of Queensberry in 1895, he confronted charges of sexual misconduct linking him to male prostitutes and petty criminals who inhabited a demimonde similar to that exposed in the earlier scandal. Queensberry's lawyers explicitly invoked Cleveland Street, portraying one of Wilde's friends as a procurer who plied his trade from

---

3 M. Holland, *Irish Peacock and Scarlet Marquess: The Real Trial of Oscar Wilde* (2003). Although it does not contradict anything in H. Montgomery Hyde, *The Trials of Oscar Wilde* (1948), the new text offers considerably greater detail of Wilde's testimony and cross-examination as well as Sir Edward Carson's closing argument for the defence. Unfortunately, Holland does not account for the provenance of his find.

4 *Scots Observer*, 5 July 1890, quoted in Holland, id., p. 77.

5 H. Montgomery Hyde, *The Cleveland Street Scandal* (1976); C. Simpson, D. Chester, and J. Leitch, *The Cleveland Street Affair* (1976); M.B. Kaplan, 'Who's Afraid of John Saul? Urban Culture and the Politics of Desire in Late Victorian London' (1999) 5 GLQ: a journal of lesbian and gay studies 290–301 and 'Did "my Lord Gomorrah" Smile?' in *Disorder in the Court*, eds. N. Erber and G. Robb (1998).

114

a sinister apartment in Westminster. Radical newspapers seized upon the precedent, demanding that this time the government not let privileged wrongdoers escape justice. Editorials and letters to the editor recited a litany of accusations that the defender of the new aestheticism in fact promoted urban decadence. Wilde's novel had created quite a stir with its suggestions of aristocratic libertinism, ill-defined secret immorality, and a background of London vice. By the time of his trials, detectives employed by Queensberry's solicitor had no trouble finding evidence that the writer himself had descended into such an underworld.

Wilde's 'feasting with panthers' had involved him with young men from the urban underclass whom bourgeois society would regard with fear or contempt. However, unlike Dorian Gray, who pursued ambiguous vices in the dark enclaves of London's East End, Wilde entertained out in the open at West End restaurants, clubs, and hotels. The writer and his circle had advertised themselves in extravagant dress with lilies or green carnations in their buttonholes. Wilde promoted an aesthetic approach to life hostile to middle-class respectability. The theatricality of his public performances surrounded by admiring young men recalls the promenades of Boulton and Park, middle-class cross-dressers whose prosecution for 'conspiracy to commit the felony' of sodomy had filled the papers in 1870–71.[6] These links were reinforced by evidence that some of his friends may have dressed 'in women's attire' or cavorted with those who did. Editorials explicitly invoked the Boulton and Park affair. Whereas the cross-dressers had successfully defended themselves as actors who played women's parts, Wilde's connections with the professional theatre were exploited to increase suspicion of his moral nonconformity. However, when challenged to defend 'the love that dare not speak its name' at his trial for 'gross indecency between men', Wilde invoked an older model of male friendship. One of the most distinguished products of the Oxford 'Greats' curriculum, Wilde invoked the tradition of pedagogic eros, emphasizing its spiritual purity:

> The love that dare not speak its name in this century is such a great affection of an older for a younger man as there was between David and Jonathan, such as Plato made the very basis of his philosophy, and such as you find in the sonnets of Michelangelo and Shakespeare. It is that deep spiritual affection that is as pure as it is perfect.[7]

Wilde combined high culture with lowlife in a mix that proved explosive when mercilessly exposed at the Old Bailey and in the press.

---

6 Cohen, op. cit., n. 1, pp. 73–129; N. Bartlett, *Who Was That Man: A Present for Mr. Oscar Wilde* (1988) 129–43; Kaplan, id., pp. 279–90; 'Gentlemen in Petticoats!' in *Imagined Londons*, ed. P.K. Gilbert (2002).
7 Hyde, op. cit., n. 3, p. 201. See, also, L. Dowling, *Hellenism and Homosexuality in Victorian Oxford* (1994); M.B. Kaplan, *Sexual Justice: Democratic Citizenship and the Politics of Desire* (1997) 49–62.

The facts of the case are well known, amply documented and commented on.[8] Two aspects of the Wilde affair distinguish it from the earlier scandals involving love between men: his memorable writing and his extraordinary celebrity. The efforts, first of Queensberry's defence, then of the public prosecutors, to link these factors to sexual criminality marked the trials as an event of cultural importance. They associated Wilde's aestheticism with the social phenomenon of effeminacy and with the private indulgence of prohibited desires. Sir Edward Carson, Queensberry's barrister and a classmate of Wilde's from Trinity College, Dublin, blurred the boundaries between literature and life, using Wilde's writing to cast him as a corrupt poseur from whom Douglas's father strived to save the young nobleman. Carson portrayed the lower-class youths connected with Wilde as at once utterly unsuitable companions and innocents seduced by the older man. Most of the press eagerly followed, depicting the writer as a symbol of cultural decadence, sexual exploitation, and dangerous deviance. Some commentators have seen the figure of Wilde they forged as shaping attitudes toward male homosexuality for generations to come.[9] Images of the homosexual, whether dangerous or persecuted, coalesced around the writer's personality and fate. However, conceptions of the aesthetic movement with which he was associated and of literature itself were also implicated in Wilde's trials.

Wilde was a star, perhaps the first modern celebrity. He was a poet, playwright, novelist, and editor. From the beginning of his literary career, he had promoted himself not only as a poet and playwright, but as the spokesman for a new approach to art and to life: 'I think I may say without vanity – though I do not wish to appear to run vanity down – that of all men in England I am the one who requires least advertisement.'[10] After two years at Trinity College, Dublin, Wilde had won a fellowship to Magdalen College, Oxford, where he excelled academically while making a name for himself as a witty and extravagant defender of radical attitudes towards art and life. When he arrived in London, he had already been recognized as an upcoming literary figure. Lecturing widely in England and in the United States of America, Wilde was both celebrated and reviled as the embodiment of the doctrine of 'art for art's sake' which opposed the moralizing tendencies of late Victorian society. Young Wilde had been caricatured as the poet Bunthorne in Gilbert and Sullivan's operetta *Patience* (1881); later, he became the model for Cyprian Brome in André Raffalovich's *A Willing Exile* (1890) and for Mr. Amarinth in

---

8 In addition to works by Hyde, Bartlett, and Cohen already cited, important studies of Wilde which inform this essay include R. Gagnier, *Idylls of the Marketplace: Oscar Wilde and the Victorian Public* (1986); E. Cohen, *Talk on the Wilde Side* (1993); M.S. Foldy, *The Trials of Oscar Wilde: Deviance, Morality, and Late Victorian Society* (1997). Richard Ellmann's *Oscar Wilde* (1987) remains the definitive biography.
9 See, especially, A. Sinfield, *The Wilde Century* (1994).
10 O. Wilde, *The Complete Letters* eds. M. Holland and R. Hart-Davis (2000) 321.

Robert Hichens' *The Green Carnation* (1894). Wilde had married Constance Lloyd and established the household at 16 Tite Street where they often entertained friends and raised their two sons. Still, by 1890, rumors about his personal life had begun to circulate. Even John Addington Symonds, an early defender of male same-sex desire, had reservations about *The Picture of Dorian Gray*:

> It is an odd and very audacious production, unwholesome in tone, but artistically and psychologically interesting. If the British public will stand this, they can stand anything. However, I resent the unhealthy, scented, mystic, congested touch which a man of this sort has on moral problems.[11]

Wilde had been introduced to sex between men in 1886, when he was thirty-four years old; after that, he came to revel in the company of young men. He spent more of his time away from home, entertaining at various venues in the West End. The writer attracted a following among aspiring litterateurs, while at the same time courting men of a rougher sort. The publication of *Dorian Gray* much enhanced his reputation among aesthetically-inclined undergraduates. One of these was Lord Alfred Douglas, known as 'Bosie', a student at Wilde's alma mater, Magdalen College, Oxford. The youngest son of the Marquess of Queensberry, Bosie eagerly sought an introduction to the writer. Their meeting eventually led to Wilde's trials, conviction, and imprisonment.[12]

By the spring of 1895, Wilde's ascent appeared unstoppable. He had found his métier in drawing-room comedies sparkling with witty conversation. *An Ideal Husband* was playing to full houses in the West End, with *The Importance of Being Earnest* about to open. The events leading to Wilde's disgrace, imprisonment, and early death were set in motion when Queensberry left a card at the Albemarle Club on February 18, 1895. It was inscribed: 'For Oscar Wilde, posing [as a] somdomite [sic].'[13] This gesture culminated a sustained and deliberate campaign of harassment designed to drive the two friends apart. The Marquess had called on the writer at 16 Tite Street, stopping just short of accusing them of sodomy: 'I don't say you are it, but you look it ... and you pose as it, which is just as bad.'[14] Queensberry's insults and threats led Wilde to show him the door. At the opening of *The Importance of Being Earnest* on 14 February 1895, the Marquess had planned to create a scene.[15] The police stopped him from entering the theatre. Queensberry left behind 'a grotesque bouquet of vegetables' for the author.[16] When Wilde received the offensive card left at his club, he decided to take action. Despite an expense that he could ill afford and risks of exposure that he managed to ignore, Wilde decided to prosecute

---

11 J.A. Symonds, *Letters*, vol. III, eds. H.M. Schueller and R.L. Peters (1967) 477.
12 Ellman, op. cit., n. 8, pp. 324–5.
13 Hyde, op. cit., n. 3, p. 76.
14 Holland, op. cit., n. 3, p. 58.
15 id., pp. 36, 58.
16 id., p. 59.

Queensberry for criminal libel.[17] A conviction might have resulted in the Marquess's imprisonment. Despite his reputation as a libertine and an atheist, the Marquess would cast himself as a father concerned for his son's moral welfare, fighting to protect twenty-year old Lord Alfred from the older Wilde. Whether or not he foresaw disaster at the time, Wilde later described himself as a casualty in the warfare between father and son.[18] In the letter to Douglas from prison known as *De Profundis*, Wilde would comment: 'Blindly I staggered as an ox into the shambles.'[19] He lamented an outcome that had come to seem inevitable:

> At the end, I was of course arrested and your father became the hero of the hour; more indeed than the hero of the hour merely: you family now ranks, strangely enough, with the Immortals, for ... your father will always live among the kind pure-minded parents of Sunday-school literature, your place is with the Infant Samuel, and in the lowest mire of Malebolge I sit between Giles de Retz and the Marquis de Sade.[20]

However complex his motivations (and many scholars have tried to plumb their depths), Wilde's decision to prosecute Queensberry led to personal disaster.

The case fully occupied newspapers across the political spectrum offering a confrontation between two of Victorian Britain's most conspicuous figures. It provided the spectacle of courtroom drama while allowing the press to moralize about life and art, family and friendship, aristocracy and celebrity. The libel trial was fuelled from the start by charges of harassment and persecution and counter-charges of sexual irregularity. Wilde charged that leaving the card at the Albemarle Club amounted to the publication of a 'false scandalous malicious and defamatory libel'. Queensberry had implicitly claimed that the writer 'had committed and was in the habit of committing the abominable crime of buggery with mankind to [his] great damage scandal and disgrace'.[21] Much of the argument at trial revolved around the significance of the word 'posing': Queensberry's attorney alleged that that Wilde's literary work comprised evidence of such a 'pose'. At Queensberry's first appearance in the Criminal Court, his attorney stated that his client '... thought it well for the morality of his son to put an end to the relations between the parties.'[22] This statement adumbrates the plea of 'justification' by which the defence undertook to prove that Queensberry's accusation was true and that it benefited the public to publish it. His private investigators covered the West End in search of men willing to disclose their relations with the writer. The formal plea, filed on 30 March 1895, went far beyond the Marquess's initial provocation. In nineteen paragraphs, it

17 Hyde, op. cit., n. 3, pp. 77–8.
18 Wilde to Robert Ross, November 1896 in op. cit., n. 10, p. 670 (ellipsis in original).
19 Wilde to A. Douglas, Jan–March 1897, id., p. 690.
20 id., p. 691.
21 Holland, op. cit., n. 3, pp. 285–6.
22 id., p. 22.

presented a devastating indictment of Wilde that the legal language could not obscure. A plea of justification turns the tables on the 'prosecutor' in a libel case who must defend himself against the evidence introduced by the 'defendant'. Queensberry's plea recited, in fourteen counts, multiple specific incidents, times and places where Wilde was said to 'solicit', 'incite', and even commit sodomitical or 'indecent' acts with ten named individuals and 'other boys' who had not been identified. Given the publicity with which Wilde had entertained these young men, they had not been hard to find. Would they appear to testify against him in court? Both parties to acts of sodomy or 'gross indecency' were equally guilty in the eyes of the law. Would the witnesses risk being prosecuted for sexual offences?

None of these young men was called to testify at the libel trial, which was resolved on the basis of Wilde's testimony alone. Although the writer was forced on cross-examination to confront and deny each of the allegations of sexual misconduct, the bulk of his testimony pertained to literary matters. The concluding paragraphs of the plea of justification charged Wilde with publishing:

> a certain immoral and obscene work in the form of a narrative entitled *The Picture of Dorian Gray* ... designed and intended ... and understood by the readers thereof to describe the relations intimacies and passions of certain persons of sodomitical and unnatural habits tastes and practices.

Further, Queensberry claimed that Wilde 'joined in procuring the publication' of *The Chameleon*, which included 'divers obscene matters and things relating to the practices and passions of persons of unnatural habits and tastes.... ' and as 'its first and principal contributor' published 'certain immoral maxims' entitled 'Phrases and Philosophies for the Use of the Young'. Queensberry's lawyers linked the literary to the criminal allegations against the writer. The plea alleged that:

> ... before and at the time of the said alleged libel the said Oscar Fingal O'fflahertie Wills Wilde was a man of letters and a dramatist of prominence and notoriety and a person who exercised considerable influence over young men that ... Wilde claimed to be a fit person and proper person to give advice and instruction to the young and had published the said maxims ... in the magazine ... for circulation amongst the students of the University of Oxford and that the said works entitled *The Chameleon* and *The Picture of Dorian Gray* were calculated to subvert morality and to encourage unnatural vice and that [Wilde] had corrupted and debauched the morals of the said Charles Parker, Alfonso Harold Conway, Walter Grainger, Sydney Mavor, Frederick Atkins, Ernest Scarfe and Edward Shelley ... and [Wilde] had committed the aforementioned and the said sodomitical practices for a longtime with impunity and without detection.[23]

The public interest required that Wilde's 'true character and habits' be exposed to deter him from further offences and from 'further corrupting and debauching the liege subjects of our said Lady the Queen.' Wilde's public

23 id., 290–1.

119

status as a literary figure transformed a series of sordid sexual allegations into a trial for 'corrupting the youth' – a charge as ancient, and potentially lethal, as that for which the Athenians convicted Socrates.

The literary dimension of the case focused on three separate subject areas, each of which presented the writer with distinct hazards: *The Picture of Dorian Gray*, published in *Lippincott's Magazine* in 1890 and separately in expanded and revised form in 1891; *The Chameleon,* edited by an Oxford undergraduate, which included Wilde's 'Phrases and Philosophies', Douglas's poems, and an anonymous story, 'The Priest and the Acolyte'; and a letter from Wilde to Douglas, which had been published as a 'prose poem.' Perhaps to deflect the element of surprise, Wilde's lawyer had placed in evidence a letter from the writer to Bosie that had been the subject of a failed blackmail attempt but had been copied and circulated in theatrical circles. The prosecution later introduced another letter from Wilde to Douglas. As a result, the literary arguments concerned not only Wilde's publications but also his private correspondence. Famously Wilde defended the first letter as a work of art. He had written it in response to some poetry that Bosie had sent him. Their shared commitment to writing helped shape the friendship. Douglas had edited *The Spirit Lamp,* which published a French translation of Wilde's letter.

These facts increased the urgency of issues about the relationship between literature and life, ardent prose and indecent conduct. Carson pressed Wilde vigorously on his conception of art and its relation to morality, relentlessly implying that the writer's aestheticism masked a thoroughgoing immoralism. William A. Cohen observes:

> In the legal battle over interpretation, Wilde avers that all his writing is literary, even when it appears explicitly erotic; the opposing counsel portrays it all as sexually coded, even when it seems legitimately literary.

However, Wilde's position on the interpretability of literary work, as developed in his aesthetic essays, works to his disadvantage:

> Yet the ambiguity for which Wilde affirmatively stakes a claim also reinvigorates the moral suspicion with which literary culture had long been regarded, now through its association with criminal homosexuality. The reason why something is going unsaid may well be that its is unspeakable – which is to say, sexual.[24]

As the 'conflict of interpretations' developed, these general impulses were inflected by social class. This potential was exposed at the very beginning when Wilde's counsel addressed the jury about the letter:

> Now, gentlemen, the words of that letter appear extravagant to those who are in the habit of writing commercial correspondence or those ordinary letters which the necessities of life force upon one every day ...[25]

24 Cohen, op. cit., n. 1, pp. 213–14; O. Wilde, *The Artist as Critic*, ed. R. Ellerman (1968).
25 Holland, op. cit., n. 3, p. 33.

This distinction leads the attorney to assure his middle-class, respectable jurors that Wilde says:

> ... as an artist and poet that letter is an expression of poetical feeling and has no relation whatever to the hateful suggestions – hateful to him as to all of you -which are made with regard to him in this case.[26]

The barrister asserts the right of the poet to his own mode of expression while identifying his moral position with that of the jury. Similarly, after summarizing the plot of Wilde's novel, he insists on the distance between the author and his eponymous hero:

> ... it hints at and suggests, for it does not describe, vices and weaknesses of which Dorian Gray is guilty, but to attack Mr. Oscar Wilde as being addicted to this sort of offence, because in the book he states that the person in the book is a vicious creature in all ways, is surely the most strange inference.[27]

The barrister insists that the novelist or playwright has not only a right but also a duty to 'describe the passions and vices of life if he desires to produce any work of art which, while idealizing reality, may be artistic in the sense of harmony and beauty and truth.'[28]

Sir Edward Clarke anticipates the positions which his client will elaborate on the stand as he defends the autonomy of artistic work from moral judgments. Most famously, Wilde contends 'there is no such thing as an immoral book.' Interrogated about 'The Priest and the Acolyte', which chronicles with apparent sympathy a doomed affair between the eponymous characters, the writer steadfastly refused to condemn the piece as 'immoral' or 'blasphemous', but insists: 'Worse, it was badly written. (*Laughter*)'.[29] Queensberry's counsel sought to establish Wilde's guilt by association with *The Chameleon*: 'I am asking you, supposing a person had been connected with the production or had approved of it in public, would you say he was posing as a sodomite?' To which the writer replied, 'I should say he had very bad literary taste.'[30] Carson pressed him further about Lord Alfred's poems, 'In Praise of Shame' and 'Two Loves', which had also appeared there. He described them as 'exceedingly beautiful poems'. Queensberry's counsel implied that they contained 'improper suggestions', quoting the last line of 'Two Loves': 'I am the love that dare not speak its name.' Asked about its meaning at his first criminal trial, Wilde would rise to heights of eloquence in the defence of pedagogic eros quoted above. Here he simply denied the suggestion of impropriety.[31] Despite Wilde's minimal participation in *The Chameleon*, Carson was able to use it seriously to impugn the writer: he emphasized that Wilde's

26 id., p. 34.
27 id., p. 42.
28 id., p. 43.
29 id., p. 69.
30 id., p. 72.
31 id., pp. 67–8.

'Phrases and Philosophies for the Use of the Young' might be taken as an endorsement of the other work by the Oxford undergraduates among whom the journal circulated. Even more damaging, he used the writer's endorsement of Douglas's poems as legitimating Queensberry's suspicions about Wilde's influence on his son.

Carson mounted his assault on the moral import of Wilde's writing by confronting him with extended passages from *The Picture of Dorian Gray*. He telegraphed his major themes early in his cross-examination reading from a hostile review:

> The story – which deals with matters only fitted for the Criminal Investigation Department or a hearing in camera – is discreditable alike to author and editor. Mr. Wilde has brains, and art, and style; but if he can write for none but outlawed noblemen and perverted telegraph boys, the sooner he takes to tailoring (or some other decent trade) the better for his own reputation and the public morals.[32]

Carson exploited this reference to the Cleveland Street affair in examining the writer about his cross-class associations. His young companions were identified as servants or clerks, often out of work; some of them would admit to occasional blackmail as well as prostitution. Although Wilde consistently denied any sexual improprieties, he passionately defended his attraction to youth: 'I like the society of young men. I delight in it.'[33] The writer tried to deflect with wit Carson's efforts to pin him down about their ages: 'I don't keep a census.'[34] In the background, of course, was another youth outside the writer's social class. When Wilde admitted taking eighteen-year-old Alfonso Conway to Brighton for a stay at the Albion Hotel, Carson asked if he had ever taken 'another boy' to that hotel. Wilde replied that he had stayed there with Lord Alfred Douglas.[35]

The relation between older and younger men was the subject which Queensberry's counsel pursued most vigorously in relation to *Dorian Gray*. He focused his questions primarily on three long passages, describing respectively the impact on the painter Basil Hallward of his first glimpse of the young hero; Basil's later confession of his feelings; and the impression made on Dorian by his reading of 'the yellow book' sent him by his sophisticated friend Sir Henry Wotton. The painter had told Wotton of his first sight of Dorian:

> I knew I had come face to face with someone whose mere personality was so fascinating, it would, if I allowed it to do so, it would absorb my whole nature, my whole soul, my very art itself.[36]

Asked whether these words described 'a moral kind of feeling for one man to have for another much younger than himself', Wilde insisted: 'I say it was a

32 id., p. 77.
33 id., p. 164.
34 id.
35 id., p. 151.
36 id., pp. 84–5.

122

the feeling of an artist toward a beautiful personality.'[37] The writer defended the artist's emotional prerogatives further when faced with Basil's confession to Dorian:

> It is true that I have worshipped you with far more romance of feeling than a man usually gives to a friend. Somehow I have never loved a woman ... Well, from the moment I met you, your personality had the most extraordinary influence over me. I quite admit that I adored you madly, extravagantly, absurdly. I was jealous of everyone to whom you spoke. I wanted to have you all to myself.[38]

Carson again raised the question whether these feelings were 'normal' or 'natural' for one man to have in regard to another. When Wilde again deflected the insinuation by treating the language as expressing an aesthetic response to a 'remarkable personality', his adversary became more personal, asking whether Wilde himself had ever had such feelings for another man. The writer quibbled with the lawyer over precise words until finally denying any personal investment: '... it is a fiction I am describing.'[39] Wilde asserted that he had never had the feelings he attributed to Basil but had 'borrowed' them from Shakespeare's sonnets. Asked if he had written an essay arguing that these were 'practically sodomitical', he replied: '... I wrote an article to prove that they were not so.'[40] His defence of the purity of the sonnets was motivated by a desire to reply to those 'people in the world who cannot understand the intense devotion and affection and admiration that an artist can feel for a wonderful and beautiful person, or a wonderful and beautiful mind.' Carson pressed on: 'And these unfortunate people who have not that high understanding that you have, might put it down to something wrong? ... And sodomitical?'[41] Wilde's reply exposed further the gap between his aesthetic theories and ordinary readers: 'I am not concerned with the ignorance of others.'[42] However, Wilde had admitted earlier, he made no effort to limit the circulation of his works to an educated audience, but sought their widest circulation – and sale. The writer was perhaps more successful in deflecting the implication that the book which Dorian read was 'sodomitical' or that his secret vice with which he corrupted others was sodomy. He insisted on the indeterminacy of immorality in the novel and on the impossibility of either a book or an individual exercising external 'influence' on the character of an adult. One is what he makes of himself. Eventually, Wilde's counsel would buttress his testimony on this score by introducing into evidence the writer's reply to the review cited by Carson:

37 id., p. 86.
38 id., p. 87.
39 id., p. 90.
40 id., p. 93.
41 id.
42 id., p. 94.

It was necessary, sir, for the dramatic development of this story to surround Dorian Gray with an atmosphere of moral corruption. Otherwise the story would have had no meaning, and the plot no issue. To keep this atmosphere vague and indeterminate and wonderful was the aim of the artist who wrote the story. I claim, sir, that he has succeeded. Each man sees his own sin in Dorian Gray. What Dorian Gray's sins are no one knows. He who finds them has brought them.[43]

Wilde's hermeneutic principles here left him with the choice of writing only for an educated elite or accepting responsibility for the impressions of a democratic readership. Indeed, the writer's effort to control the interpretation of his texts conflicts with his own commitment to aesthetic indeterminacy.

Focusing on the allegations of misconduct with young men, Carson relentlessly exposed and underlined class differences. Conway had either sold newspapers or just hung around at the pier in Worthing; Charles Parker and his brother were an unemployed valet and groom; Edward Shelley was described as an 'office boy'. Wilde rejected these characterizations, insisting that Parker (like others among his young companions) had aspired to perform in music halls and Shelley (uniquely among them) to pursue a literary career. However, Carson continually referred to them in invidious terms. The writer had defended his literary work against prurient and moralizing interpretation by insisting on the distance between those who appreciate art and an uncultivated philistine majority. Now Carson asked again and again what the aesthete might find to discuss with youths who were mostly idle and uneducated. Wilde did not deny that he had sought out these young men, wining and dining them at restaurants and clubs in Soho and the West End, lavishing gifts upon them, and occasionally giving them money. Pressed to say what enjoyment he could find with men whose interests were neither literary nor artistic, Wilde affirmed: 'The pleasure of being with those who are young, bright, happy, careless, and amusing.' When Carson interrupted, he went on '(emphatically): I don't like the sensible, and I don't like the old.'[44] These questions culminated in this famous exchange:

> *Wilde*: Well, I will tell you Mr. Carson, I delight in the society of people much younger than myself. I like those who may be called idle and careless, I recognize no social distinctions at all of any kind and to me youth – the mere fact of youth – is so wonderful that I would sooner talk to a young man half an hour than even be, well, cross-examined in court. (*Laughter.*)
> *Carson*: Then, do I understand that even a young boy that you would pick up on the street would be a pleasing companion to you?
> *Wilde*: Oh, I would talk to a street Arab if he talked to me, with pleasure.
> *Carson*: And take him to your rooms?
> *Wilde*: If he interested me.[45]

In protesting so vigorously, the writer may have revealed too much.

43 id., p. 221
44 id., p. 166, parenthesis in original.
45 id., p. 175, parenthesis and italics in original.

Carson was more interested in houses of ill repute than in street pickups. In his opening statement, Queensberry's counsel argued that 'Alfred Taylor is the pivot of this case.' The writer admitted that he had visited Taylor's rooms at 110 College Street for tea-parties with his friends. Wilde admitted that he had met as many as seven or eight men through Taylor, including five named in Queensberry's plea as his partners in 'indecent practices'. The writer insisted that Taylor was 'a young man of great taste and intelligence, and brought up at a very good English public school.' Unlike the men to whom he introduced Wilde, 'he was very artistic, extremely intellectual, and clever, and pleasant.'[46] Taylor had inherited and quickly run through a large fortune from the family cocoa business. Wilde denied that his friend had been expelled from prestigious Marlborough School, although he had not graduated. His accomplishments included playing the piano for his friends. When Carson sought to exploit the implications of Taylor's 'artistic' propensities in decorating his rooms, Wilde defended his 'good taste', denying that they were luxurious or that dark curtains were always drawn against the light of day. Carson sought to portray the house where Wilde met his young companions as exotic, even sinister, 'strongly perfumed'. For Wilde, it was 'charming perfume': 'He was in the habit of burning perfume, as I am in my rooms.'[47] Details of Taylor's unorthodox style associated him with Boulton and Park: 'Did you know whether Mr. Taylor had a lady's costume there? ... Did you ever see him with a costume on – a lady's fancy dress?'[48] Wilde denied ever having seen, or heard of, such a thing. However, the cross-examination (supported by testimony at the criminals' trials) portrayed Taylor's rooms as a cross between 19 Cleveland Street and some of the more exotic scenes in *Dorian Gray*.

Carson had woven the potential evidence about Wilde's conduct and associations together with a reading of his letters and publications into a net with which to snare the writer. It is hard to imagine he would have escaped even if he had not adopted such a provocative 'pose' in court. The lawyer's speech made explicit the strategy that had guided his cross-examination, moving deftly back and forth between Wilde's literature and his life. Carson portrayed his client as being in the right in his efforts, however extreme, to end the relationship between Wilde and Lord Alfred. Again and again, the lawyer asked the all-male jury: what would you have done if you had been a father in Queensberry's position? Wilde's writings were used to support the charge of 'posing', independent of any evidence as to the writer's sexual conduct. Carson argued that they alone show their author to be 'either in sympathy with, or addicted to, immoral and sodomitical habits.'[49] The lawyer capitalized on Wilde's insistence that the interpretation of literary

46 id., p. 159.
47 id., p. 156.
48 id., p. 158.
49 id., p. 255.

125

works depended on the audience. It was enough that the writer had admitted that Dorian Gray's sins *might* be read as including sodomy or that Basil Hallward's adoration of Dorian *might* be read as sexual desire. He implied that the young and impressionable men who admired Wilde might be especially prone to these readings. The lawyer emphasized the widespread distribution and sale of the novel regardless of the cultural qualifications of its readers. Similarly, he argued that *The Chameleon* was directed at inexperienced undergraduates who would read 'Phrases and Philosophies for the Use of the Young' alongside 'The Priest and the Acolyte' and Douglas's poems praising 'the other love'. Wilde's 'prose poem' addressed to Bosie encouraged the production of his questionable verse. Thus, Wilde's publications, even if ambiguous as their author asserted, should sound the alarm for an attentive parent. Carson identified a single thread running through the fiction, letters, and poetry: 'a man using towards a man the language which men sometimes use, and perhaps legitimately use, towards women.'[50] Equally damaging, he found a theme common to 'The Priest and the Acolyte', *Dorian Gray*, and Wilde's letters: the domination of a younger by an older man. Carson argued that this was the key to the writer's connection with Bosie: '... have you the slightest doubt that the same kind of mind that wrote this *Chameleon* wrote these letters to Lord Alfred Douglas?'[51] The lawyer read the jury an extended passage from *Dorian Gray* describing the impact of his first conversation with the worldly and cynical Lord Henry Wotton on 'this innocent young man': 'Life suddenly became fiery coloured to him. It seemed he had been walking in fire. Why had he not known it?' Watching, the older man '... was amazed at the sudden impression that his words had produced'.[52] For Carson, *Dorian Gray* prefigured Wilde's influence on Douglas:

> ... it is the story of a man corrupted by another man and who by such corruption is brought to commit, or the book suggests he has committed, this sodomitic vice of which we will hear a good deal more, probably, before this case closes.[53]

Bosie's poem 'The Two Loves' might stand alone as justification of Queensberry's 'frightful anticipation':

> ... there is no difficulty in seeing in it that the whole object and the whole idea of it is to draw the distinction between what the world calls 'love' and what the world calls 'shame', one being the love that a man bears toward a woman, and the other being the unholy shame that a man ought to have if he ventures to transfer that kind of love and that kind of passion to a man. That is the idea all through Lord Alfred Douglas's poem, and is it not a terrible thing to think that a young man, upon the threshold of his life, having been these several years in the company, aye, under the domination of and adored by Oscar Wilde as

50 id., p. 256.
51 id., p. 257.
52 Quoted, id., p. 260.
53 id., p. 261.

would appear from these letters that have been given here – is it not a horrible thing to think that there to the public he makes known the results of his education and the tendencies of his own mind upon this subject, the frightful subject of the passion of man for man?[54]

Carson reads Wilde's letter to Bosie as expressing his 'vile abominable passion towards this young man': 'I want to know, when that letter has been written by Wilde to Lord Queensberry's son and Lord Queensberry protests, are you going to send Lord Queensberry to gaol?'[55] The reiteration of the Marquess's title three times underlines the improbability of this outcome to the libel trial.

Wilde's own road to 'gaol' may have been paved by his literary production, but he traveled it as a result of his conduct and associations. Early in his speech, Carson targeted Alfred Taylor as 'the pivot of the case', describing him as 'practically the right-hand man of Wilde in all these orgies with artists and valets.' Carson uses Taylor's rooms to evoke the brothel on Cleveland Street and to suggest the perils of aestheticism:

> You will hear the kind of life this man Taylor lived, the extraordinary den that he kept in Little College Street with its curtains always drawn, the luxurious hangings of his windows, the rooms gorgeously and elaborately furnished with the perpetual changes of varied perfumes and the altogether extraordinary life that he was leading there; the daylight never admitted: always the shaded light of candles or of lamps or gas.[56]

Carson's description suggests the steamier passages in *Dorian Gray*. Even more importantly, he identifies the contradictions between Wilde's pronouncements on art and on social class:

> ... when you come to confront him with these curious associates of a man of high art, which no one can understand but himself and the artistic but his case is that he has such a magnanimous, such a noble such a democratic soul (*laughter*) that he draws no social distinctions, and it is exactly the same pleasure to him to have a sweeping boy from the street – if he is only interesting – to lunch with him, as the best educated artist or the greatest *littérateur* in the whole kingdom.[57]

Carson characterizes the writer's position as 'utterly irreconcilable,' but offers his own damning resolution of the apparent paradox: there was 'something unnatural, something unexpected' in his relations with these young men.[58] Wilde had met the Parker brothers when Taylor brought them to share his birthday dinner. Carson was unrelenting in his insistence on the 'unnaturalness' of this cross-class socializing. Why did Taylor bring as his guests 'a groom and a valet. ... if he knew that Wilde was moral and upright and the artistic and literary man that he undoubtedly was?' The lawyer's

54 id., pp. 257–8.
55 id., p. 270.
56 id., p. 253.
57 id., p. 254.
58 id., p. 274.

127

answer is that Taylor was Wilde's procurer. His ridicule is as much social as sexual:

> ... Wilde addressing the valet as Charlie, and Parker addressing Wilde, the distinguished dramatist – whose name was being mentioned, I suppose, in every circle in London for the distinction he had gained by his plays and by his literature – and, just fancy, the valet at the dinner addressing him as 'Oscar'.[59]

Carson portrays Wilde's transgression of social boundaries as a pursuit of personal pleasure rather than an expression of altruism or solidarity. The lawyer walked a fine line between treating the writer's companions as symptoms of his degradation and as victims of his influence:

> ... let those who are inclined to condemn these men for allowing themselves to be dominated, misled, corrupted by Mr. Oscar Wilde, remember the relative positions of the two parties and remember that they are men who have been more sinned against than sinning.[60]

He underlined the asymmetries in these relationships:

> ... they were not one of them really educated parties with whom he would naturally associate; they were none of them his equal in years; and there was... a curious similarity in the ages of each and every one of them.

Acknowledging the writer's fascination with the young, Carson asked: 'Has Mr. Wilde been unable to find more suitable companions... in youths of his own class?'[61] Then he closes in for the kill. Referring to his 'theories of putting an end to social distinctions,' he argues that Wilde was not motivated by 'a very noble and a very generous instinct'. If he had wanted to help his young associates, he could have found work for them or assisted in their education. Instead, Wilde had bought them silver cigarette cases and entertained them in a fashion that they could never afford. Carson insists that when he gave money to some of the men, the writer was paying for incriminating letters or buying silence about his own sexual conduct. When Wilde admitted he had given Alfred Wood money to move to America, Carson treated it as an attempt to get the blackmailer out of the way. When Wilde bought Alfonso Conway new clothes for a trip to Brighton, Carson depicted it as an effort to disguise his class origins: '... he dresses him up like a gentleman and he puts some of these public school colours on his hat and he makes him look as if he were a proper person to be associating with him.' Queensberry's attorney condemned the writer for taking his young friends out of their 'proper sphere' in a manner which 'in the future [they] could never expect to live up to.'[62] As Carson moved toward the conclusion of his speech and the introduction of his witnesses, he had outlined a damning indictment of Wilde for 'corrupting the youth' – not only through

---

59 id., p. 275.
60 id., p. 273.
61 id., p. 274.
62 id., p. 279.

sexual misconduct and literary subversion, but also through exploitation of the working classes.

On the third day of the trial, Wilde did not appear while his lawyers tried to withdraw the case with the least damage to their client. They conceded that, based on the literary evidence alone, the defence had shown that Wilde had *posed* as a sodomite, without admitting any sexual wrongdoing. However, Queensberry stood firm: the judge directed a verdict in his favour, a finding that his accusation was true and had been published in the public interest. The press which had done so much to promote Wilde's reputation now trumpeted his fall and the end of the aesthetic movement:

> The obscene imposter, whose prominence has been a social outrage ever since he transferred from Trinity Dublin to Oxford his vices, his follies, and his vanities, has been exposed, and that thoroughly at last. But to the exposure there must be legal and social sequels. There must be another trial at the Old Bailey, or a coroner's inquest – the latter for choice; and the Decadents, of their hideous conceptions of the meaning of Art, of their worse than Eleusinian mysteries, there must be an absolute end.[63]

After Wilde's conviction at his second criminal trial and his sentence to two years' imprisonment with hard labour, one paper editorialized:

> No sterner rebuke could well have been inflicted on some of the artistic tendencies of the time than the condemnation on Saturday of Oscar Wilde at the Central Criminal Court.

The long piece concerned itself only with the implication of the writer's disgrace for the literary and cultural movements with which he was associated:

> ... there has lately shown itself in London a contemporary bias of thought, an affected manner of expression and style, and a few loudly vaunted ideas which have had a limited but evil influence on all the better tendencies of art and literature.

As a self-constituted representative of these tendencies, Wilde had used his 'considerable intellectual powers and unbounded self-assurance' to 'dazzle and bewilder' those younger and less experienced. The editorial particularly criticizes the doctrine of 'art for art's sake':

> ... because art is held to be an independent thing, with its own laws, its own rights, and its own sanctions, we advance to that fatal separation between it and morality which has done so much to degrade and vilify its best work and its choicest aims.[64]

Adopting the jury's verdict and judge's sentence as a warrant for its cultural position, the paper announces triumphantly: 'And if such a reaction towards simpler ideas be called Philistinism, then let us all be Philistines, for fear of

---

63 *National Observer*, 6 April 1895, quoted in Hyde, op. cit., n. 3, p. 156.
64 *Daily Telegraph*, 27 May 1895, quoted in J. Goodman, *The Oscar Wilde File* (1989) 133.

national contamination and decay.'[65] Few dissenting voices were heard. One, however, wrote to the republican *Reynolds' Newspapers* asking them to 'modify their sweeping denunciation of Mr. Wilde's writings'. T.G. Roy quoted extended passages on the need to eliminate poverty from Wilde's 'The Soul of Man Under Socialism'. His letter was published under the headline, 'Oscar Wilde and the Democracy'.[66] Clearly Wilde's conviction had set back more than just his own personal fortunes or the social status of same-sex desires; it marked a containment and moralization of the critical force of literature as such. Rather than the end of a nineteenth-century aesthetic movement, we might see the Wilde trials as beginning the culture wars that marked the twentieth century and have not concluded yet.

65 id., p. 134.
66 *Reynolds' Newspapers*, 12 May 1895, 5.

JOURNAL OF LAW AND SOCIETY
VOLUME 31, NUMBER 1, MARCH 2004
ISSN: 0263-323X, pp. 131-41

A Fragment on Cnutism with Brief Divagations on the Philosophy of the Near Miss

PETER GOODRICH*

This fragment is taken, mid-sentence as it were, from a longer discourse. It is plucked in process from a discussion of friendship for ideas. It is part of a longer journey through the annals of amity. The fragment also examines a fragment, a gloss on a text, a marginal comment, a handwritten note, which is taken to constitute the modern origin of Cnutism.

All of which makes me inordinately fond of the most nodal of spaces, that of the near miss. It is the zone of failures that come close to success, of successes that mingle, as they always must, with their own demise. It is the domain of the brief flaring or momentary venture in which we glimpse, but no more than glimpse, the recognizable presence of a friend. You know the sort of thing. The flush of fellow feeling, the sense of common critical apprehension, of shared insight, or elective affinity, and then it suddenly gets pulled up short. The friend votes with the opposition, or gets distracted and marries, or expresses affection for someone else, moves on, fails to write, or lets you down by posting someone else's letters rather than writing you their own. So let's think about these momentary relational modes, these fleeting flashes of amicable connection, these near misses.

The near miss implies both nearness and missing. Take your pick, but amity involves both. There is closeness and there is the lateral and often less visible sense of missing, of being to the side of where you wish to be. Friendship has always had a marginal site. In the French tradition, it has tended to be located in spaces that exist in between other things: the alcove, the *ruelle* or bedside, the dressing chamber, as well as the salon or *chambre bleu*, the blue room. We find it also in spaces of solitary connection. In the study, or the library or the laboratory, on a map, or inside an envelope, on a

* *Cardozo School of Law, Yeshiva University, Brookdale Center, 55 Fifth Avenue, New York, NY 10003, United States of America*

Many thanks to Lauren Berlant, Richard Collier, Drucilla Cornell, Marinos Diamantides, Peter Rush, and Pierre Schlag for offering comments and suggestions. An especial thanks to Ed Mussawir, for providing the Cnutist fragment. Thanks to Adam Gearey for suggesting publication. Especial thanks to Linda Mills for seeing it through.

131

postcard, between the covers of a book. Or we encounter it more mundanely in cafes, bars, tea rooms, botanical gardens, chat rooms, restaurants, galleries, cinemas, and the like. Take these last and more normal examples. They are all transitional spaces, sites on the way to something, to eating, to seeing a movie, or to getting drunk, whatever that happens to mean to you. They are sites of passage both in the sense that there is something to be consumed and in the connotation of spaces of leisure.

If I am right – and who are you to think I am not? – then these variable architectural and scriptural spaces of amity place the friend by and large amongst beautiful or desirable things. Amongst things that we maybe love. Amongst relics, artworks, or culinary creations, or good wines. It is as if we imbibe friendship, through the mouth or through the eyes, but as a mechanism of risk avoidance we also tend to locate, and take it in with something else. The risks would otherwise be too great. That seems to be the case in all this embroidery and ornamentation of amity with leisure, with down time, with the ease of objects or images that can be consumed along with the friend. Perhaps it simply indicates that we want to eat the friend. Freud thought that, but whatever it is, it illustrates also that we cannot wholly have, or absorb, or ingest the friend. There is a degree to which we have to come close and miss. We have to mark our difference and in my case I need to tell the inside story.

Nietzsche described friendship through the metaphor of two ships in the night. The depressed Derrida talked about his 'all out friendship' for his dead friends.[1] They both thought of friendship as a paradox, it was a sharing of solitude, it was the sighting of a face in the dark. It was a near miss. I agree but I want to give the near miss a more positive twist. It is our best, our all, our fate. Call it eloquence. I think of it as the moment of thought, the surprise of resistance. Like a caress that doesn't have to lead to anything more, like an intensely shared line from a poem or song, a frisson of recognition, a beautiful face glimpsed through a half open window, and then back to your meal or the movie or the next room in the gallery. A near miss is an intense hit. Excitations and animations all.

. . .

Here is a secret, though it won't be a secret for very long. Yesterday I received an email from a colleague in Australia. He attached a chapter from a doctoral thesis that he is supervising. It is an essay on my work. Early in the chapter, the author, one Ed Mussawir, and I like him a lot though I haven't met him yet, tells a story. Wittily discussing whether or not I have lived up to my name, he intersperses the following anecdote about me, or more specifically about the first book that I published:

1 The reference to 'all out friendship' comes in an encomium for Jean-Francois Lyotard, in J. Derrida, *The Work of Mourning* (2001) at 214–15. I discuss that and other instances in P. Goodrich, 'The Immense Rumor' (2004, forthcoming) *Yale J. of Law and Humanities*.

132

It was not without a certain degree of irony for example that while reading Melbourne University's copy of *Legal Discourse* I discovered on page seventy eight the inscribed comment of an apparently frustrated reader: 'This book is written by a cunt of a bloke. Fucked if I can understand it!'[2]

Straight off, I have to admit that I have tended to have an ambivalent relation to commentaries and critiques of my work. I basically read them very inattentively. The critic has to work to get my attention. So, initially, my response is a little defensive. Sure, I marvel at how direct Australians can be, but then I find myself thinking something along the lines of:

> Hell, the book is the publication of my thesis and it was written for my examiners. One was bald and prone to wearing a kilt, a skirt, but he had a Latin title, Regius Professor, and was formidably well qualified and successfully learned in things that I did not dare even approach. And the other one still had hair, he is dead now, but his early books were so esoteric and incomprehensible that I could only pretend to have any idea of what he had written on. And I had no choice. I had to publish the book to get the job.

And that seems a pretty convincing answer to me. My antipodean tormentor would surely lay off if he knew all that. I am guessing it was a male. Kind of a stab in the dark, but it fits stylistically. I think one can say that it offers a male position and expression. Not so much a tone as a dose of testosterone.

I have to admit, however, that it is not that simple. I may have been scared and a little bit traumatized, but still I was doing the verbal equivalent of preening my feathers or polishing my armour or fixing the gaps in my chain mail. It may seem strange that my Australian glossator couldn't see that straightaway. And I could also point out that if this critic had actually written a thesis himself, he would also know that there is no way that one is going to rewrite it. Not for publication. Not for anything. Not after ten solid years before it finally got written and presented within a traumatic whisker of being out of time. And hey, I wrote that twenty years ago and since then I have changed. I am on to the next best thing.

Anyway, back to my being named after a colloquially invoked female body part. Thus, 'a cunt of a bloke' and then rapidly on to a post-coital state: 'Fucked if I can understand it'. Sit with the synecdoche, if you will, and then ride with the metalepsis. It is strong stuff. And, even if you are slow like me when it comes to facing my critics, it fairly soon occurs to you that this gloss on the text, the marginalia to page 78, is pretty sexualized, and quite full of desire. I am not saying that it is in and of itself flattering, though one could say that, but more that it needs to be understood in terms of desire and frustration. Both poles are important. One is pushed towards viewing it as a critical case, and excuse the grammar but it is in the service of a bad pun, of *lector interruptus*. He really wanted to finish and it was most frustrating to pull up short and not

---

2 E. Mussawir, 'Portrait of a Legal Playwright: A Linguistics of Dramatisation' unpublished manuscript, 3.

be able to do so. For him, it would seem to be a case, to coin a phrase, of bad textual intercourse. A near miss.

There is also the flip side. According to the usual modes of sentence construction, the two quoted clauses seem to imply that it is the author of the book who is invaginated, but it is the reader who is fucked. What kind of sense does that make? It is certainly messing with the usual stereotypes of sexual action and of textual function. It is also an earthy figure from a seeming literalist. I am even willing to imagine that he viewed the whole reading experience as an unwarranted tease, that he wanted more and got less. But for me, the passion is the thing. The steam in the stacks. The fact that the reader left a commentary. That the student became an author and let rip his feelings isn't nothing. To borrow a phrase from *Pulp Fiction*, the reader got medieval if not with my ass, at least with my text. That is undoubtedly something.

Well, I think I have probably said enough to convince you that despite my modesty I am in fact both attentive and responsive to my critics. Indeed I am not above changing my style, if I really have to. But that is a separate issue. I am on to a different question. I don't think my Australian glossator, the author of the interlinear interposition, really liked the book. I think it is safe to say that he didn't rush out of the library to buy a copy, although I hasten to add that he still could, I have quite a few copies left, and it can be purchased from Amazon.com in the United Kingdom, in case you are interested.

So the reader wrote me a letter. It took anything up to twenty years to arrive. It followed a very indirect path, but it is Slavoj Zizek's theory that the letter always arrives. In his rather morbid opinion the letter is like a bullet with your name on it. You can maybe postpone its arrival – by changing your address, by having it sent *poste restante*, by running, who knows – but in the end it is going to find its way to you. Apparently there is an epistolary equivalent of the maxim that you can run but you can't hide. That is just how it is, and in this case, and rather unusually in my opinion, S.Z. has a good point. Here I am, in fact discussing the marginal commentary and so I cannot avoid the conclusion that the letter arrived. Not only has the letter arrived, but on the surface at least it seems pretty critical, in fact rather negative.

Here is the thing. It arrived somewhat late in the day. It was a near miss. I had already changed my ways. I was already busy writing this. But it was a friendly act. A corrective correspondence. An honest expression, a heartfelt declaration of critical sentiments, a gloss in the margin of the law. I doubt that the author particularly cared if I saw it. But I also think that he would be happy to learn that I did. He would think it might help me shape up or write better. And if other students saw it, then they might be spared some frustration or released from their pain. No small thing, especially if you take into account the augmented suicide statistics for libraries. Okay, I made that last bit up, it is purely anecdotal, and just a figure of speech, a way of trying to keep your attention on my argument. Which goes as follows.

The humanist legal tradition was all about the margins and the between the lines or interlinear spaces of the text. Lawyers were called glossators. They were trained to write in the margins and between the lines and at the top and the bottom of the page. And here, many centuries on, a student of law, though not necessarily a law student, glossed my text. It is powerful stuff, and if the punchy phrase sticks, that is also because we have already encountered the margin, the preface, the various thresholds and peripheries where affect and amity, emotion and enmity are invariably placed.

It is as simple as this. The margin is where the reader writes. The lateral and the interlinear are the nodal spaces in which the text encounters the living. They are the moments and the maps of law application. And here is precisely the space of amity and enmity, of correspondence, of handwritten familiar letters. This is the space where stuff gets done and it is truly sad and dysfunctional that we keep looking away. We ignore the marginalia and we overlook the near misses. And that way, truth to tell, unhappy to report, life passes us by or gets put in the hands of lawyers.

As a culture we tend to pay rather little attention to the peripherally visible. Frankly we are more likely to lock it up, or bomb the hell out of it, than pay attention, rest with it, and enter dialogue. And by that token, the near miss is a threat and a failure, an absence of presence soon likely to be turned to rubble. And then we have to add to that the curious yet real sense in which the metaphoric attribution of the characteristics of female genitalia is viewed as offensive or negative. I don't have to tell an auditor as sophisticated as you that the Latin for vagina means shame. But who reads Latin anymore? Could we not rather say that the genitalia are also erogenous and erotic, that sex is fun, and that if you got fucked by a book then talk to your therapist about your pattern of object choice.[3]

I confess that the last line is a bit too easy. In fact I think it is what we often do. We throw the criticism back, we get aggressive or dismissive, pompous, long-winded or sarcastic in the face of negative commentary. We are not comfortable with the difficult stuff that gets placed in the margins. We skitter at the sight of dirty words. We play like Teflon when reading criticisms of our work. We just don't like it. It is not amicable in the easy and fatuous sense in which we think of working amity and tend to define it as an invisibly tight bond of repetitive affirmation, or as the reoccurrence of the self in someone else.

Back fleetingly and perhaps finally to the critical marginalia and to my interpretation of it. This may come as a surprise. It was a surprise to me and I

---

3   Just as an aside, the analysis could get pretty complicated. Imagine how it would go: 'my lover is a Lacanian and so he refuses to say his own name'; 'she follows Zizek and only ever allows me to look at her genitalia'; 'I know he is besotted with Irigaray but please help us through the differences'; 'he has been reading Judith Butler and now he is convinced that he has to fake all his orgasms'; 'he is a deconstructionist and so whenever we arrange to meet it is never in the same place'; 'he's an old fashioned Sartrean and only loves me for what I am not'; 'she's a Levinasian and will only make love to my face'.

think its pretty good. My intermediary, Ed Mussawir, has this to say of Goodrich the name, because he has never met me: 'But having been called a "cunt of a bloke", I dare say, he may never be the same again . . .'.[4] And that is the point. The criticism matters. Even if I hadn't read it at that point in time when it was sent, I was changed already, in anticipation, by prolepsis.

The correspondence was sent to me. The letter arrived and I read it. And it did cause me thought, engaged me in dialogue, put me in touch with a different reading and view. I am even willing to go a bit further. I think that the marginal, and here I fear sounding too like the literary critics, is key. It is just a fragment but it got through. It was hard on me but that is precisely the space of dialogue, of amity and enmity. And I can offer one further example, another interpretation of it as a near miss.

Looking back it was a difficult text. I had been under the impression, you will recall, that I needed a lot of fancy theory to get by my examiners. It worked. I looked all scientific and serious. When I met people for the first time they expected someone with a pipe, gray hair, a tweed jacket, and roughly eighty years old, back hunched from all the texts that he was carrying inside. And I was able to shock them, look at the picture, long thinning black hair, fine aquiline nose, impertinent eyes, and youthful gait. A near miss between the name and its current incumbent, between the text and the bloke who wrote it.

Yet that is not in the end my point. There is another near miss, a mix up of the middle two letters in the word cunt. I don't think the critic necessarily meant what we on the East coast would mean by cunt. I think there was a transposition of the n and the u. Quite understandable. Easily done. Happens a lot. It is the figure of *synchisis* or confusion of letters. And, of course, the u is an n upside down. All of which is to say that the word that fit was Cnut. A Cnut of a bloke, meaning a fossil, an archaism, and the equivalent of King Cnut. It is pronounced Canute but spelled Cnut. He was the Anglo-Saxon King, you will undoubtedly recall, who got so fed up with the sycophancy of his courtiers that he decided to prove to them that he was not a God. He devised a radical demonstration of his all too human frailty. He was carried on his throne to the sea at low tide. There on the edge of the incoming water, he regally ordered the tide to stop but the sea came on in anyway.

King Cnut was trying to prove something or other to his followers. As I said, I think the point of the myth and of the scenic ritual was to show the limits of sovereignty and the absurdity of worshiping the King. If that was the purpose then you might think he would have made the point better if he had walked to the sea but we have to allow for the paradoxes. After all he was King, and being human is not a disqualification for sovereignty even today. He wanted to share the fact that he had his failings, his flaws, his near misses. Like, for instance, he couldn't stop the tide.

4 Mussawir, op. cit., n. 2, p. 8.

Me neither. Though it was not the sea but rather the law that I was ordering to stop, *ex cathedra*, with all my Latinate words. And so my interpretation of a Cnut of a bloke, of a Cnutist, is someone who is addicted to the positivity of failure or, put it like this and in the positive, to the semiotic significance of the impossible. In that form it is a pretty witty apothegm and not without its accuracy. After all, what was *Legal Discourse* the book? It was the work of a left-leaning, rather shy, English doctoral student that offered a theory of legal language as the prosaic equivalent of a dominatrix. Aged twenty-three, and with rather less sexual experience than your average second millennium mid-teen, he was arguing for the radical dismemberment of law. And why not stop the tide coming in as well? So what do you think? A touch of Cnutism? I guess so.

Don't worry. I am not planning on starting a school or a movement. Nothing like that, though 'the Cnutists' does sound fun and kind of risky. Just a transposed letter away from a reference to what Leonard Cohen calls a highly prized five inches of flesh. It is also just a c ahead of a nut. But let's just say that Cnutism describes me back then, and a lot of my colleagues now, pretty well. And on top of that, it just remains to say that I will leave it to others, to Kim or Pierre, Patricia or Jack, or just possibly D.K. and Professor D. to point all that out to the lumpen professoriat.

. . .

So, talking of near misses, Cnutism captures the narrow window of the near miss quite excellently. It also, incidentally, proves that there is no phrase nor turn of words that cannot be improved upon with a little serious interpretation. But first off, I want to acknowledge that I owe my sense of the concept or rite of Cnutism to my critic, and to a productive misreading of a seemingly acerbic fragment meant at least in part for me. So let me just note that the concept of the near miss derives from an interruption and expresses that interruption. It refers to a break in the pattern, a missed beat, a gloss to the side of the text.

Next, I need to point out that the Cnutist makes a virtue of failure. Cnut turned his impotence into a powerful lesson. There is an exquisite closeness and a didactic miss. And part of the lesson was obviously that failure is something to learn from and specifically that we need to recognize who we are. There are a lot of things, sovereign or subject, Cnutist or Marxist, liberal or feminist, that we just cannot do. Sooner or later you are going to have to face up to your near misses. And perhaps surprisingly given how little account history has paid to Cnutism, it turns out to be quite an optimistic enterprise.

Suddenly you can examine your apparent failures in the light of the successes that can be derived from them. You can look at failure as part of a bigger picture. Think of it like this, or maybe just think of what happened to Cnut. He didn't just float off, though he could have. The tide came in and his suite or following or courtiers or whoever rescued him and carried him out of harm's way. So he lived to prove his lesson and maybe the courtiers got a

137

little bit more real about who he was. More than that, had everyone waited long enough, had they been as patient as they should have been, then the tide would eventually have gone back out. Come dusk, and Cnut's order would actually have been repaid in spades: the tide would not just have stopped, it would have receded. He would by that point in time have been waving to the withdrawing waters over the dusky horizon. Which is quite a thought. Actually, I like to think of that moment as a Cnutist triumph though it is also possible that he had misread the tidal schedule.

And then, of course, rapidly on its heels, the tide would be up again. That is just how things are. But it does bear pointing out that when the tide comes in again, Cnut would be proving his hypothesis. So in the longer term, he would be right both ways. That is what my therapist would probably call the bigger picture. The long term perspective on tidal flow. The deeper point, however, or more accurately the temporally enlarged point is that none of the above depends in any way upon Cnut's proclamation. His law, because what the sovereign says is in fact the definition of law (ask Austin if you have any doubts on that), has nothing to do with what happens. Or rather it has few direct effects, many near misses.

Another way of saying the same thing, would be that my book *Legal Discourse* had absolutely no direct impact upon the making of law. In a way we know that already. As an innominate Australian critic put it, the book was written by a Cnut of a bloke. And as he also pointed out, it wasn't that easy to understand. Nor, to be absolutely honest, would I ever have expected it to have persuaded lawyers or lawmakers. Back then in fact we were busy planning on overthrowing the lawyers, toppling the law, as it were, and at the very least, if revolution wasn't on the cards, we were going to ignore the law. That would show the ruling class what was what. And that kind of an attitude doesn't usually lead to a constructive conversation although my leftist peers seemed happy enough that we were talking amongst ourselves.

Returning to me, which after all is my fate, and I can't in the end help it, I wouldn't be looking for the practical impact of a theoretical treatise, written as a doctoral thesis in philosophy of law, such as *Legal Discourse*. Funnily, though this helps explain the Australian critic's frustration, the book was used on a number of courses in legal theory and in socio-linguistics. It sold quite well. Got reprinted a couple of times. And if I wanted to assess its impact, I would look to the margins. I would try to find out whom it upset as much as whom it pleased. I would ask about conversations, as well as citations and quotations and all those more frontal but less significant accolades and apprehensions. I would try to find out what happened in the alcoves, what got said under the stairs, in the corridor, to the side of the hallway, or behind closed office doors. Indeed that is the thing with us Cnutists. We look to the long term. We read footnotes. We are happy to wait. We don't need to be that important. Which is lucky, actually, because in fact we are not very important, not that significant at all except that we realize it and are willing to display our unimportance through curious but occasionally memorable feet wetting rites.

138

Staying with continents beginning with the letter A, here is another story. There is a judge on the High Court in Cape Town who also teaches at the Law School there. He teaches *Legal Discourse*, as it happens, and he says that the students find it pretty hard going but he persists. I am not sure why. Can't remember. I don't listen that well to that sort of conversation, but I do seem to recollect that he had a reason. Maybe he thought I was right. After all, it is not impossible and he was a leftist. Still is, so he claims. In any event, I am arguing that to understand what happens we need to look to the margins, the near misses, the influence and animus of friends.

So he told me that he was sitting on a case brought under the new South African Constitutional provision guaranteeing economic rights, including housing. The case was being heard shortly before the end of term and the beginning of the Christmas vacation. A group of women and children came to Court and tearfully argued, through their representatives, that the new Constitution required the state to house them. And otherwise they would all be sleeping rough over the holidays. Which is not a bad argument, rhetorically speaking.

My friend, let's say Judge Dennis D., who told this story quite openly at a conference I attended, wanted to be able to interpret the Constitution to require the state to provide housing. But he knew that if he couldn't persuade the senior judge then it wasn't going to happen. Try as he might, the senior judge just wasn't buying it. Prospects were bleak until the end-of-term office party or whatever the High Court equivalent happens to be. At the party, Judge Dennis D. happened upon the senior judge's wife. He told her about the case, and about the women and the children who might be living outside over the holidays. The weather forecast wasn't good. That sort of thing, and he must have been pretty eloquent, and she must have been quite moved. I say that because the next day, according to Judge Dennis D., the senior judge came in and said something like 'it is time to settle this, I am going to vote with you'.

From a Cnutist perspective, that is another margin accessed and analysed. That is how it goes. Those are the lines of power, the incidents of amity, even amongst those who are not the best of friends. Put it like this, it was a near miss but it worked out quite well. He couldn't persuade the senior judge but he managed to persuade his best friend, the queen of his friends according to the old Christian manuals on amity, his wife. And that did the trick. If you cannot persuade the judge, persuade a friend of theirs, or in Platonic terms, persuade them through ideas with which you know them to be friendly. Your near misses, or indeed your talk with the misses, may end up getting the job done.

. . .

I could lard all of this with a bit more theory. I could cite the very chipper Kipnis on marital confinement and the erotics of office amity. Or I could dazzle you with quotations on desire and lack, love and impossibility from Jacques Lacan. I find him pretty funny, but come to think of it he probably actually was a cunt of a bloke. That is going by the sounds of it, in that his

139

daughters' books on their father aren't too flattering at all. Or there is always Zizek, S.Z. as I think of him, on cultural trends in waxing pubic hair, the trajectory from the bikini line to the Brazilian. But it would be just so much additional lard. We Cnutists are far more into the practicalities.

The philosophy of the near miss simply poses an old fashioned question in a twisted yet optimistic way. So here is the thesis. Essential, I would say, but placed in the margins, there are feelings of amity and enmity that basically determine what gets done. It is here, in the epistemic alcove that the manipulations of reason and the armature of slogan and spin get set up. It is the zone of near misses, because close and warm though the margin may be, these amicable and animated affects don't make it into the text. That is a start, but there is more to it.

The philosophy of the near miss is an attempt to capture the ambience of our times. Let's say that the times they are a-rolling. I don't simply mean that obesity is on the up, though it is. I am thinking also of near misses, the fads, the trends, and the paranoia. Postmodernism came and went by the turn of the century. Y2K, the millennial computer virus never took. Didn't bite. The love bug e-mail of May 2000 caught the business world with its pants down, but what's a few billion dollars here or there? The 'sobig' email worm, like most such size-based claims, proved to be an exaggeration. Feminism is finally fading, and the political scene is frighteningly retro. So there is a contemporary catalogue of near misses. Nothing new in that. You can figure out your own list. From bull to bear you have got to admit that the near miss captures that sense in which nothing is entirely certain. We come close but we neither control, nor possess, nor fully consume the local events that make up our lives. It is time to turn our attention to them. They are the anthropological key.

Here goes: physical anthropology has long observed that like other species, when humans feel strongly about each other they will literally put their heads together. Think of Don Zimmer screaming at Pedro Martinez.[5] He was right in his face. And if you are falling in love or having an office affair or you are simply French it won't be long before one or other of you says 'shut up and kiss me'. You will go head to head. You will touch, taste, smell the other head. But you won't be able to get inside. The analytic philosophers, not that I care about what they have to say, used to talk of this in terms of the problem of the other mind. Fair enough, though I would prefer the possibilities of the other mind. In either event, you cannot be the person you love. You cannot erase the person you hate, at least not without facing the danger of immortalizing him. And you wouldn't want that.

5 There are some who would probably say that sports metaphors don't help. In fact I am not sure if either of the names is correct. So you can change them as you wish. It could be Bill O'Reilly shouting, spinning out of control, thug that he is, with Barney Frank. Or Dick Cheney finally getting to meet Al Franken, or Bill Clinton and Ken Starr on the same page. Kitty Mackinnon debating Camille Paglia is another possible. Or go with a great love. Clark Kent and Lois Lane. Jason the Argonaut and the Sirens. Whoever. We are talking a whole load of near misses.

140

We cannot wholly know, or feel, or be the other person. That is how it is. We can get close. We can even be marginally inside each other and as a best possible outcome we can share what Nabokov termed a 'little death'. But there is still the barrier of the body, the weight of the unconscious, the fact that as often as not we are living out the philosophy of the near miss. It is a matter of the pragmatics of Cnutism. I will put it like this, a radical formulation, the maxim of the near miss: there are feelings that just don't have an epistemic equivalent.

Like all good maxims, that one is a little opaque. But I don't want to be upsetting my Australian reader; I can take a hint in the margins as well as the next Brit, and so I will try to translate. I think it means that we get ahead of ourselves. When things get hot and heavy, when we light up or burn away, we are way in front of our rational selves. We are making out or letting go. It is what tennis players call being in the zone. It is a great feeling, it's super cool, and it doesn't last. But us Cnutists, we like to think that it is important. We think that what happens matters.

When you go head to head, when you want to be inside the other person, to convert them or to love them, there comes a point when you realize, friend or enemy, that it's not going through. It is the moment of the *Lysis*, of the untangling, of sitting back in pleasure or pain, doesn't matter, and apprehending that this is all there is: a painful proximity, an exquisite flush, a near miss, that comes along with passing through.

141

JOURNAL OF LAW AND SOCIETY
VOLUME 31, NUMBER 1, MARCH 2004
ISSN: 0263-323X, pp. 142-48

Dominions: Law, Literature, and the Right to Death

PETER FITZPATRICK*

The 'curious right' attending modernity and revealed in Blanchot's 'Literature And the Right to Death' could be readily reduced to that sovereign right to take life which ultimately subordinates law. Yet, so the argument runs, with that same curious right law surpasses sovereignty. And it does so by way of its similarity to literature. What will uncover that surpassing by law, and by literature, will be a pervasive concern with death as the horizon of the law.

DEATH AS THE HORIZON OF THE LAW

Nothing that is not there and the nothing that is.[1]

The affinity between law and death is usually put in terms of law's pretension to finality. Taking indicative *aperçus* from Blanchot, this is law as 'the end', as antithetical to 'life itself'.[2] And in a way Blanchot would go so far as to subordinate law to death for, so he finds, law is 'less the command that has death as its sanction, than death itself wearing the face of law'; this 'death is always the horizon of the law'.[3] The thought is hardly original. When death is seen as something like a constituent limit of law, this is law in its avowal of certainty and predictability, law 'in its origin, in its very order'.[4] Yet it is revealing, and this is a point I will come to later, that the

* School of Law, Birkbeck College, University of London, Malet St., London WC1E 7HX, England

As with so much else, this paper was generated in discussions with Adam Thurschwell and Colin Perrin. My precarious belief in it was sustained by Carrol Clarkson, Hillis Miller, and Johan van der Walt. Costas Douzinas provoked further thought on sovereignty.

1 W. Stevens, 'The Snow Man' in *Selected Poems* (1965) 7.
2 M. Blanchot, *The Madness of the Day* (1981, tr. L. Davis) 16; M. Blanchot, *The Infinite Conversation* (1993, tr. S. Hanson) 225.
3 M. Blanchot, *The Step Not Beyond* (1992, tr. L. Davis) 24–5.
4 J. Derrida, 'Force of Law: 'The Mystical Foundations of Authority' in *Acts of Religion* (2002, tr. M. Quaintance) 276.

142

association between law and death is so often seen in terms of an ultimate or final assertion that is sovereign, either the law itself as sovereign or law as an 'instrument' of sovereignty, a giving effect to 'the right of death of the sovereign'.[5]

Almost in spite of all this, death is also for Blanchot the horizon of the law in quite another way. Again, this thought does not put a great strain on originality, even if it will prove to be a more productive one. Here the horizon does not simply contain but, rather, connects integrally with what is beyond, marks some commonality with what is beyond, or the possibility of it. The horizon thence becomes not only the condition and quality of law's contained and distinct existence but also an opening onto all that lies beyond and is other to that existence. It is in this way that, for Blanchot, death 'raises existence to being', that 'death becomes being'.[6] This death 'is man's possibility, his chance, it is through death that the future of a finished world is still there for us'.[7] And this is death as a liberated 'nothingness', a nothingness which 'is the creator of the world in man'.[8] Death as horizon here is not only the end but also the beginning, the opening to and making possible of all that can come from being to existence: death is 'the Other'.[9] For death as this horizon of the law, however, what we have with Blanchot is not now an explicit affinity between death and law but, rather, parallel descriptions. So, law for Blanchot is (also) that which is quite 'lacking' in fixity, quite uncontained and unsubordinated, a self-affirmation made 'without reference to anything higher: to it alone, pure transcendence'.[10] This law takes its instituted existence from a being beyond. 'Let us grant', says Blanchot, 'that the law is obsessed with exteriority, by that which beleaguers it and from which it separates via the very separation that institutes it as form, in the very movement by which it formulates this exteriority as law'.[11] Such law is the same as what Blanchot would also see as the law of the law, see as 'a responsibility ... towards the Other' that is 'irreducible to all forms of legality through which one necessarily tries to regulate it' but which ultimately 'cannot be enounced in any already formulated language'.[12]

---

5 J. Locke, 'The Second Treatise of Government,' in *Two Treatises of Government* (1965) 308; I. Kant, *The Metaphysical Elements of Justice* (1965, tr. J. Ladd) 331–3; M. Foucault, *Discipline and Punish: The Birth of the Prison* (1979, tr. A. Sheridan) 49; and, for the quotation, M. Dean, *Governmentality: Power and Rule in Modern Society* (1999) 105.
6 M. Blanchot, 'Literature And the Right to Death' in *The Station Hill Blanchot Reader: Fiction & Literary Essays* (1999, tr. L. Davis) 391–2.
7 id., p. 392.
8 id., pp. 398–9.
9 M. Blanchot, *The Writing of the Disaster* (1995, tr. A. Smock) 19.
10 Blanchot, op. cit., n. 3, p. 25.
11 Blanchot, op. cit. (1993), n. 2, p. 434.
12 M. Blanchot, *The Unavowable Community* (1988, tr. P. Joris) 43.

143

Thence, the achingly simple point of this paper becomes that, no matter how 'necessary' this regulation, for law to be law nothing can be placed before it. Or that which is placed before it can only be nothing.[13] This nothing is for Blanchot 'the savage freedom of the negative essence' that emerges from speech being insufficient 'for the truth it contains', a truth always denied in the enounced.[14] This truth has its revenge, so to speak, in the constant corruption of the enounced, in the 'ruin' of any 'work', in the 'sickness' of words, a sickness which is also their 'health' – the generative condition of their relation to the world, of their constituent connection to the nothingness of being.[15] Likewise, law for Blanchot, that law 'obsessed with [an] exteriority' which 'institutes it as form' and from which it wrenches existence, such law 'exists only in regard to its transgression-infraction'.[16] In its 'ruin', its 'rottenness', borrowing now from Derrida, the realized law continually slides into this unrealizable exteriority, an exteriority which in turn must be 'cut' into for law's 'necessarily' contained existence.[17]

What we have here, in sum, are two laws or two deathly horizons of the law. One is the law inseparable from the nothingness of 'its' exteriority, the law which, as Cixous says, 'does not exist', 'has no material inside'.[18] This is a law which can only ever 'be' other than what it 'is', always dying in its deliquescence. But not yet. What still insists is the invariant law which in its determinate existence cannot be other than what it is, dying in a desolate stasis. This ambivalence provokes a search in-between its two dimensions, a search for the domain of Blanchot's 'literature', that literature which 'is the work of death in the world'.[19]

LAW LIKE LITERATURE

Such literature is an 'opening' to what is beyond, to alterity and possibility, to 'what is when there is no more world', or 'to what would be if there were no world', to 'the void'.[20] But this void is of the kind encountered by Blanchot's protagonist in *The Madness of the Day* for whom it was disappointing, a void which inexorably becomes 'a presence' and protean: 'one realizes the void, one creates a work'.[21] Between the realized and the

13 Compare H. Cixous, *Readings: The Poetics of Blanchot, Joyce, Kafka, Kleist, Lispector, and Tsvetayeva* (1991, tr. V.A. Conley) 21.
14 Blanchot, op. cit., n. 6, p. 382.
15 id., p. 368.
16 Blanchot, op. cit., n. 3, p. 24; Blanchot, op. cit. (1993), n. 2, p. 434.
17 Derrida, op. cit., n. 4, pp. 252, 273.
18 Cixous, op. cit., n. 13, p. 18.
19 Blanchot, op. cit., n. 6, p. 393.
20 id., p. 388; and see C. Fynsk, *Language and Relation . . . that there is language* (1996) 238–9.
21 Blanchot, op. cit. (1981), n. 2, p. 8; Blanchot, op. cit., n. 6, p. 395; and Fynsk, op. cit., n. 20, p. 238.

unrealizable, between the appropriated and that which is still 'ours for being nobody's', there is a 'shifting', a 'passing', a 'movement' impelled by 'a marvellous force' which is the impossibility of the movement being otherwise.[22] This is an activity always situated, an emplaced 'affirmation', 'an operation' which cannot be separated 'from its results'.[23]

Literature for Blanchot is a work like any other – he instances building a stove – even if it is such 'to an outstanding degree'.[24] Law and literature, it could now be said, share the same ambivalence between existent instantiation and what is ever beyond yet incipient in it.[25] The comparison between law and literature more usually points to their opposition of course. Literature's realms of the imagined and the possible oppose the all-too-solid certainty of law – the law-confounding power of Plato's poets, for example.[26] Yet it is exactly the aspect of literature to which Plato would object, to its illimitable inventiveness and its quality of fiction, which impels law's making, for law is only called upon to affirm some certainty in the face of uncertainty. And despite the incessant jurisprudential efforts to render law as fact, society, economy, and so on, it refuses being in 'a world sapped by crude existence'.[27] Peremptorily, the legal fiction can illustrate the formative location of law beyond existence, for with the fiction the enounced content of the particular law remains the same whereas operatively, and by way of the fiction, that content has changed to its opposite. So, and for example, in enounced Roman law, certain litigation could only be initiated by a Roman citizen but foreign litigants were able to do the same because of a fiction deeming them to be citizens for the purpose.[28] Thus, in Blanchot's terms, a fiction is 'truth and also indifference to truth'.[29]

LAW'S ENABLING

What Blanchot's 'literature' does not give us and what law does is a characteristic conceptualization of that which is in-between being, with its possibility, and a worldly existent. Granted, in its vacuity, in its rejection of any determinant anteriority, law dependently absorbs the concepts taken from its 'context'.[30] Yet law invests these concepts with the imminent

22 Blanchot, op. cit., n. 12, p. 29; Blanchot, op. cit., n. 6, pp. 363, 365, 369, 387, 389.
23 Blanchot, op. cit., n. 6, pp. 365, 397.
24 id., p. 371.
25 For a pointed and brilliant account of the similarity see P. Tuitt, *Race, Law, Resistance* (forthcoming) ch. 5.
26 Plato, *The Laws of Plato* (1980, tr. T.L. Pangle) para. 656c.
27 Blanchot, op. cit., n. 6, p. 395 for the quote.
28 H. Maine, *Ancient Law* (1931) 21.
29 Blanchot, op. cit., n. 6, pp. 396–7.
30 Thus the law in Blanchot's *The Madness of the Day* is totally dependent on the protagonist but she, the law, 'treacherously' elevates him only to elevate herself above him: Blanchot, op. cit. (1981), n. 2, pp. 14–16.

145

possibility of a being otherwise so that they are not, even in their own explicit terms, exhausted by presence.

Let me take, with inexcusable brevity, some of what could be called law's enabling concepts so as to show how in them the nothingness and the possibility of being subsists with the determinate and the actuality of existence. Taking equality, equality before the law: in law's irreducible openness, in its not being tied to any existent differentiation, there is ever within it an incipience of equality. That 'pure' equality can only be before or anterior to the law made determinate, for with the coming to determinate existence differentiation and inequality will always supervene. Thence equality endures in a shrunken life of 'more or less'. Impartiality as an enabling concept can be seen in the same way. Law's lack of ties to the existent inclines towards a lack of attachment in law's 'application'. But what is, in Locke's terms, law's being needful of 'a known and indifferent Judge' is not finally feasible since the disregard of difference becomes inexorably compromised when judge and judgment are made known in the determinate scene of application.[31]

Another telling example comes from the requirement that laws be 'general'. Because of this requirement, it used often to be said that a decision confined to a particular determination does not count as law.[32] Yet the ultimate way in which law is made determinate is in the decision, and the decision will always be specific. Neither the decision nor the circumstances provoking it will ever be exactly repeatable or repeated. Yet, if the general cannot find itself in law's determinate existence, it cannot be so general that it falls completely into nothingness and has no bearing on anything specific, no operative content at all. Hence the common and paradoxical requirement that law's 'generality must be specific'.[33] Perhaps the ur-instance of an enabling concept in law could be that of 'responsibility' and I will draw on that as a bridge back to Blanchot's concept of a responsibility which 'is' the law of the law, that responsibility or, in an archaic usage, responsability 'towards the Other' which is 'necessarily regulated' in the making of the determinate law.[34] In this inexorable narrowing there is a setting of law's responsive range. Yet law must, to be law, remain responsively open to what is within and beyond that range. For law ultimately to deny that responsiveness by inflicting death would be law's antithesis.

31 Locke, op. cit., n. 5, p. 396.
32 For example, id., p. 409; J.-J. Rousseau, *The Social Contract* (1968, tr. M. Cranston) 82.
33 F. Neumann, *The Democratic and the Authoritarian State: Essays in Political Theory* (1957) 28.
34 Blanchot, op. cit., n. 12, p. 43.

Which brings me, with a touch of inevitability, to Blanchot's 'right to death'. This is 'a curious right' which emerges when the void, or the nothingness of being carried by literature, by law, has 'in *absolute* freedom ... become an event'.[35] The voiding of existence is somehow made existent. He instances the Reign of Terror in the French Revolution. Here the generality of right has become universal, 'pure abstraction' – a universality which for the citizens comes to 'negate the particular reality of their lives', which fills possibility so completely that 'in the end no one has a right to his life any longer, to his actually separate and physically distinct existence'.[36] To be a citizen in this totalized event, to be a carrier of this strange or estranged right, is to be absolutely, is to lose the materiality of one's distinct being. Totality realized allows of no being apart from itself. There remains no space for our own, our singular life. There 'death is sovereign'.[37]

Here, then, is a seeming affinity, even identity between death and sovereignty which would go to confirm the sovereign 'right to death', the right to stop our existence, even the right to our existence. And classically, sovereignty, like literature and like law, assumed a determinate, an emplaced existence yet would extend to all possibility. This marvellous combination was effected, after a fashion, through a transcendent reference joining specific rule to deific scope. Without that reference, sovereignty persists as what Derrida calls a 'secularized theological concept'.[38] This sovereignty 'throned behind/Death ... heeds but hides, bodes but abides ...', borrowing from Hopkins.[39] With its claim to a completeness yet specificity of power, this is a sovereignty to which law has proved susceptible. Law's constituent imperative that nothing can be placed before it leaves it a vacuity. It must ever respond to and depend on an 'outside' for its contents and, in much philosophical and in even more jurisprudential thought, sovereignty has been assertively advanced as that which endows law with content.

All of which would seem to wrap things up and you, dear reader, may be almost as relieved as I to conclude at that, but there would remain the problem that the right to death imports the exact opposite. It is 'each person', 'every citizen' who 'has a right to death', and not the sovereign.[40] For Blanchot, a 'sovereign amplitude' does 'nothing'.[41] We may discern what the sovereign may do positively or determinately by filtering the right to

---

35 Blanchot, op. cit., n. 6, p. 375 his emphasis; and compare p. 379.
36 id., p. 376; compare Blanchot, op. cit. (1993), n. 2, p. 225.
37 Blanchot, op. cit., n. 6, p. 378.
38 J. Derrida, 'A Discussion with Jacques Derrida' (2001) 5 *Theory and Event* 49, <http://muse.jhu.edu/journals/theory_and_event/v005/5.1derrida.html>.
39 G.M. Hopkins, 'The Wreck of the Deutschland' in *The Poetic Works of Gerard Manley Hopkins* (1990) 127.
40 Blanchot, op. cit., n. 6, p. 376.
41 Blanchot, op. cit., n. 12, p. 32.

death through 'a simple and redoubtable logic', borrowing the phrase, if not the confidence, from Nancy.[42] For 'each person', each particulate in its 'absolute' and 'free' completeness, to be-with other persons, being still distinct yet in common, each would have to be the same as the other. Distinctness would thence be lost. Alternatively, if the 'absolute' distinctness of each is to be preserved, then there would be as many operative versions of what is in common as there are particulates, and thence the utter dissipation of commonality. The seemingly paradoxical price, then, of the distinctness of each in their relation to each other is the existence of *some* determinate being-in-common inhabiting and limiting each 'in' their very distinctness.

This commonality enabling distinct being, a commonality which is a determinate or determinable being-in-common, does provide a place for sovereignty. It is, however, a place that has been effectively occupied by other modes besides a monadic sovereignty. Sovereignty is but one specific mode of rule. As such it depends integrally on law, reversing now the standard ascription of law's dependence on sovereignty. Granted there can be sovereign acts apart from law, acts sustained, for example, by commitment to such neo-sacral entities as nation, commitment unto death, yet if sovereignty is to endure beyond the evanescence of the act, if it is to extend indefinitely yet enclose itself, if it is to subsist determinately yet traject to what is beyond its existence 'for the time being', sovereignty has to be bound to law. The condition of being sovereign is a claim of or to right. No amount of asserting the existence of a sovereign condition can make the qualitative leap to being-in-right. And what the sovereign condition always lacks in being stretched between determinate existence and the possibility that is within being has always to be constituently integrated into it. Law is the amenable means of so doing, of sovereignty's thence being sustainedly within the world. The sovereign ability to come adaptively to '[a]ll things counter, original, spare, strange', borrowing from Hopkins again, is an ability carried and sustained by law through its intrinsic inability to be bound to any pre-existent, its generative incompleteness and labile openness.[43] Yet if law carries sovereignty through Blanchot's 'night' of nothingness and possibility, it also and 'necessarily' returns it to the 'day' of an 'enounced' existence, and of this returning there can be 'no end' for 'there is no possibility of being done with the day, with the meaning of things, with hope ...'. [44]

---

42 J.-L. Nancy, *The Inoperative Community* (1991, tr. P. Connor) 4.
43 G.M. Hopkins, 'Pied Beauty' in Hopkins, op. cit., n. 39, p. 144.
44 Blanchot, op. cit., n. 12, p. 43; M. Blanchot, *The Work of Fire* (1995, tr. C. Mandel) 8.

JOURNAL OF LAW AND SOCIETY
VOLUME 31, NUMBER 1, MARCH 2004
ISSN: 0263-323X, pp. 149–58

Beyond Otonomy, or Beyond the Law of Law's Ear

Julia H. Chryssostalis*

Can the relationship between law and literature be thought in terms of conversation? Can the law still 'hear' the voice of a writing that has come before it, yet outside the frame of the 'hearing' and the rules of 'standing'? And when literature speaks, what does it say? Perhaps what the law has always known ...

SCENES OF WRITING AND OF REWRITING

Show us a trace of justice.
What is thy law?[1]

In a law and literature context, Antonio Tabucchi's book, *The Missing Head of Damasceno Monteiro*[2] – a tale of police corruption and abuse and the criminal justice system's unwillingness to deal with the brutality of its legal apparatus – is an interesting case on several levels, not only because its text offers a number of opportunities to explore the relation between law, society, and literature but also because it is a text which could be said to explicitly inscribe itself in that relation. Let me try to explain what I mean by this.

Two scenes from the book's 'life-story' might help here. The first concerns the scene of its writing. Tabucchi wrote the book in 1996 *in response* to a particularly shocking set of events from earlier that year: the

---

* School of Law, University of Westminster, 4–12 Little Titchfield Street, London W1W 7UW, England

I would like to thank Patrick Hanafin for his patience, gentle prodding, and generous support.

1 G. Ungaretti, 'La Pietà', in *The Penguin Book of Italian Verse*, ed. G. Kay (1958) 376; tr. my own.
2 A. Tabucchi, *La Testa Perduta di Damasceno Monteiro* (1997); in English, *The Missing Head of Damasceno Monteiro* (2000, tr. J.C. Patrick). All references in the text are to the Italian edition. Where a direct quote is provided the translation is my own.

149

killing of a 25-year-old Portuguese man, Carlos Rosa, in a police station of the Republican National Guard in the outskirts of Lisbon. His body was subsequently found in a park, headless, and bearing clear signs of torture. Tabucchi felt revolted by the incident[3] and wrote *The Missing Head* around it. Yet, why should this be important in this context? After all, Tabucchi's is not the first book based on actual events. Here is what I suggest.

Taken together with Tabucchi's views about the writer's role *in* the world[4] and his view of literature as a form of knowledge,[5] it means that the writing of *The Missing Head* cannot be read simply as a writer's personal reaction to a set of events that have profoundly moved him, or as the fictional treatment of a brutal and ugly actual incident. It should be also read as *a response* in the most literal sense: as a gesture, which occurs in return, as replication, folding back, or re-ply – in short, as both repetition and answer. For at stake in *The Missing Head*, is not so much writing's (or literature's, or fiction's) rootedness in the emotional state of the writer or the world it is set in – that is, the social and legal world it redoubles. It is, rather, writing's (or literature's, or fiction's) *return* to this (social and legal) world in order to engage it, challenge it, interrupt it, present back to it what it does not want to know – in short, in order to speak. Or perhaps, put differently, at stake in *The Missing Head* might be precisely that the *con*nection between writing (or literature, or fiction) and the world is not only one of *con*text but also of *con*versation.[6]

Now, the second scene from *The Missing Head's* 'life' I want to bring up allows for a different view of the text's inscription in the relation between society, law, and literature. Crucially, it concerns the text's reception, and interestingly it involves *The Missing Head's* rewriting. The story goes more or less like this. When the book came out in Portugal, the reaction to it was mixed. And not surprisingly perhaps. The issues the book deals with are difficult, the incident it is based on was somewhat 'taboo', and parts of the media did not quite appreciate a 'foreign' writer probing into it. So let's just say that Tabucchi did not get many interviews.[7] Yet the media were also very reluctant to give any substantial coverage to the actual trial of the sergeant that had killed and

3 In a recent interview with Asbel Lopez, Tabucchi talks about the way he felt when he first learned about the incident. See A. Lopez, 'Antonio Tabucchi: A Committed Doubter' at <http://ww.unesco.org/courier/1999_11/uk/dires/txt1.htm>.
4 This role is marked by, what in Italian is called *impegno*: a word, which weaves together notions of duty, obligation, engagement, involvement, regard, concern, commitment, and care. Interestingly, Tabucchi provides in this connection an emblematic figure. On a more general level, and the sort of work involved in a new politics of literature, see <www.autodafe.org>.
5 A. Tabucchi and A. Chrysostomides, *A Shirt full of Stains. Antonio Tabucchi in Conversation With His Translator, Anteos Chrysostomides* (1999, in Greek) 130. See, also, A. Tabucchi, *La Gastrite di Platone* (1997/98).
6 Drawing from this point, one could perhaps further argue that the status of literature to the world is not meta-static but ec-static, in the full Heideggerian sense of that term.
7 Lopez, op. cit., n. 3, pp. 2–3.

decapitated the young burglar in his custody. Why? Maybe because the Republican Guard continues to yield significant power in Portugal. Or maybe because, as Antonio Cassese notes,[8] police stations in general, along with prisons, barracks, detention centres, and psychiatric hospitals constitute 'the *sancta sanctorum* of each state ... in other words those places where national sovereignty is given its overpowering yet most recondite expression'.[9] Still, in this climate of general numbness, suddenly, the day after the sergeant's testimony, everything changed. Radically. So, what was it that the sergeant had said? Trying to explain how it had all happened, the sergeant told the court: 'He [Carlos Rosa] told me things that offended me, and I placed my gun at his temple; and at that moment the gun went off, even though I did not mean to fire it'. At which point, the judge said: 'Fine. Let's suppose that what you are saying is true. Why did you then cut his head off?' And the sergeant replied: 'Your Honour, when I saw the dead body on the floor, I got so frightened I just lost my head'. The following day, one of the tabloids came out with a headline which read 'The Missing Head of Sergeant Santos', taking over and practically rewriting the title of Tabucchi's book. The headline caused a real stir and the overall climate changed completely.[10] In the end, Sergeant José Dos Santos was sentenced to seventeen years' imprisonment. An apt ending? No doubt. But also an ending which in a certain sense had 'rewritten' itself. For in so far as *The Missing Head* had already scripted an end to the story before the actual story had ended,[11] the ending of the actual story could only either 'follow' *The Missing Head*'s 'script' or rewrite it. And it rewrote it.

8 In A. Cassese, *Inhuman States: Imprisonment, Detention and Torture in Europe Today* (1996), Cassese provides an account of his experiences (covering the years form 1989 to 1993) with the European Committee for the Prevention of Torture and Inhuman or Degrading Punishment, an international group of inspectors whose job is to investigate, on behalf of the Council of Europe, the conditions of detention in the states that have joined the Convention for the Prevention of Torture and Inhuman or Degrading Punishment. On the Convention, see, further, A. Cassese, 'A New Approach to Human Rights: The European Convention for the Prevention of Torture' (1989) 83 *Am. J. of International Law* 128; and on the activities of the committee, M. Evans and R. Morgan, 'The European Convention for the Prevention of Torture: Operational Practice' (1992) 41 *International and Comparative Law Q.* 590. Also see, generally <www.cpt.coe.int>.
9 id. (1996), p. 1. *Sancta sanctorum* is expressed as *holy of holies* in English, which initially referred to the inner chamber of the Jewish tabernacle. It also corresponds to the Greek *adyta tôn adytôn*, where *adyton* means literally a place that is inaccessible or out of bounds, and designates both the most sacred (in the case of a temple, or a church) and the most secret (like the depths of one's heart or soul) of places.
10 The account provided here follows Tabucchi's own account in Tabucchi and Chrysostomides, op. cit., n. 5, pp. 123–4.
11 In the book, the responsibility of the National Guard is split between the Sergeant and two other Guards. The 'real' culprit is of course the Sergeant, a corrupt and sadistic creature, who nonetheless manages to get away with it. The Court in the end declares him innocent with regard to the murder of Damasceno Monteiro. In the book, the court 'buys' the story of the National Guard, which, in its basic contours, is the story Sergeant Santos will tell the actual court a few months later: 'it was an accident; when I saw the body on the floor, I panicked; and so I cut off the body's head'.

Now, the 'rewriting' of *The Missing Head* just described is no doubt an extraordinary event, which seems to confirm the idea proposed earlier that the relationship between literature, law, and society could be thought in terms of conversation. For if *The Missing Head* (and by extension, writing, literature, or fiction) could be said to constitute a response, a reply, a return to the (social and legal) world in order to speak, then it is also possible to think that the (social and legal) world could respond back. In other words, the rewriting of *The Missing Head*'s title by the tabloid as well as the rewriting of its ending by the court – that is, ultimately literature's rewriting by the social and the legal worlds respectively – could constitute a counter-response in the context of an on-going conversation.

At this point, the following question arises: if literature comes to the (social and legal) world to speak, what does it come to say? On this, let's start with *The Missing Head*.

FROM THE MYSTERY TO THE ENIGMA OF THE MISSING HEAD

(Re)locating the events of the story away from Lisbon to the northern city of Oporto,[12] Tabucchi uses the conventional plot of the murder mystery to produce a double narrative, a narrative which, in recounting the murder investigation, also gradually secretes the narrative recounting the crime. In the investigating role, he places Firmino, a young reporter working for a Lisbon tabloid while also researching the influence of Vittorini in the post-war Portuguese novel in his spare time. The *motto* of the paper Firmino works for, *The Event* (*O Acontecimento* in Portuguese), is 'what the citizen must know', but this, in this case, seems to refer exclusively to the gory detail of sex scandals and brutal murders. The discovery of a headless body in the outskirts of Oporto, means that Firmino is swiftly dispatched there to 'cover' the story – and *uncover* the mystery (of both the missing head and its missing identity). In Oporto, Firmino is 'stationed' at a small bed-and-breakfast, whose owner, Dona Rosa, seems to have all the right connections. It is she, for instance, who sets up for him a meeting with Manolo, the old gypsy who had found the body in the first place, and from him Firmino learns that the dead man was wearing a T-shirt with 'Stones of Portugal' written on it. This eventually leads him to the place where the dead man used to work and to find out his nickname. Then, the missing head is fished out of the river – and of course the fisherman knows exactly where to find Firmino, who thus gets 'exclusive' pictures for his paper – while the following day Firmino also finds the dead man's name. Summoned by a disembodied voice to the phone, he is told that the name is Damasceno Monteiro. Firmino

12 Although it is clear that, as far as the events of the story are concerned, the setting itself is not crucial. It could have been anywhere in Europe, or, for that matter, the so-called 'civilized' West.

152

arranges to meet his 'source' and the rest of the 'mystery' quickly unravels: Damasceno, who worked at an import-export company, one day stumbled upon a heroin smuggling ring and decided to steal a drug shipment. He enlisted one of his pals for the job, the one who has lived to tell the story, but things went horribly wrong, when the arch-dealer surprised them by arriving on the scene. It turned out he was Sergeant Titanio da Silva, a sergeant of the Republican Guard, who needed to find out about another of his shipments that had gone missing, and, convinced that Damasceno was his 'man', he 'arrested' him, took him to the police station and the rest is 'history'.

Now, from all this, it should have become quickly clear that, although the 'unravelling', or the 'uncovering' of the 'mystery' of (Damasceno's) *Missing Head* makes for a gripping read, at the same time, there is not much from what is uncovered that we do not already know one way or another. Take, for example, the two things that take Firmino half the book to find out: the identity of the victim and the identity of killer. The former *we* know even before opening the book. The latter we 'learn' early on from Manolo. From his account, it transpires that the police are withholding evidence, in other words, trying to deceive 'us', which suggests precisely that they might have something to do with the killing. Thus, *The Missing Head* presents us with a rather perplexing situation: a murder *mystery* which is not much of a mystery; an 'investigator' who seems more ignorant about the 'mystery' than we are;[13] and an 'investigation' which does not solve the 'mystery', because the 'mystery' is both 'half-solved' anyway and also seems to solve *itself*. Firmino simply pushes it towards its solution, bearing witness to, as well as reporting back to his readers, every turn and development. He does not actually *provide* the solution, that is, he does not reach the solution either by reasoning or by intuition as in the classic murder mystery/detective story. Instead, Firmino seems to have always the good fortune to stumble at the *right time* on the right piece of information or lead, which then incrementally produce the solution.[14] Which also means that the full narrative of the 'murder' is gradually produced as the 'investigation' progresses, and not retroactively as a renarration at the end, while things are still 'hanging', left unexplained.

13 At the same time, one needs to accept that Firmino looks much more like the naïve, everyday companion of the 'classic' detective than the detective himself. He is an ordinary, average person, with nothing of the detective's notorious perspicacity, full of prejudices, 'who embodies what we could call the field of *doxa*, spontaneous common [or, in this case, public] opinion.' S. Zizek, 'Two Ways to Avoid the Real of Desire' in *Psychoanalytic Literary Criticism*, ed. M. Ellman (1994) 125, fn. 7.
14 And it has to be said here that this is something profoundly frustrating for the reader who is thus denied one of the most basic pleasures of the murder mystery/detective story, namely, the certainty that the 'investigator' will solve the case. Here, not only does the case 'solve' itself, it also turns out that the reader knew the 'solution' all along, and thus the position of innocent ignorance from which the reader *enjoys* the murder mystery is no longer available. On the role of the 'investigator' as guarantee of meaning in the detective story, see, further, Zizek, id., pp. 116–17.

Yet, in addition, *The Missing Head* seems to be structurally different from the 'classic' murder mystery/detective story. There, as Slavoj Zizek explains, we start with:

> a void, a blank of the unexplained, more properly of the *unnarrated* ('How did it happen? What happened on the night of the murder?'). The story encircles this blank, [and] is set in motion by the detective's attempt to reconstruct the missing narrative by interpreting the clues. In this way, we reach the proper beginning only at the very end, when the detective is finally able to narrate the whole story in its 'normal', linear form, to reconstruct 'what really happened,' by filling in all the blanks. At the beginning there is thus the murder – a traumatic shock, an event that cannot be integrated into the symbolic reality because it appears to interrupt the 'normal' causal chain ... [From this moment] everyday reality becomes a nightmarish dream as the 'normal' link between cause and effect is suspended. This radical opening, this dissolution of symbolic reality, entails the transformation of the lawlike succession of events into a kind of 'lawless sequence' ... Suddenly 'everything is possible', including the impossible. [Thus] the detective's role is precisely to ... resymbolize the traumatic shock, to integrate it into symbolic reality, [while his sheer presence] guarantees in advance the transformation of the lawless sequence into a lawful sequence; in other words, the re-establishment of 'normality'.[15]

In *The Missing Head*, on the other hand, we have neither the narrative nor the role of the 'investigator'/detective working in this way. We never have, that is, free-floating, unsymbolized clues waiting for the investigator's interpretation. We never have the sense of 'reality' happening as a lawless sequence – only that *this is* a 'lawless' reality, where the law enforcer yields the most lawless force. Plus, as noted above, neither do we have an 'investigator' whose role is to 'solve' the case, since the case is partly already solved and partly solves itself. Thus, the role of Firmino's presence is not to guarantee the 'solution' of the 'mystery', so that life can become normal again, but to tell a story – a story, which might interrupt normality.

Thus, we reach here the rather obvious yet unavoidable question. Given that the mystery was not much of a mystery after all, and that we knew (perhaps not in detail, but still we knew) right from the start what it was that had happened to the head of Damasceno Monteiro, what is the point of having a murder mystery if there is not much of a mystery to be had? The answer here might be that perhaps all along we have been busying ourselves with the wrong thing or, rather, with the wrong blank. That is to say, the 'void', the 'unexplained blank' at the root of the story of Damasceno Monteiro is not the question 'How did it happen?' or 'Who killed Damasceno Monteiro?' or even 'What happened to his head?'. As the figure of Firmino shows, all these are 'blanks' that can be easily 'filled' by anyone. In other words, they are questions that one does not need to be Sherlock Holmes, Hercule Poirot or Miss Marple in order to answer them. The 'void' to be explained at the basis of *The Missing Head* is, rather, a different one: not 'How *did* it happen?' but 'How *could* it

15 id., p. 117

154

happen?'; 'How *could* a head just go missing?'; 'How *could* someone be murdered, while in police custody?'; 'How *could* all this be allowed to happen?'. These are clearly not the questions of a mystery. They are, rather, the questions of an enigma – an enigma placed both before each one of us and before the law.

INTERLUDE: THE REST OF THE STORY

So let us resume our story. After the revelations concerning the role of the police in Damasceno's murder, *The Event* decides to back Damasceno's family in a lawsuit against Sergeant Silva and the other officers involved. So Dona Rosa puts Firmino in touch with a lawyer, Fernando de Mello Sequeira, nicknamed 'Loton' (after Charles Laughton), the last descendant of an aristocratic family, who is famous in Oporto for defending the victims of social and political injustice – seeking to redeem thus his family's aristocratic past. In the days that follow, Firmino helps Loton put together the case against Silva and gradually gets to know him. A fascinating character, 'Loton' is a man who abandoned his studies in legal theory to dedicate himself to the practice of law, yet someone who can talk with the same ease about the structure of Swiss train timetables and the structure of the universe; tripe cooked-the-Oporto-way and French literature; or his grandmother and Kelsen's Grundnorm – and Kelsen's Grundnorm is something he talks a lot about, as he has been obsessed with it for years (he even abandoned his studies in Geneva to follow Kelsen's lectures at Berkeley in the early 50s).

Eventually, the day of the trial arrives and it does not take long before the outcome becomes clear. For while the court asks all other witnesses – the gypsy who discovered the body, the fisherman who found the head, and the victim's friend and accomplice – only to confirm their initial statements; it is willing to listen uncritically to the Republican Guards' entirely fictional version of events. Damasceno's death was an 'accident', and the court gets to hear how upset and desperate he was; how the guards took pity on him and went to make him some coffee, leaving him alone for a few minutes; how they were startled by a gunshot, only to discover that Damasceno, using the gun that one of the officers had accidentally left behind, had killed himself; how everything got too much for Sergeant Silva, who had to rush home to get his migraine tablets, leaving the two guards on duty to clear up the mess; and how they, in their panic and ignorance, decided to cut off Damasceno's head, throw it in the river and leave the body in the woods.

The guards' account of events – totally absurd, and at the same time totally predictable – has a strange effect. After it, the trial seems to have already ended. Nothing seems able to make any difference – neither Loton's questions about the cigarette marks on Damasceno's body, nor his courageous closing speech counterposing our programmatic commitment to human life and the way in which we allow people denied their liberty to be treated, and connecting Kafka's terrible penal machine and Kelsen's Grundnorm, the abstract principle of law's legality. When the court reaches finally its decision there are no surprises. Silva is absolved of the murder, but gets a six-month suspension from his duties for leaving his post, and the two guards are sentenced to two years' imprisonment for defiling a corpse and for committing a grave omission in the course of their duties.

KELSEN WITH KAFKA, OR WHAT, ACCORDING TO LOTON, LAW CAN LEARN FROM LITERATURE[16]

Kelsen with Kafka? Isn't that an unlikely pairing? What could possibly connect Hans Kelsen, the theoretician of the 'pure theory of law' and Franz Kafka, the writer of the *Penal Colony* and its flesh-fed machine? Isn't Loton's association of the two somewhat far-fetched? And isn't it an outrageous thought that behind the *Grundnorm* one could find Kafka's vampiric apparatus? Perhaps, but not as much as one may initially think. We could start considering the connection between the two by looking at another unlikely pair, Kant and Sade. That is, the Kant of the *Critique of Practical Reason*[17] and the Sade of the *Philosophy in the Bedroom*.[18]

In his essay, 'Kant with Sade',[19] Jacques Lacan maintains that the *truth* of the Kantian moral law (in its classic formula, 'act in such a way that the maxim of your action may be accepted as a universal maxim') is to be found in the Sadian natural law – which, being set up as an 'anti-morality', adopts as norms the exact opposite 'of what was considered up to that point as the essential minimum of a viable and coherent community'.[20] Of course this might seem strange at first. For isn't the Sadian law a point-by-point 'reversal of the fundamental imperatives of the moral law, extolling incest, adultery, theft, and everything else you can think of'?[21] And if this is the case, in what way can it provide the truth of Kantian ethics, where the definition of the good rests on its universal value rather than on the feelings, interests, or passions of individuals? What is crucial to understand here is that Lacan sees the connection between the two not in any substantive terms but in the fact that Sade advances his position by reference to entirely

16 Tabucchi, op. cit. n. 2, p. 217: 'allow me a literary reference, for literature also helps to understand the law'.
17 I. Kant, *Critique of Practical Reason* (1957).
18 M. de Sade, *The Complete Justine, Philosophy in the Bedroom, and Other Writings* (1956). Here, the relevant text is the pamphlet, 'Frenchmen, one more effort to become republicans!'.
19 J. Lacan, '*Kant avec Sade*' (1971) II *Ecrits* 119. See, also, J. Lacan, *Seminar VII. The Ethics of Psychoanalysis*, ed. J.-A. Miller (1992) especially 76–80.
20 Lacan, id. (1992), p. 78.
21 id., pp. 78–9.

Kantian criteria of ethics.[22] In other words, the link between them is that the Sadian moral universe is possible through Kantian rules. For the Sadian maxim, according to which 'everyone has the right to *enjoy* any other person whatsoever, as the instrument of their pleasure' is acceptable on Kant's own criteria: that is to say, it can be universalized and is empty of any particular content or desire.[23] Thus, as Lacan points out:

> If one eliminates from morality every element of sentiment, if one removes or invalidates all guidance to be found in sentiments, then in the final analysis the Sadian world is conceivable – even if it is its inversion, its caricature – as one of the possible forms of the world governed by a radical ethics, by the Kantian ethics as elaborated in 1788.[24]

Two further points need to be made here. The first concerns the implications for the ethical subject of this *katharsis* of sentiment, this radical emptying of interest, marking the universalization of the moral law in Kantian-Sadian ethics. For, as Lee notes:

> [t]he law, by demanding that the will be empty of particular content in effect situates the human subject in relation to a world devoid of particular qualities or attributes. Things of this world are stripped of all their characteristics, their good and their evil, and find a place within ethical theory only as bare existences ... In other words, the moral subject relates not to a world of objects but to the real Thing for which all these objects are symbolic or imaginary substitutes or both, and where 'even the bare existence of the remaining unqualified things ... symbolized in Sade's narratives by the apparently deathless victims of torture – is finally utterly negated.[25]

The second point, which Lacan brings up in his *Seminar*, concerns again the implications of the moral law but from a different point of view. We saw earlier how the moral law in Kantian-Sadian ethics is marked by the emptying of all sentiment. However, in both the Kantian and the Sadian ethical universe there still exists '*one* sentient correlative of the moral law in its purity, and strangely enough, it is nothing other than pain itself'.[26] It is enough to turn here to the third chapter of the *Critique of Practical Reason*, where Kant, says:

> Consequently we can see *a priori* that the moral law as the determining principle of will, by reason of the fact that it sets itself against our inclinations, must produce a feeling that one could call pain. And this is the first and perhaps only case, where we are allowed to determine, by means of a priori concepts, the relationship between a knowledge, which comes from practical pure reason, and a feeling of pleasure or pain.[27]

At this point we can return to the Kelsen-Kafka pair. Don't we find in the Kelsenian project for a 'pure theory of law', that is, a *theory* 'free of all

22 id., p. 78.
23 Lacan, id. (1971), p. 125.
24 Lacan, id. (1992), p. 79.
25 J.S. Lee, *Jacques Lacan* (1990) 166; quoting Lacan, id., p. 131.
26 Lacan, id., p. 80; emphasis in the original.
27 Kant, op. cit, n. 16.

157

ethical-political value judgements'[28] and purged of all considerations of morality, politics, and history, the same Kantian-Sadian gesture of emptying the object from all 'pathological' content? Don't we find in the Kelsenian insistence on the distinction between the *formal validity* of the legal order, which is a logical question, and the *content* of particular laws, which is a political, or moral, or theological question, the same basic formalist gesture also marking the Kantian-Sadian strategy of distinguishing between the empty universal Law and its particular content? And isn't it precisely that which makes the Sadian universe a Kantian one, as well as opening up the possibility for envisaging the Kelsenian world as one of distinctly Kafkaesque contours? For, after all, by what is Josef K. crushed if not by the sheer force of empty rules? And isn't it the case that the possibility of the monstrous apparatus of the penal colony as a *legal* machine arises only with the insistence that the determination of the legal is merely a logical operation, which depends on nothing else but a basic, empty rule? And isn't it that basic rule which ultimately means that the marks the machine makes on the flesh of its victims is legal writing?

'EVERYTHING THAT I HAVE KNOWN,
YOU WILL WRITE TO ME TO REMIND ME, WITH LETTERS ...'[29]

---

28 H. Kelsen, *The Pure Theory of Law* (1967), 352.
29 F. Hölderlin, 'Wenn aus der Ferne' in <www.hoelderlin-gesellschaft.de/texte/wenn_aus_der_Ferne.html>; the translation is my own following the one in Tabucchi, op. cit., n. 2, p. 127.

158

JOURNAL OF LAW AND SOCIETY
VOLUME 31, NUMBER 1, MARCH 2004
ISSN: 0263-323X, pp. 159–62

Endnote: Untoward

PETER GOODRICH*

A plethora of readings. Indeed a brace of Readers, two Lecturers – the word a base Latinity for Reader – and a name which is but a double 'r' away from Booke. The sum of which is a thoroughly literary endeavour, a bookish event, a series of textual exhalations. The first question to be asked, untoward though it may be, is what have the Readers been reading? The rest will follow from the answer to that question.

The initial answer is that the configuration 'Law and Literature' allows for a reading of literary texts. Aside from the innominate marginal scribble that Goodrich reads, the gathering of texts analysed, interpreted, and brought to law are entirely literary. There is a little hedonism, a touch of reverie, as well as an expansive gesture toward accessibility, in the selection of books being read. Melanie Williams turns to W.H. Auden and questions the trauma that motivates specific, nominate, theories of law. Her concern is with the 'unconscious trends', the patterns and repetitions that lead from 'September 1, 1939', a poem which Auden wrote in New York at the outbreak of World War II, and September 11, 2001. If there is a motif it is a line that Auden changed from 'We must love one another or die' to 'We must love one another and die'.

Melanie Williams conjures a trauma that is perceived as external to law but which is in fact internal to legal thought. The poet's concerns with crisis, the failure of reason, with love and war can be traced in displaced form in the history of jurisprudence. She offers a reading that is against the grain, a subtle and untoward interpretation that Adam Gearey picks up in analysing the words of Desmond Tutu and of the Truth and Reconciliation Commission. He also plays upon a contrary or untoward grain, a legal

* Cardozo School of Law, Brookdale Center, 55 Fifth Avenue, New York, NY 10003, United States of America

Editors' note: Due to missed deadlines, timelags, and delays, Peter Goodrich was unable to read the contributions by Peter Fizpatrick, Morris Kaplan, and Julia Chryssostalis. The editors regret this inconvenience to the reader, but this chance interruption in the unity and coherence of the volume seems emblematic of the need to resist any final word.

poetics, an aesthetic jurisdiction, a yearning for an outside that finds muted expression, a whisper internal to law: 'And yet/Through glass and bars/Some dream a wild sunset/Waiting stars.'

The paradox of Truth and Reconciliation was that of a law that was not law. Its function was to tell a truth that could never be present. You need in some degree to be a poet to understand an unknowable justice or to glimpse a truth that is untoward or marked by indirection. Adam Gearey wishes 'to tell it slant'. He punctures the normality of legalism with a competing text and law, and the prize – if reading can produce a prize – is a poetic confrontation as much as it is a confrontation with poetry. In Patrick Hanafin's term, offered in the course of a reading of Blanchot, it is an act of insubordination. For him, literature rebels against law in a profoundly political manner. Literature, as he argues here and elsewhere, is the pharmakon, both poison and remedy, source and cure of the malady of law. Literature is here the resistance, the residue of failed dreams, the call to arms, the political hope of making law anew. In his version, literature is untoward in that it calls away from the boredom and stasis of legalism, it seduces and garners a literary community that will 'unwrite' and so cure the law.

If Patrick Hanafin is a little untoward, or locally insubordinate, Piyel Haldar provides a trope that offers an epoch and a whole continent of salacious indirection. The jurisprudence of travel literature goes wholly against the grain. He reads a genre of commentaries upon despotism as the oriental mode of law. He portrays a vast myth, a juggernaut of juristic fantasms, a radically subversive look at the inside of Western law as it stares out at Eastern practices. The imperialistic complacency of what Selden dubbed 'dulling custom' and the immemorial practice of common law, is juxtaposed to descriptions of the bedevilled aberrations, the monstrosity, the luxury and excess, the sheer deadly pleasure, the salacious cruelty of despotism.

Haldar's point is that there is as much desire as there is disapproval in the excessively detailed depictions of oriental life. There is as much projection as there is objection. To borrow a wordplay of Hanafin's, the obsession with harems and sudden death does not so much inscribe as describe or unwrite the Western law that so enjoys detailing the pleasures of the East. Suffice to say that in all of this there is a most untoward thread of hedonism, of motive force, of the contrary and cutting. Literature objects to law as it is currently written. The literary can play with law, and in the longer term literature can come to play the law or at least teach lawyers to write differently.

I cannot make much of that last remark here. This is an endnote, though of course it is neither an end nor a note, just something untoward. So I will fulfill that indirection by looking finally at the Booke. If the topic is law and literature, then there is presumably no reason to exclude the possibility of a contribution from a literary scholar or, as it happens here, from Brooker. In fact Brooker's contribution is emblematic. In one sense that is because he is

160

assisted by knowing what he is talking about, literature being his discipline, his profession, and his institutional love. In another sense he personifies the untoward. The lawyers in this volume all engage with literary texts as a way of challenging the stylistic, textual, and hedonic limits of law. They argue in variable forms that literature represents a fracture, a crisis, a puncture of the legal restraint of the text. They use poems, fictions, insubordinate acts, and wild writings as a way of getting outside of the norm of legal writing and so bringing to consciousness the politics of law's inscription.

Brooker is wise to all of that, and as a lone literary scholar he holds the mirror to the maundering of law. He takes as his text a literary law and analyses the judgments handed down by a court of voluntary jurisdiction, the invention of Flann O'Brien (or Nolan, or na gCopaleen). His question is: what constitutes a positive law of literature? O'Brien's wit and wordplay produce a satirical law, a better-written and infinitely less inflated text. It is a version of the slanted reading that Adam Gearey sought in the Truth and Reconciliation Commission report, a truth that undoes itself in the very moment of its enunciation, a law that recognizes that it is also lawless, a written judgment that mimics the legal and yet is literary and far from entirely serious.

The crux of Brooker's essay, his most untoward moment, comes in the form of a Menippean instance of satirical play. A defendant confesses to his failure to abscond. The grounds are linguistic. Had he not appeared then 'too well I knew that my bail would not be *confiscated*. Neither would it be *impounded* (Here defendant became moved.) Neither would it be *declared forfeit* – or even *forfeited*. It would not be *attached*. It would be ... (Here defendant broke down and began to weep.) ... My bail would be ESTREATED.' Brooker cunningly comments that the term 'estreat' is recondite. No question about that. It is positively untoward and definitely in need of a little explanation.

Estreat, we are told in Rastell's *Termes de la Ley* 'is a figure or resemblance, and is commonly used for the copy or true note of an original writing, as estreats of amerciaments'.[1] So the estreat ironically concerns the truth of a writing that has been misplaced or at least is not available in the original. It is a fiction in the sense that the estreat is legally true and yet in fact unverifiable. Fitzherbert's *Natura Brevium* lists the estreat under the general title of a writ of *moderata misericordia*, or moderate mercy, a writ that seeks to limit the amount of damages. The estreat, and even Flann O'Brien would be hard pressed to concoct quite such a baroque fantasia of juridisms, was used 'where there are many plaintiffs named, and they amerced, the clerk hath forgotten, and cannot shew how the usage hath been to make the estreats against them ... For it cannot properly be said that a man hath mercy shewed and offered unto him if he shall pay, or shall be put to more charge for the offence of another person, which himself hath not

1 J. Rastell, *Les Termes de la Ley* (1566, 1812 edn.) at 208.

161

done.'[2] It is lost in translation, but broadly means that the party estreated is legally proven to be the party amerced, or the one who owes the damages.

O'Brien's defendant might well weep at being estreated. He is being named, interpellated by the law. Estreatment, in other words, is the punctum, the moment when the law leaves the Booke and interrupts life. In its more modern definitions, the estreat is precisely the moment of collection, the instance of leaving the chain of records and enforcing the fine.[3] The estreat, however, also testifies to the imperfection of the record and the necessity of mercy or equity because of the failure of memory, and the infinite regress of writing. A record only ever refers to something absent but noted and in a similar vein what is written will always refer to other writings, and here to absent texts. By the same token, this precariously literary quality of law provides the possibility of interruption, whether pathological, hedonistic, serious or satirical.

So here is my hypothesis and envoi: the function of the literary is that of estreating the study of law. Literature does not treat law, it estreats law, which means that it plays with the law so as to reinforce or subvert or amend or destroy as occasion warrants. Literature moves beyond the law, it makes a fictional, and so, imperfect copy and then indicates or alludes to the fact that copies are all that we have. The estreat is a reference to the necessary disjunction between record and recollection, and the estreatment of law by literature means travelling beyond the record, taking law outside itself, so as to go back in. In the jargon of Hollywood you need a treatment to pitch a movie. The treatment gives you the basic image of the movie: let's say Atlantis filmed in the Arctic to which the studio types would say 'no way, there would be white out'. The estreatment is a similar accounting of the image of a law: let's say the Irish Constitution, and O'Brien, the head of fiction, calls it 'desperate and dark of hue' or simply terribly written. If that is the case, if it is poorly inscribed, then tear it up, whether text or law or constitution and write it anew.

---

2   A. Fitzherbert, *Natura Brevium* (1514, 1793 edn.) at 75–6.
3   As, for example, *Black's Law Dictionary* (1999, 7th edn.) at 572.

Printed and bound by CPI Group (UK) Ltd, Croydon, CR0 4YY

09/06/2025

14686137-0005